AS **10**

Third

Other A-level Law titles

Contract Law (second edition), by Mary Charman

Criminal Law (second edition), by Tony Storey and Alan Lidbury

Tort Law (second edition), by Sue Hodge

AS Law

Third edition

Mary Charman
Bobby Vanstone
Liz Sherratt

WILLAN
PUBLISHING

Published by

Willan Publishing
Culmcott House
Mill Street, Uffculme
Cullompton, Devon
EX15 3AT, UK
Tel: +44(0)1884 840337
Fax: +44(0)1884 840251
e-mail: info@willanpublishing.co.uk
Website: www.willanpublishing.co.uk

Published simultaneously in the USA and Canada by

Willan Publishing
c/o ISBS, 5824 N.E. Hassalo St,
Portland, Oregon 97213-3644, USA
Tel: +001(0)503 287 3093
Fax: +001(0)503 280 8832

Contents

Introduction to the third edition

This new edition of *AS Law* builds further on the success of previous editions. Its role as a textbook for study at AS-level has become clear, bridging the gap between GCSE and A-level. There is a definite demand for a book which makes a complex academic subject accessible, and we have taken this into account in formulating the style of writing; but equally we have borne in mind the needs of all, including the most able students, in providing depth and accuracy of content, whilst remembering the nature of the examinations at AS-level. This edition of *AS Law* therefore meets the need of those who wish to study the subject for just one year and those who continue into the second year to study for the full A-level.

Subject content covers the specifications of both AQA and OCR, particularly in an expanded section on practice questions to suit both examination boards. However, the book will also be useful for students studying law for other qualifications at this level. One of the authors served on the QCA committee that set the subject criteria for Law, and all of the authors played a significant role in the development of the major specifications

Material has been updated to incorporate the findings of the Auld Review which considers developments in the criminal process, and the changes which have taken place in the civil process since the Woolf Report and the Access to Justice Act 1999. Regarding police powers, the content includes the Code for Crown Prosecutors (2000) and principles from *Bibby v Chief Constable of Essex Police* (2000). Consideration of Human Rights includes high-profile cases, such as that of Michael Douglas and Catherine Zeta-Jones in *Douglas and others v Hello! Ltd* (2001), and consideration has been given to the increasing involvement of politics with the legal system.

Law making/Sources of Law is clearly an important area of study to both examination boards, and in support of this the practice material has been changed and updated, with help provided in approaching the use of sources to answer questions. This is a key issue for OCR candidates, since the Sources paper for that board carries substantial marks. Similarly, the chapters on the substantive areas of Criminal Law and tort have been revised and updated, and new-style questions have been included to take into account recent changes to the examination format for the AQA examination board. The section on key skills provides specific suggestions to help teachers and students in preparation of portfolios.

The use of diagrams has been increased in response to demand from users, in order to help revision and to aid memory of key facts and cases.

Activities are included in the form of 'thinking points' to help with critical analysis and practical tasks to help reinforce theoretical study. These have proved to be helpful in setting the legal rules into the wider context of society, and in encouraging consideration of issues of justice and morality. They also provide opportunities to develop communication skills in reading, writing, discussing and presenting, and information technology skills in research and presentation.

As in the previous edition, the book does not provide complete answers to the questions asked, now includes new-style examination questions for both AQA and OCR, with *outline* answers, to (a) give reassurance that an answer is on the right lines, and (b) to help those unfamiliar with examination format to make a positive start. Students are thus encouraged to develop a well-constructed, yet individual, answer, enabling the development of skills needed for current examinations and for later extended essay work. It should always be remembered, however, that a number of different answers and approaches may be equally good.

Those of you following the OCR specification will find excellent examples in the later chapters to illustrate some of the English Legal System topics and, will, we hope, enjoy a taste of what is to come in the second year of your A-level studies. We wish you well in your studies, success in your examinations, and hope that you will be inspired to continue to the full A-level in Law.

Acknowledgements

We have many people to thank for their support, including the users, both teachers and students, who have made positive and helpful comments, and Sue Hodge for her expertise in the chapter on Torts. We also acknowledge with gratitude the support of the major examination boards and, of course, would again like to thank Brian Willan and the production team for their patience and expertise.

The publishers are indebted to OCR (Oxford Cambridge and RSA Examinations) and AQA (Assessment and Qualifications Alliance) for permission to reproduce specimen questions.

Table of legislation

European legislation

Table of cases

Part 1

Law-making: sources of law in the English legal system

Why do we obey law? Where does it come from? How did we arrive at the laws which operate in our country today? How do we create new laws?

These questions are all are part of the study of sources of law – really this is an investigation into where the laws which regulate our lives come from and how they apply to us. There are some very ancient sources of law which, although interesting historically, are beyond the scope of A-level study. In this section of the book, however, we will look at the major sources of the law operating in our country now.

The main sources of law to study for examination purposes are:

- European law – arguably the most important at present, since it is growing very quickly indeed.
- Statute law – Acts of Parliament, how they are passed and how they are interpreted by courts.
- Judicial precedent – how cases follow each other in court, creating new law.

We will also examine two further areas briefly (you should know a little of these for the examination):

- the influences on parliamentary law-making;
- the general issue of law reform (the methods by which the law can be changed, or a new law introduced).

Sometimes these areas of law conflict, and then we need to decide which law to follow. For example, there may be a judgment in a case on an issue over which either Parliament has since created a statute, or where there is a statute which applies, but since the statute's creation European law has introduced a regulation. We will see that where European law is formed on an issue, this *must* be followed, even if it conflicts with existing national law. In this sense then, European law could be said to be the most important modern source of law, so we will examine this first, before looking at the more traditional sources.

1   European law

Introduction

Do *you* feel European? Most people would usually describe themselves as British, English, Welsh, French, Indian, American or whatever happens to reflect most accurately their personal nationality. However, everyone resident in one of the 15 countries which form part of the European Union is also bound legally by the laws of that body of member states, and is therefore, at least in the legal sense, European. This presents all sorts of openings for individuals and organisations, and can be viewed with promise and excitement. New opportunities exist for travel, employment and business dealing; and rather than taking a leap into the dark, EU citizens can make the most of these opportunities knowing that there is a legal framework for their protection.

Figure 1.1

In the past, the United Kingdom has had a tendency to take a rather insular approach to being an integral part of Europe, possibly because:

- our geographical location of being separated by water from other member states created a feeling of division, especially when travelling;
- political and economic strength over a long period of our history allowed a degree of independence from other European countries;
- divisions caused by war in the past have taken a long time to heal.

The legal system, and judges in particular, were no exception to this reluctance to move away from total patriotism, but gradually over a period of time both the courts and society generally are realising that the European

Union, with its own legal structure, is here to stay, and that the United Kingdom can benefit from being an integral part of it. In fact, it will be seen from the material that follows, that the United Kingdom plays a large part in forming the laws which are created under European law, and is therefore a relatively influential member of the European Union.

Your study of European law will involve four main issues:

- The development of the European Union (briefly).
- The institutions of Europe – an investigation into exactly who makes European laws.
- The effect of the European Union on national sovereignty – in other words, how much being part of Europe affects the individual status of member states.
- Legislation and its effect on national law – how European law operates in our own country.

Development of the European Union

The original idea of forming a group of states was not based on an aim to be one integrated legal entity, but on economics. It was felt that there would be considerable advantages in countries joining together to manage large commodities, such as coal and steel. Today, the European Union is one of the world's largest trading units. This can be seen as an exciting opportunity to form an ideal civilised body of people and organisations – almost like playing a strategy game, such as Sim City, but in reality! However, unlike a strategy game, people and member states are all very different, and many practical problems arise – as we will see.

Some of the aims of the present European Union, which are now much wider than the original economic ideal, can be seen in Article 2 of the Treaty of Rome (amended by later treaties):

> The Community shall have as its task ... to promote throughout the Community a harmonious and balanced development of economic activities ... a high level of employment and of social protection, the raising of the standard of living and quality of life ...

These are some of the important stages of development:

1952 A European Coal and Steel Community was formed, the forerunner of the present day European Union.

1957 The Treaty of Rome was formed, creating the legal status of the European Union.

1972 The United Kingdom joined what was then known as the European Economic Community. This was achieved by by passing the European

Communities Act 1972, which incorporated the Treaty of Rome into English law. This came into effect on 1 January 1973.

1986 The Single European Act of 1986 was passed, which became effective in 1992, and amongst other things gave much more freedom of movement to workers.

1992 The ratification of the Maastricht Treaty, and under the Treaty of European Union 1993 the European Community changed its name to the European Union.

1999 The Treaty of Amsterdam added a new Article to the Treaty of Rome to 'take appropriate action to combat discrimination based on sex, racial or ethnic origin, religion or belief disability, age or sexual orientation'.

The Articles of the original Treaty were renumbered, so, for example, the former Article 177 is now Article 234.

2001 The Treaty of Nice makes provision for enlargement to include new member states, more qualified majority voting and different voting.

Thinking point

Why do you think that the aims of the European Union have changed from the purely economic origins to embrace issues such as standards of living and, more recently, issues of equality and non-discrimination?

European institutions

The Commission

The Commission has responsibility for running the European Union on a day-to-day basis, and is the executive branch of the Union. It could be likened to the civil service, and has thousands of employees. The role of the Commission is as follows.

- To propose ideas for discussion to the European Parliament, and to draft formal proposals for changes in European law to the Council. Under the Treaty of Amsterdam, national Parliaments are given notice of Commission proposals six weeks before those proposals are discussed by the Council. The European Parliament may request the Commission to make a proposal to the Council.

- To implement the EU budget and take general responsibility for administration within the European Union.

- To ensure that member states obey the rules of the European Union. The Commission has the power to take a member state to the European Court of Justice for infringement of a law or failure to implement it.

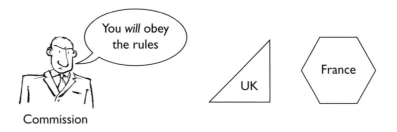

Figure 1.2

The 20 Commissioners serve for a renewable term of five years. There is one Commissioner from each of the smaller member states and two from each of the larger ones (the United Kingdom is one of these larger states). A Commissioner's duty is to serve the interests of the European Union, not the interests of an individual member state.

The European Parliament

This is sometimes known as the Assembly and, surprisingly, is not the legislative body of the European Union. It does not make law directly, but acts as a discussion forum. It is made up of over 600 Members of European Parliament (MEPs) who are elected directly every five years by the citizens of the member states. Seats are allocated to member states in proportion to their population. Issues which are proposed by the Commission are discussed by the European Parliament and are then passed back to the Commission for formal drafting.

Practical task

Find out who has been elected as your Member of European Parliament, and try to discover a little of their background. Find out what geographical area he or she represents and compare this to the area represented by your Member of Parliament.

The European Parliament has been criticised for not having any real power. However, note the following:

- It has a right to be consulted about legislation and on some matters, under the co-decision process in the Treaties, its consent is required.
- It has powers with respect to a limited proportion of the EU budget.
- It has investigative powers, and can ask questions to ensure that the Council and the Commission are fulfilling their obligations under the Treaties.

- The European Parliament can dismiss the whole Commission and it has a right of veto over new members appointed by the member states. In 1999 it exercised this right of dismissal when fraud was discovered within the Commission. The entire Commission resigned but, confusingly, all the Commissioners stayed in their jobs until a new Commission was appointed months later, and in addition, the new Commission included people who had previously resigned.

The Council

The Council is the legislative, or law-making, body. Politically, therefore, it is the most powerful of the institutions. It is composed of a representative of the government of each member state. This is often the Foreign Minister, but could be any appropriate minister. The composition for a particular meeting depends on what is to be discussed, so, for example, the Minister for Transport may attend if a transport issue was to be discussed, or the Minister of Agriculture if the debate concerned agricultural policy. The person who attends must have the authority to make decisions which will be binding on his or her country. When the heads of the governments, e.g. the Prime Ministers, meet to discuss wider or very important issues, then the Council meeting is known as a summit.

As the Council consists of people who get together only for meetings and have heavy responsibilities elsewhere, much of the day-to-day work of the Council is done by COREPER (the Committee of Permanent Representatives), a permanent group of officials. The Council tries to make policy by unanimous agreement. If this is not possible, decisions are made by majority vote or by a qualified majority. The qualified majority system gives larger states more votes than smaller states, and the use of this kind of voting was increased by the Treaty of Amsterdam. The Treaties govern whether a particular decision needs to be unanimous or a majority. In certain circumstances a member state has a power of veto when an issue is of 'very important interest' to their country.

The European Court of Justice

This court sits at Luxembourg and consists of the president plus one judge from each of the member states. All the judges sit in a full court hearing with one of the judges acting as president, but there are also hearings in chambers with fewer judges. The Treaty of Rome states that judges 'shall be chosen from persons whose independence is beyond doubt'. The Treaty also sets out the function of the European Court of Justice. It is to 'ensure that in the interpretation and application of the Treaty the law is observed'. As well as judges, the European Court of Justice (ECJ) has Advocates-General, who advise the court on the law.

Judges

Advocates-
General

European Court of Justice = 15 Judges + 9 Advocates-General

Figure 1.3

If a point of European law is involved in a case that comes before an English court it is dealt with by that court just as if it was a point of traditional English law. If there is a doubt over the meaning of a European law, or over whether it applies to the case before the court, the court may refer the issue to the ECJ. If the court responsible for hearing the case is the highest court in the national system – in the United Kingdom this is the House of Lords – then under Article 234 the court *must* refer the point of law to the ECJ. This is necessary to make sure that there is only one authoritative interpretation of each point of European law, which will bind all the courts in all member states. If the highest court in each country could make its own decisions on points of European law, there could be different interpretations in different countries, creating inconsistencies and possible unfairness.

Article 234 says:

The Court of Justice shall have jurisdiction to give preliminary rulings concerning:

(a) the interpretation of this Treaty;

(b) the validity and interpretation of acts of the institutions of the Community ...

.... Where such a question is raised before any court of tribunal of a member State, that court or tribunal may, if it considers that a decision on the question is necessary to enable it to give judgment, request the Court of Justice to give a ruling thereon.

It can be seen from the wording of the Article that it is the choice of the court, not the individual, whether to make a reference to the ECJ. The parties can request it, but not require it. Once the ECJ has decided the point of law the case is referred back to the court from which it came. The court then applies the decision of the ECJ to the issue in hand. The following is an example of a case brought by a member state and heard by the ECJ.

UK v EU Council (1996)
The UK challenged a directive on working hours, claiming it had been made under an inappropriate Article of the Treaty. The UK claimed that another Article should be used, requiring a unanimous vote by the Council rather than a majority vote. The European Court of Justice decided against the UK, upholding the legality of the directive.

As well as being the interpreter of European law, the ECJ hears cases brought by the institutions of the European Union, member states or individuals alleging infringements of European law. Cases brought by individuals may be heard by the Court of First Instance, which was created in 1988 to ease the burden on the ECJ and deals with less technical issues, largely turning on questions of fact.

In many cases, of course, the application of European law will be quite clear, and where a national court is able to interpret and apply a point of European law before it, there is no need to refer to the ECJ. This is known as the doctrine of *acte clair*. It is an important doctrine, because while Article 234 is very useful in ensuring consistent and uniform application of law, if it were used as a matter of course on every query, the ECJ would not be able to cope with the number of cases.

The value of the *acte clair* is to spare the ECJ from an impossible work load, and also to encourage national courts to improve their awareness and expertise in interpreting European law. On the other hand, there is always a risk that national courts will go too far in interpreting European law in a way which reflects national views too strongly, especially as there is no rule of binding precedent in European law as there is in English law.

Bulmer v Bollinger (1974)
Lord Denning discussed the use of this Article by English courts, and said that a reference was unnecessary where the point raised was 'reasonably clear and free from doubt'.

However, the benefit of the ECJ making the decision on a difficult or ambiguous point, rather than a national court, was stated by Bingham J as follows:

> *Customs and Excise v Samex* (1983)
> It [the ECJ] has a panoramic view of the Community and its institutions, a detailed knowledge of the treaties ... and an intimate familiarity with the functioning of the Community market which no national judge denied the collective experience of the Court of Justice could hope to achieve.

Table 1.1 A summary of the institutions of the European Union

European institution	Membership	Function
Council of Ministers	Ministers from member states	• makes policy decisions • issues regulations directives and decisions
Commission	Commissioners from member states	• day-to-day running of the European Union and can bring action on member states not complying with European law • formally proposes legislation
Parliament	Members of European Parliament elected from member states	• a discussion forum • may request legislation and amend legislation • has investigative powers, but overall powers are limited • has a right to be consulted
European Court of Justice	15 judges (one from each member state) and 9 Advocates-General to advise on the law	• rules on cases referred under Article 234 • interpretation of legislation

Practical task

Find out more about the institutions of Europe from the Internet and from CD-Roms (available in libraries and very good for reports from newspapers such as *The Times*). In particular watch for the effects of the Treaty of Nice on voting rights in the institutions.

Legislation created by European law

The Treaty of Rome is the foundation of European law (refer back to the development of the European Union). It is the fundamental treaty which forms the basic rules for the European Union and is the basis of the European laws that are in force now. The Treaty of Rome outlines the various forms of legislation which can be created as follows:

> In order to carry out their task, the Council and the Commission shall, in accordance with the provisions of this Treaty, make regulations, issue directives, take decisions, make recommendations or deliver opinions.

- *Treaties themselves are, of course, law, and as they are fundamental, are said to be a primary source and apply automatically to member states.*

The following types of law, then, are created under the Treaty, and said to be secondary sources:

- *Regulations have general application and apply to all member states.*
- *Directives can be binding on each member state to whom they are addressed, but the way in which they are implemented is left to the national authorities.*
- *Decisions are binding on those to whom they are addressed.*
- *Recommendations and opinions, more minor sources, are not binding at all, but should be considered by courts in forming their own decisions.*

Terminology

We have already used a number of new terms in European law – the types of law, for instance. However, there are some further terms which must be understood in order to read cases and Articles on European law. The main new expressions are as follows:

- European law is said to be **hard** or **soft** depending on whether it binds a national court.
- European law is said to be **directly applicable** when a person can use the rule to bring an action or defence in a national court.

  To be directly applicable a provision must:

  (a) be clear and precise;

    (b) not be subject to the choice of the member state whether to imple-
        ment it;

    (c) not need implementing measures by the member state.

- The term **vertical effect** means that an individual can use European law
  against a state or a body closely associated with a state (a body 'ema-
  nating from the state').
- The term **horizontal effect** means that an individual can use European
  law against another individual.

Treaty Articles

Treaty Articles are of direct effect, horizontally and vertically, and are hard
law (binding).

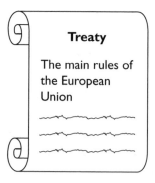

Treaty

The main rules of
the European
Union

Figure 1.4

    It was held in the case of *Van Gend en Loos v Netherlands* (1962) that a
Treaty Article could have direct effect; and in the case of *Van Duyn v Home
Office* (1975) – see page 13 below – it was said that a Treaty Article gave
right to freedom of movement. The following case shows how useful the
Treaty can be to an individual.

Macarthys v Smith (1980)
Wendy Smith was paid less than men who had previously done the
same work. She was not able to sue successfully under English law
because the men were not employed at the same time. However, under
European law her employer was held in breach of the Treaty in not
treating male and female employees equally.

The ECJ has since found a large number of Treaty provisions to have direct
effect, for example in free movement of goods and persons, and in various
aspects of discrimination.

Barber v Guardian Royal Exchange (1990)
Mr Barber was made redundant aged 52, but was not allowed to receive the company pension until 55. A woman would have received the pension at 50. The Treaty, which was directly effective, was held to prohibit sex discrimination in this way.

Directives

These are of direct effect vertically and are, therefore, said to be hard law. There is a time limit within which a directive should be implemented and, because it is the role of the state to implement a directive, if an individual suffers damages because of failure to implement, the state may be liable to the individual.

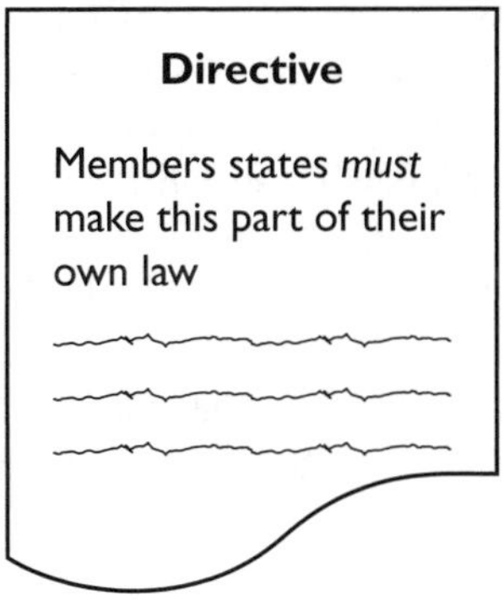

Directive

Members states *must* make this part of their own law

Figure 1.5

Francovich v Italy (1991)
A successful claim was made for failure to implement, and it was suggested that this formed a new 'Eurotort'. A business became insolvent, and a directive provided that employees of insolvent companies should be entitled to compensation for unpaid wages and salaries. The Italian government had failed to implement the directive and the ECJ held that in such circumstances the state was liable to pay damages to individuals affected by the failure.

In the following case the use of a directive is seen in refining the provisions of a Treaty.

Van Duyn v Home Office (1975)
Miss Van Duyn was refused entry to the United Kingdom on the grounds that she belonged to the Church of Scientology (the Home Secretary had previously announced that such people would not be admitted). The Treaty provides for free movement of workers, but allows

limitation to this on grounds of public policy. Directive 64/221 states that this policy will be based on personal conduct of the individual.

The ECJ held that an individual should be able to rely on this directive, against a member state, without further implementation. On this occasion the Home Secretary was justified in banning Miss Van Duyn's entry as the ban was based on personal conduct.

The vertical effect of directives is apparent in case law, and is well illustrated in the following situation.

Marshall v Southampton Area Health Authority (1986)
Helen Marshall was compulsorily retired at the age of 62. Male employees were entitled to work until they reached 65. An unimplemented directive provided for equal retirement ages for men and women. The ECJ held that Miss Marshall was entitled to rely on the directive because the defendant was, in effect, the state and it would not be fair to allow the state to defend itself by relying on its own failure to implement a directive. However, this rule only applies if the defendant is the state or an emanation of the state. The ECJ made it clear in *Marshall* that a directive cannot give an individual rights against another individual.

So, in the slightly later case of *Duke v GEC Reliance* (1988) it was held that the plaintiff could not rely on an unimplemented directive because the employer was not in any way a part of the state. Another way of putting this is to say that once the time limit for implementation has expired a directive has vertical direct effect but it does not have horizontal direct effect (it works upwards – against the state – but not sideways against other individuals or organisations).

Thinking point

Is it fair that someone working, for example, in a state hospital could enforce rights concerning equal treatment under European law, but a similar person working in a private nursing home could not do so?

Does this not contradict the idea of equality?

Of course, the decision in *Francovich* (see page 13 above) would help by giving a person the right to sue the state for damages if they sustain a loss because the state has failed to implement a directive. This ECJ decision, which obliges governments to pay money to the victims of a state's failure to implement directives, not only provides compensation for individuals but also gives governments an incentive to make sure that directives are implemented within the time limits. The Consumer Protection Act 1987 is largely the result of the effect of European directives, and is a good example of Parliament implementing a directive by passing legislation.

Thinking point

The issue of whether an individual can sue another individual or organisation is obviously an important one. Can anything be done if a directive is not being given vertical effect by a state?

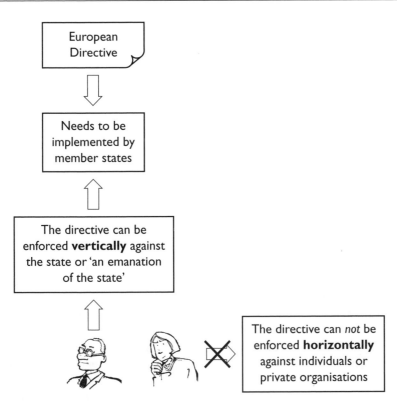

Figure 1.6

Von Colson v Kaman (1983)
The two women plaintiffs claimed that the German prison service had rejected their job applications in favour of lesser qualified men and that this was in breach of the Equal Treatment directive. The ECJ required the German state to interpret their national law in the light of the wording and purpose of the directive, even though it had not yet been implemented in Germany. This decision, then, would give rights to any employee in a prison in Germany, through an unimplemented directive.

The case of *Foster v British Gas* (1991) showed how unjust it would be if a directive was not available to an employee, just because the employing organisation had recently been privatised. It was held that the employer would be *treated as* an emanation of the state. This raises the question of what exactly is an 'emanation of the state'. It is certainly arguable that the UK system of judicial precedent (see Chapter 6) operates in such a way that once a case has been heard in court on an issue, it then applies to other cases in United Kingdom since the judges are bound, legally, to follow precedent. In the case of *Marleasing SA* (1990) it was suggested that directives should possibly be of horizontal direct effect because of the duty now on courts to interpret domestic law in the light of European law.

Figure 1.7

Regulations

Regulations put flesh on the bones of the Treaties. For example, the Treaty of Rome lays down the *principle* of free movement of workers between member states, but it is regulations that give the workers the *rights* they need to make this freedom a reality. For example, if an individual moves countries for work reasons, they have the right to the same tax and social advantages as nationals of the member state to which they have moved – such as housing and education rights. These are the things that make working in another state a practical possibility. When a regulation is passed it immediately and automatically becomes law in all member states, so it is directly applicable and is, therefore, hard law. It is said to be self-executing, so comes into effect without further national legislation. Providing that the regulation is clear and unconditional, and that no action is required by European or national authorities to give rights to individuals, it is said to be directly effective. This means that a regulation gives rights to individuals who can sue in national courts to enforce those rights.

Castelli v ONPTS (1984)
Regulation 1612/68 provides that a migrant worker is entitled to the same social and tax advantages as national workers. In this case, an Italian woman was widowed and went to live with her son in Belgium.

As she had a right to live with her son, it was decided that she was entitled to receive the payment of a guaranteed income paid to all old people in Belgium.

Note that the widow's right came from the regulation – the domestic Belgian law on the subject was irrelevant.

Decisions

Decisions are binding on those to whom they are addressed (state or individual) and are hard law. A decision is not a piece of legislation that affects people in general. It is made by the Council or the Commission and addressed to a state, individual or company. It obliges them to do whatever the decision requires. Thus, it is a method of dealing with particular situations which are seen as infringements of European law. Decisions are particularly useful in implementing European competition laws as the Commission can investigate practices of a company, or several companies, and issue a decision telling them to stop or to modify what they are doing.

Recommendations

Recommendations are not binding, but a court must take them into consideration. They are therefore said to be soft law.

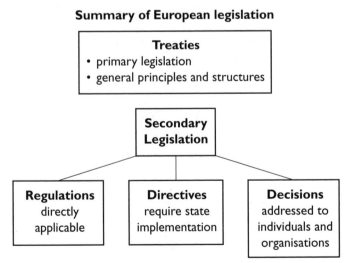

Summary of European legislation

Figure 1.8

The effects of the European Union on national sovereignty

Article 2 of the Treaty of Rome states the object of the Treaty as being:

> to promote ... a harmonious development of economic activities ... and closer relationships between states.

The idea of the European Union is that it is a supra-national body, hovering over the member states, affording them security and economic advantage. Section 2 of The European Communities Act 1972 submits the United Kingdom to following European law, and requires English law to be subject to European law. Therefore, in passing this Act it must be argued that some loss of sovereignty has occurred. However, it has happened willingly, as the Parliament which agreed to this also has the power to withdraw from the European Union if it so wished, by passing another Act.

It could also be argued that the United Kingdom has not actually lost sovereignty, but merely traded the insular nature of its sovereignty for the greater security of the European Union. After all, the United Kingdom has voting powers and representation, along with other member states.

It is now beyond doubt that European law takes precedent over domestic law, as the following case shows.

Costa v ENEL (1964)
The ECJ held the Italian courts bound by European law, saying that, 'the member states have limited their sovereign rights ... and have created a body of law which binds both their nationals and themselves'.

The overriding nature of European law is seen clearly in the following series of cases, where an injunction was allowed to be used against the Crown to prevent it from enforcing an Act which conflicted with European law.

Factortame cases (1990–2000)
The cases concern the issue of Spanish boats fishing in UK waters, the name being taken from one of the main companies involved. The Merchant Shipping Act 1988 was passed to deal with the problem of 'quota hopping' – foreign-owned boats registering in the United Kingdom simply to gain access to the UK fish quota

allocated by the European Union. The Act was designed to ensure that such boats were UK-owned and managed. Application was made by the High Court under Article 234 to see if the Act contravened Treaty provisions regarding discrimination on nationality, and an interim order made disapplying the Act provisions.

On appeal regarding the interim order, the Court of Appeal held that UK courts had no power to disapply a statute.

The case then went to further appeal to the House of Lords.

Meanwhile the ECJ held that the Act did contravene the Treaty, and ordered it to be suspended pending a full trial. In 1991 the ECJ decided that the Act was contrary to European law. Lord Bridge said:

> Some public comments ... have suggested that this was a novel and dangerous invasion by a Community institution of the sovereignty of the United Kingdom Parliament. But such comments are based on a misconception. If the supremacy within the EC of Community law over the national law of member states was not always inherent in the EEC Treaty, it was certainly well established in the jurisprudence of the Court of Justice long before the UK joined the Community. Thus, whatever limitation of its sovereignty Parliament accepted when it enacted the ECA 1972 was entirely voluntary.'

Despite a certain amount of hostility to European law amongst English judges Lord Denning suggests that we should gain inspiration from it.

Bulmer v Bollinger (1974)
'The treaty is like an incoming tide. It flows into the estuaries and up the rivers. It cannot be held back.'

The effects of membership have been widespread and practical, e.g. preventing unlawful restrictions on imports of potatoes and UHT milk and discriminatory taxation on wine, and the requiring of tachographs to be fitted in lorries. As a result of the ECJ decision in *P v S* (1996), Parliament was forced to pass the Sex Discrimination (Gender Reassignment) Regulations 1999 to allow the Sex Discrimination Act 1976 to apply to transsexuals. In the case of *Thoburn v Sunderland* (2002) a greengrocer was forced to recognise that implementing a directive to use metric weights and measures took priority over previous English statute law.

The Treaty of Nice will almost certainly result in wider membership (27 countries have applied to join the EU). European law is bound to have an increasingly important impact on English law, and a member state cannot afford to be insular in its approach.

Summary

Background
- Currently 15 member states (applications from other states pending).
- Treaty of Rome 1957 – foundation of current legal status, building on economic unity.
- UK membership based on European Communities Act 1972.

Institutions
- Commission – day-to-day management, proposes ideas for discussion in Parliament and drafts formal proposals for legislation; ensures member states obey European Union rules; implements European Union budget.
- European Parliament – discussion forum with elected members and investigative powers.
- Council of ministers – legislative body, contains representatives from members states; some work done in committee (COREPER); heads of states in council known as summit.
- European Court of Justice – the court of the European Union; one judge from each member state plus Advocates-General; hears referrals from member states under Article 234; limited role as court of first instance.

Legislation
- Treaties – fundamental, primary source, apply automatically to member states: *Macarthys v Smith* (1980), *Francovich v Italy* (1991).
- Regulations – general application, apply to all member states: *Castelli v ONPTS* (1984).
- Directives – binding on member states to whom addressed, but must be implemented: *Marshall v Southampton Area Health Authority* (1986).
- Decisions – binding on those to whom they are addressed.
- Recommendations and opinions – minor sources, not binding, should be considered.

Sovereignty
- Arguments – UK entered by statute and can therefore withdraw membership by statute; UK has full voting rights; UK is now part of more powerful body. However, general effect is that domestic law must take account of European law; if conflict arises, European law prevails: *Costa v ENEL* (1964), *Bulmer v Bollinger* (1974), *Factortame* (1990–2000).

Tasks

1   Make sure that you understand any words used in connection with European law which may be new to you, especially these:

Treaty   horizontal effect
Directive   vertical effect
Regulation   domestic law

You can check the meaning of the words in the glossary.

2   The 'composition' of a body means who the members are (not by name, but what qualifies them to be members). The 'function' of a body means what its responsibilities are and what it does. Describe the composition and function of each of the following European institutions:

(a) the Commission
(b) the European Parliament
(c) the Council of Ministers
(d) the European Court of Justice.

3   Explain how each of the following kinds of European law affects individuals in member states:

Treaties
Directives
Regulations
Decisions.

4   Consider the effect which European law may have had on English sovereignty.

5   Explain the effect on English law of an Act of Parliament which conflicts with European law.

6   Look for newspaper reports and Internet accounts about developments in the European Union following the Treaty of Nice.

2 Domestic legislative processes and institutions

The UK Parliament

The UK Parliament makes our national laws. We can use the word 'national' very loosely to mean law which applies to England and Wales, but since the growth of European law, it is now more correct to refer to domestic legislation. By 'domestic legislation' we mean laws made by Parliament in the United Kingdom, or with its authority. They are 'domestic' because they only apply within the United Kingdom, or part of it, and do not apply to other European countries. 'Parliament' is used here to mean the Parliament sitting at Westminster. This is made up of the House of Commons and the House of Lords. Both of these parts of Parliament, and the Queen, must give consent to create a new statute.

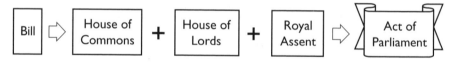

Figure 2.1

Parliament makes law for England and Wales. It can delegate powers to the Welsh Legislative Assembly. Scotland has its own Parliament to deal with some issues, while others are still governed by Parliament in London. Parliament consists of two Houses: the House of Commons and the House of Lords.

The House of Commons

The House of Commons has 659 members, known as Members of Parliament or MPs, each of whom is elected, on a simple majority of votes cast, to represent a constituency (a geographical area). Anyone can put themselves forward to be elected, but it is rare for a person who is not the candidate of one of the major political parties to succeed in becoming an MP. A general election must be held at least once every five years, but it happens more frequently than this. The Prime Minister decides when to call an election and it is timed so that people are likely to vote for the party in government at the time the election is called. If an MP dies or retires, or is otherwise unable to continue to serve, a by-election is called, where the voters in that particular MP's constituency vote for a replacement. Otherwise MPs remain in office until there is a general election. This system results in MPs having divided loyalties:

- they owe their success to the people who voted for them and they have a duty to represent everyone in the constituency;
- however, they would not have stood any chance without the support of a political party and their future political career rests on pleasing people within that party, both in Parliament and in the constituency.

The House of Commons in its modern form has existed for over a hundred years. Its roots go back much further, but the majority of the male population did not vote until the end of the nineteenth century and women did not vote on equal terms with men until the 1920s. Now, almost every British citizen over 18 has the right to vote, the exceptions being hereditary peers, prisoners and some mental patients.

The House of Lords

The second chamber has also been in existence for hundreds of years, but until recently it had not changed much during those centuries. The House of Lords was made up of over a thousand people, most of whom were:

- hereditary peers, or
- life peers.

Most of them had the right to membership because they had inherited that right. During the mid-twentieth century it was decided that it should be possible to give the right to sit in the House of Lords to individuals who had proved their worth to society in some way – sometimes in politics, sometimes in other fields. These life peers, as their name suggests, cannot pass the right to sit in the House of Lords to their children, but they become members of the House of Lords for the rest of their lifetime.

In 2001 the Wakeham Commission recommended that one-third of the members of the House of Lords should be elected rather than hold their seats by hereditary right, and that appointment should be through an independent Appointments Commission rather than the Prime Minister. In response, a Government White Paper appeared in 2001 proposing 20 per cent elected members, 20 per cent selected by the Commission and the rest nominated by political parties. This would allow the House of Lords to be seen to be democratic, but should one elected House be set against another? It could be questioned whether an elected House of Lords could effectively challenge an elected House of Commons.

Thinking point

- What problems might arise if different political parties hold majorities in the two Houses, for example, if there was Conservative majority in the House of Commons and Labour majority in the House of Lords?
- Discuss whether there is a need for a second House.

It is a good idea to focus first on what a second House is for – to keep a check on extreme ideas of the first house, and to ensure that any law passed really does reflect the needs of society generally. Assuming that there is a second House, discuss how its members should be chosen and how long each member should be entitled to sit. Should it be for a specified period or for life?

The legislative process

Acts of Parliament are created by the House of Commons, the House of Lords and the Queen, and originate in two different kinds of Bills.

Public Bills

An Act begins as a Bill, which is the word given to a formal proposal put to Parliament for discussion. Most Bills are introduced by the government and are called 'Public Bills'. The government is formed by the political party with the greatest number of MPs in the House of Commons. The most senior members of the government form a Cabinet, headed by the Prime Minister, and it is the Cabinet which decides what Bills will be put before Parliament. Each member of the Cabinet has responsibility for an area of government and for the department which runs that area of government on a day-to-day basis. Most of the work is done by civil servants, who are full-time paid officials and who generally stay with one department throughout their careers. The Cabinet minister tells the civil servants what the policy of the government is and senior civil servants will tell the Cabinet minister what needs to be done.

Between them, they agree what changes to the law are necessary and put these forward to the Cabinet as a whole. Each department has different priorities and there is never time or resources to do everything, so a Cabinet committee decides which ideas will go forward to Parliament. Once the decision to create a Bill has been made the civil servants responsible for it work with government draftsmen called Parliamentary Counsel. Parliamentary Counsel are specialists in drafting. It is their job to make sure that the Bill will mean exactly what it is intended to mean. This is more difficult than it might sound – see Chapter 5. The Bill is sent to one of the Houses (usually the House of Commons if it involves public expenditure or is at all controversial), and it will then have three Readings.

Figure 2.2

First Reading

The First Reading is a formality. The title of the Bill is read out and this informs MPs what the Bill concerns, and that it is ready and beginning its passage through Parliament.

Second Reading

The Second Reading is the most important stage politically. The minister responsible for the Bill explains its purpose to the House and the opposition spokesperson responds. There is then a general debate on the Bill and the House decides, in principle, whether it wishes to legislate in this way on this subject. If the government has a large majority in the House of Commons it would be most unusual for a Public Bill to fail to pass its Second Reading. If a Bill is not on a controversial issue – some legislation is routine or covers an issue about which there is little disagreement between politicians – then the Second Reading may be made by a Second Reading Committee. This saves the time of the House of Commons as a whole.

Committee stage

A Bill which passes its Second Reading then goes to a Committee stage. This will usually be in a Standing Committee, which is made up of about 18 MPs who have an interest in and knowledge of the subject matter of the Bill. The Committee consists of MPs from different parties in the same proportions in which those parties are represented in the Commons – so every Standing Committee will have a majority of MPs from the party in government. Their job is to look at the Bill in detail. They may make amendments which could either be accepted or rejected by the House of Commons at the Report Stage. Occasionally Bills will go to a Committee of the Whole House (just as its name suggests, a Committee of which every MP is a member, used for very important issues) or a Select Committee (which is more usually concerned with investigations into matters of government).

Third Reading

The Third Reading is, like the first, something of a formality. At this stage there can be no changes to the substance of the Bill, but errors can be corrected. It may be, for example, that something which made sense in the Bill as originally drafted no longer makes sense because other parts of the Bill have been amended. A Bill which has passed through all its stages in the House of Commons will then go through a similar process in the House of Lords. The House of Lords does not use Committees, so the Committee Stage is taken by a Committee of the Whole House. Any amendments the Lords wish to make will be effective only if they are agreed by the House of Commons.

The major function of the House of Lords is to invite the House of Commons to reconsider. If agreement is not reached, the Commons may send the Bill for Royal Assent after a year. The Lords have no power to amend Money Bills (those which are largely concerned with finance).

Royal Assent

The granting of Royal Assent is a pure formality, not even undertaken by the monarch in person. Traditionally Royal Assent is not refused, not necessarily because the Queen agrees with everything, but because the House of Commons and House of Lords act as a 'sifting' process. Whatever reaches the Royal Assent stage should reflect the general will of the people. However, the fact that Royal Assent is needed shows the historical power of the monarch, and acts as a restraint on very extreme proposals becoming law.

The legislative route

The route usually taken by a Bill is passage through the House of Commons, then the House of Lords and then Royal Assent.

A Bill that is not particularly controversial may begin in the House of Lords, then pass to the House of Commons. An example of a type of Bill that frequently does this is a Bill appended to a Law Commission Report (see Chapter 4 for an explanation of the work of the Law Commission). More surprisingly, perhaps, the Human Rights Bill was introduced into the House of Lords because it was the responsibility of the Lord Chancellor's Department, even though it introduced a very important constitutional change. Once a Bill has been through all its stages in both Houses and has received Royal Assent it becomes an Act of Parliament, so the Human Rights Bill became the Human Rights Act 1998.

The legislative route

Green Paper	discussion / consultation document
White Paper	government's proposed new law
Bill	debated and approved by the House of Commons
Bill	debated and approved by the House of Lords
Royal Assent	given by the Queen
Act of Parliament	a new law is formed

Figure 2.3

Practical task

(a) Devise a flow chart, based on Figure 2.3, showing the progress of a Bill through the legislative process.

(b) Use the flow chart to help you prepare a short presentation on the progress of a Bill. Try to find a specific example of a Bill currently passing through the process.

Private Members' Bills

So far, law created by Parliament has largely concerned issues that the government of the day wishes to deal with as a matter of policy. It is very important that there is also a way in which issues raised by the people themselves can be debated. These issues may be introduced to Parliament by individual MPs (remember, they represent the people in their constituency).

About 12 Acts are passed each year that have not been Public (government) Bills, but which were introduced as Private Members' Bills. Any MP may enter into a ballot. Names of MPs are drawn at random and those whose names come out first may introduce a Bill on any subject they choose. The Bill goes through the same stages as a Public Bill, so it does need a certain amount of government support if it is to succeed. Governments will give support to ideas they like but which might be regarded as too controversial to form the subject matter of a Public Bill. More usually, a government will agree to introduce a Public Bill on the subject once a Private Member's Bill has demonstrated that there is considerable support for the proposed change in the law. This was the case with the Protection from Harassment Act 1996, which provided specific criminal offences to deal with the problem of stalkers.

Parliamentary supremacy

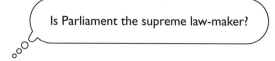

Is Parliament the supreme law-maker?

Figure 2.4

The constitutional theory is that Parliament can make any law it chooses. Certainly, the courts regard their role to be the application of what Parliament has decided to be the law to the facts of the case before the court. A person who rests their case on the argument that an Act is illegal is not likely to get very far, as can be seen from the following case.

> *Cheney v Conn* (1968)
> The plaintiff objected to his tax assessments on the ground that the government was using some of his tax for making nuclear weapons. He argued that this was illegal under the Geneva Conventions. The court applied the Finance Act 1964, under which the tax assessment was made, in preference to the Geneva Conventions Act 1957, on the basis that where there is a conflict between two Acts the later Act prevails. The judge commented: 'It is not for the court to say that a Parliamentary enactment, the highest law in this country, is illegal'.

The European Union and Parliamentary supremacy

So is Parliament supreme as a law-making body? Does it have overall control of the legislative process?

We have seen in Chapter 1 that there is a potential problem when Parliament passes an Act which conflicts with European law. The decision reached in the *Factortame* cases was that European law prevails (see p. 18). It is argued that this is because that was the intention of Parliament in passing the European Communities Act 1972.

> **Thinking point**
>
> We saw from the case of *Cheney v Conn* that when a court is faced with two Acts which conflict, it follows the later Act.
>
> Does this mean, in theory at least, that if Parliament was to pass an Act that stated 'It is the intention of Parliament that this Act prevails over any provision of European Law', then that Act would be effective and would overrule the European law?

The courts are also obliged to give effect to the clearly expressed intention of Parliament, and are most unlikely to accept an argument that Parliament has acted beyond its powers. Whatever the legal position might be, it is clear that this situation would result from a political decision and would be unlikely to arise unless the government of the day was prepared to leave the European Union. In the *Factortame* situation it seems reasonable to assume that Parliament did not realise, when it passed the Merchant Shipping Act 1988, that its provisions conflicted with European law.

It is sometimes said that Parliament has delegated the power to make law on certain subjects to the European Union. This view supports the argument that Parliament remains supreme, in that it can always take back a delegated power.

Delegated legislation and Parliamentary supremacy

Delegated legislation – where Parliament passes on some of its power to make law (see Chapter 3) – can be seen as a limitation on Parliament's powers in so far as law is being made by some other body, not by Parliament itself. It can be argued, however, that Parliament may, if it chooses, remove the power it has granted – so that Parliament still remains the supreme law-maker.

The Courts and Parliamentary supremacy

In theory, Parliament is always supreme over the courts, and if an Act is passed that conflicts with a decision of a court, the Act becomes the law. However, many points of difficulty arise when thinking about how the courts *really* view the position of Parliament.

- In areas of law governed by Acts of Parliament the judges make it very clear that it is their job to give effect to the will of Parliament, even if the judge or judges concerned do not agree with the law that Parliament has created.

- As you will see in Chapter 5 (Statutory Interpretation), the judges still have to decide what it was that Parliament intended and it is arguable that their personal views might colour their judgment on that point.

- There are large areas of law for which there are no statutes. This is known as 'common law' and is made by judges in the course of deciding cases (see Chapter 6). If Parliament has not made rules, then the judges have to do this. Some people argue that this places too much power in the hands of the judges. However, Parliament can still pass an Act to change the law made by judges, so any exercise of power by the judges is, to an extent, controlled by Parliament in so far as they can change laws they do not like.

Human rights and Parliamentary supremacy

It is argued that there are certain fundamental rights that are possessed by every human being. Logically, it might be argued that any law which took away such rights would be invalid. In English law this is not the case, and in theory Parliament could pass any law it wished to pass, however immoral that law might be. If the statute is clear, the courts would be obliged to apply that immoral law.

The Human Rights Act 1998 came into force in October 2000. This delay in bringing an Act into effect is very common. In this case, the time between the Act being given Royal Assent and when it became law was considered necessary to allow for judges to be trained and for government departments to consider the implications of the Act for their areas of responsibility. The Act makes the European Convention on Human Rights part of English law, but does not give it a status that is any higher than an ordinary Act of Parliament. A person who believes that his or her rights under the Convention have been breached by any public authority may sue and could be awarded damages, but the main aim of suing would be to obtain a declaration from the court that the public authority had acted wrongly. An example is seen here.

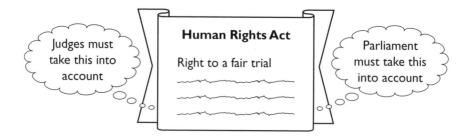

Figure 2.5

The Convention gives a right to a fair trial. A person who believed they had been denied that right in a criminal case because the procedural rules governing their case operated unfairly against them might sue under the Human Rights Act. What the claimant would really want is their conviction set aside and, perhaps, a change in the rules so that others could have fair trials. If the court found that a domestic statute contained a provision that amounted to a breach of the Convention, the Human Rights Act says that the judge may point out the conflict between domestic law and the Convention. The appropriate minister then has power under Section 10 of the Human Rights Act to change the statute using an Order in Council (a type of delegated legislation).

The minister can choose not to change the domestic law. Section 19 of the Act says that all Bills must contain a statement saying either that the Bill is compatible with the Convention or that it is not and that the intention is to pass incompatible legislation. This means that the Human Rights Act does not prevent Parliament passing laws that take away fundamental human rights. All it does is to require Parliament to address the issue of what it is doing.

Lord Hoffmann explained some of the problems of Parliamentary supremacy in a recent case.

> *R v Secretary of State for the Home Department,* ex parte *Simms and another* (1999)
>
> Parliamentary sovereignty means that Parliament can, if it chooses, legislate contrary to fundamental principles of human rights. The Human Rights Act 1998 will not detract from this power. The constraints upon its exercise by Parliament are ultimately political, not legal. But the principle of legality means that Parliament must squarely confront what it is doing and accept the political cost. Fundamental rights cannot be overridden by general or ambiguous words. This is because there is too great a risk that the full implications of their unqualified meaning may have passed unnoticed in the democratic process. In the absence of express language or necessary implication to the contrary, the courts therefore presume that even the most general words were intended to be subject to the basic rights of the individual. In this way the courts of the United Kingdom, though acknowledging the sovereignty of Parliament, apply principles of constitutionality little different from those which exist in countries where the power of the legislature is expressly limited by a constitutional document.

Political reality and Parliamentary supremacy

The House of Commons is made up of people who are voted into power. The House of Lords now has little real power. In practice, therefore, 'Parliamentary supremacy' tends to mean supremacy of the political party having for the time being a good majority in the House of Commons. The leaders of that party, the Cabinet, decide what legislation will be introduced. Members of Parliament are instructed when and how to vote by the party whips. The limit on what Parliament can do is, therefore, in reality set by the views of the Cabinet as to the best political decision. Having said that, a great deal of law is not at all political in content and similar rules would be constructed no matter which political party was in power.

In reality, whatever law is created, whether it be made by Parliament or through case law, the judges are likely to have the last say on how it is implemented. This point was made strongly in the case *R v Home Secretary ex p Anderson* (2002) when the House of Lords, sitting as a court of seven judges, stated that it is up to the courts, and not the Home Secretary, to set appropriate sentences. This follows an ongoing dispute over the lengths of sentences of life imprisonment given to murderers. The dispute is likely to end now since heed must be taken of the Human Rights Act 1998 which gives the right to a fair hearing by an impartial tribunal – likely to be interpreted as the judiciary, not a politician. This must, to some extent, weaken the sovereignty of Parliament in relation to the courts.

Summary

UK Parliament
- House of Commons – composition and role.
- House of Lords – composition and role; consider whether there is a need for a second House.

Legislative process
- Public Bills – the political impact on law-making; personnel and organisation; the three readings, committee stage and royal assent.
- The legislative route; Private Members' Bills.

Supremacy
- The constitutional theory of supremacy; the effect of European Union membership; delegated legislation; the relationship between Parliament and the courts (especially consider the role of the courts in (a) interpreting statutes, and (b) enforcing the Human Rights Act 1998.

Political issues
- The relationship between Parliament's political role and its legislative role.

Tasks

1 Find from the newspaper or the Internet a Bill that is going through Parliament at the moment.

   (a) What stage has it reached?
   (b) Is it a Public Bill or a Private Member's Bill?
   (c) What is the purpose of the Bill?

   If you can do this for one or two Bills during your course they would be good examples to show that you understand the legislative process.

2 Write a brief explanation of the following words and phrases. Use the glossary to check your answers:

legislation	Bill
constituency	controversial
hereditary	constitutional
interim	ambiguous

3 What does the expression 'Parliamentary supremacy' mean? How far is it true to say that Parliament is 'supreme'?

3   Delegated legislation

The nature of delegated legislation

One of the major problems with law-making by Parliament is the purely practical consideration of limited time. When the Cabinet decides which proposals will go forward to be drafted as Bills and put before Parliament they are not able to proceed with everything they regard as desirable – they have to prioritise. This problem with time became more pressing during the mid-twentieth century when the role of government in everyday life increased. For example, the provision of a health service, education and social services funded by taxation means that Parliament must lay down the rules, both for the services and their finance. One solution to the problem of lack of parliamentary time is to cut down on the amount of detail Parliament has to deal with.

Delegated legislation is sometimes known as secondary legislation. It is where an Act of Parliament is passed giving someone other than Parliament the power to carry out tasks. The body is then acting with the authority of Parliament.

A good example is seen in the way in which child benefit is paid. If Parliament has decided the policy issue – that child benefit will be paid to parents of all children below 16 – then it is perhaps acceptable and even desirable for the detailed rules to be drawn up by a different body, especially if that body has members who are experienced in organising the payment of social security benefits.

Other examples of delegated legislation.

- Local authorities can make by-laws for the smooth running of a particular area. The power to do this comes from the Local Government Act 1972.
- Railway operators can regulate the way in which people act while on trains under the Railways Act 1993.

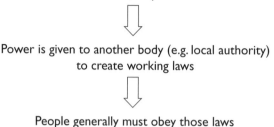

Delegated legislation

Parliament creates a 'parent' statute

Power is given to another body (e.g. local authority)
to create working laws

People generally must obey those laws

Figure 3.1

Advantages of delegated legislation

There are good reasons for Parliament delegating its legislative power to a range of bodies and individuals. The following could be seen as advantages of this system of law-making.

- Delegated legislation saves parliamentary time (probably the most important reason for using this method of law-making). Members of Parliament (MPs) are relieved of the need to spend unjustified amounts of time on routine and uncontroversial issues, and can concentrate on shaping laws needed for today's society.
- Once the broad principles of policy have been decided by Parliament, the detailed and often technical rules will be made by people who are experts in the particular field involved.
- The rules can be made, and changed, fairly quickly because they do not have to go through the parliamentary process of readings and committees in both Houses of Parliament. This speed is useful both because it allows rules to be changed as circumstances change and also because it is possible to deal with any emergencies as they happen.

Disadvantages of delegated legislation

- The major criticism of the use of delegated legislation is that it is not democratic. It could be seen as law-making by people who are not elected and therefore not directly accountable, in the way that MPs are accountable, to the electorate. This is not true, of course, if the delegated powers are given to a local authority, because this authority will be elected by local people.
- In situations where there is little accountability, there is said to be little control over the legislative process (this will be discussed in more detail shortly).

- The public are generally unaware of legislation which is created in this way.
- The Act of Parliament that gives the power to make delegated legislation, known as the 'parent Act', or 'enabling Act', often gives power to a government minister, but sometimes the rules are actually made by civil servants. This creates a further level of delegation and also conflicts with a basic principle of government – the separation of powers.

Conflict with the principle of the separation of powers

John Locke wrote in 1690 that it 'may be too great a temptation to human frailty… for the same person to have the power of making laws, to have also in their hands the power to execute them'. A Frenchman called Montesquieu took the same view in the following century. The argument is that if one group of people makes the law, a second group enforces the law and a third group decides the result of any dispute as to what the law is, then no single group of people can be in total control of society. Each group provides a check on the power of the others. Applying this principle to the United Kingdom, we have Parliament as our law-maker (the legislature), the Cabinet and civil servants as our law enforcers (the executive) and the judges to resolve disputes (the judiciary).

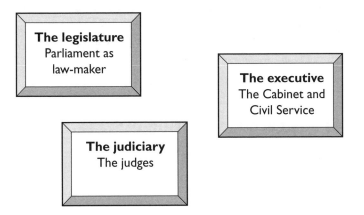

Figure 3.2

In the United Kingdom, however, the boundaries of powers are not clear cut. Many instances can be found which do not follow the idea of the separation of powers.

- Judges do make law, especially when deciding a case on a new issue, and therefore forming a precedent. They also interpret statute law which has been created by Parliament, so they greatly influence the way in which law operates in practice.

- Judges of the House of Lords have the right to sit in Parliament (although they do not generally exercise the right).

- Each government department is headed by a minister who is an MP.

- The most striking example is the role of the Lord Chancellor. He is the speaker of the House of Lords and a senior government minister, and yet he heads the judiciary and is responsible for the selection of the judges.

- As we have seen above, delegated legislation gives power to a government department or local authority to create a law, but it is then that same department or authority which is responsible for enforcing the laws it has just created.

Thinking points

It is not suggested that there is at present any aim of corruption or assumption of control, but the accusation could be made that the opportunity exists.

On the other hand there is some argument for these instances of apparent lack of control, for example it can be argued that it is necessary to have a government minister responsible for each government department, to make the departments accountable to Parliament – the minister has to answer questions put by MPs about his department.

Equally, there are times when judges make law and do it very well – see Chapter 6 on judicial precedent.

The role of the Lord Chancellor, however, is much more controversial – see Chapter 12 on the judiciary.

Types of delegated legislation

There are three kinds of delegated legislation:

- statutory instruments
- by-laws
- Orders in Council.

Statutory instruments

Statutory instruments are drafted by government departments. The power to create these laws will have been given to the minister who heads the department by the parent Act. They may also be referred to as 'ministerial regulations'. The parent Act will lay down the procedure that must be followed to bring the statutory instrument into force. There is often a duty to consult various named organisations, and then one of two procedures will be followed.

1   The normal procedure is the **negative resolution procedure**. The statutory instrument is laid before Parliament for a period of 40 days. If an MP objects to the contents of the statutory instrument the House (it may be either the Commons or the Lords), or a Standing Committee, will debate the issue and may pass a negative resolution, which will make the statutory instrument void. The statutory instrument becomes law from the date on which it is laid before Parliament – so it is possible for a statutory instrument to be law for a while before it is annulled.

2   If the power given by the parent Act is controversial, Parliament may state within the Act that the **affirmative resolution procedure** must be used. Here, the statutory instrument will become effective only if one or both Houses (as specified in the parent Act) passes an affirmative resolution.

Statutory instruments are commonly used to change regulations made under Acts such as the Road Traffic Acts and the Health and Safety at Work Act, which govern fields where there are technological, economic or other changes occurring all the time. The statutory instrument is a common method of implementing European directives.

By-laws

Parliament may give local authorities, or other bodies, the right to make law in respect of a certain area or a certain activity. The purpose of this is to allow the making of rules to suit local circumstances, for example a local council can pass by-laws to make detailed provisions with regard to car parking or the control of dogs in parks. Similarly, it is usually through by-laws that railway operators regulate behaviour on trains and at stations. By-laws have to be approved by the relevant minister.

Orders in Council

Parliament may choose to delegate the power to make changes of constitutional or other great importance to the Privy Council. This is a body of senior ministers, past and present, that meets with the monarch, and is useful as a means of bringing in powers in an emergency situation. One common use of Orders in Council is to bring an Act, or part of an Act, into effect. Few statutes or sections of statutes become law on the day they receive the Royal Assent. Most statutes provide for at least some sections to come into effect on a date to be appointed by the relevant minister.

Controlling delegated legislation

Since delegated legislation is made by bodies other than Parliament, it is important that some control exists over it. This control can be safeguarded by Parliament or by the courts.

Practical task

Find some examples of delegated legislation. Try to find:

(a) a statutory instrument

(b) an Order in Council

(c) a by-law.

Statutory instruments can be found in the reference section of larger libraries. Orders in Council will be found in the same place because they are governed by the same rules on publication. By-laws can be spotted in a range of public places (railway stations may be a good starting point).

    Explain what each piece of delegated legislation is about and note down the Act under which it is made.

Parliamentary control

There are various ways in which Parliament could be said to retain some control over delegated legislation.

- Parliamentary control over delegated legislation lies first of all in the careful creation of the original parent statutes, so that opportunities for abuse are not created. Sometimes a statute gives a minister very wide powers, such as the power to change a provision in the Act itself through the use of delegated legislation. For example, Section 8 of the Access to Justice Act 1999 provides that the Community Legal Service will be governed by a code when deciding whether to give legal advice to an individual. It sets out a range of criteria to be included in the code, plus 'such other factors as the Lord Chancellor may by order require the Commission to consider'. Thus, criteria laid down by Parliament can be added to at a later date without reference to Parliament.

- Parliament also has some control over statutory instruments in the two procedures by which these instruments are created, the negative and (affirmative) resolution procedures (see above).

- Thousands of statutory instruments are created each year. The Joint Committee on Statutory Instruments, which has members from the House of Commons and the House of Lords, scrutinises statutory instruments and draws the attention of Parliament to any statutory instrument which:

  (a) imposes a tax on the public;

  (b) is made under an Act which states that the statutory instrument cannot be challenged in the courts;

  (c) is designed to be retrospectively effective, although this is not provided for in the parent Act;

(d) has been delayed in publication or in laying before Parliament;

(e) may be outside the powers, or an unusual use of the powers, conferred by the parent Act;

(f) needs clarification;

(g) is badly drafted.

In this way, statutory instruments that are defective in some way are less likely to escape detection. The volume of statutory instruments is, nevertheless, too great to allow the Joint Committee to look at every statutory instrument.

- Having delegated power, Parliament may, of course, withdraw power. This is really the ultimate constraint on abuse of delegated power.

Control by the courts

An individual who believes that a piece of delegated legislation goes beyond the powers given by Parliament may challenge that legislation, provided he or she is affected by it. The courts will not deal with hypothetical questions, so there is a rule that any person who brings a claim must have a personal interest in it. Any delegated legislation which is made by a body which has exceeded its powers is said to be *ultra vires* (beyond one's powers) and therefore void.

The following are examples of challenges to delegated legislation made through the courts.

Kruse v Johnson (1898)
It was decided that a by-law that is 'manifestly oppressive' will be void. The defendant in this case had been charged with singing hymns in the street, contrary to by-laws.

DPP v Hutchinson (1990)
The by-laws under which women were prosecuted for entering Greenham Common RAF base were held to be beyond the powers given by the Military Lands Act 1892 because they prohibited entry onto common land. It was argued that if the by-laws had been properly drafted they could have been within the powers given by the Act and the prosecutions would have been valid. The House of Lords held that the court had the power to sever (take out) an unlawful part of a by-law or other piece of delegated legislation, leaving the remainder of it valid, if after severance the piece of legislation remained unchanged in its purpose and effect. This was not possible with the by-laws in this case, and the House of Lords

decided that they were, therefore, void. This meant that all the women who had been prosecuted over many years during the Greenham Common campaign had their convictions quashed.

Boddington v British Transport Police (1998)
The House of Lords held that a defendant to criminal charges could argue that the by-law under which he had been charged was void. Boddington was caught smoking on a train where smoking was not permitted. He argued that prohibiting smoking throughout a train went beyond the power given under by-law 20 of the British Railways Board By-laws 1965, made under s.67(1) Transport Act 1962. While the House of Lords upheld the smoking ban as lawful, they made it clear that challenging the validity of a piece of delegated legislation can be a good defence to a criminal charge. They also made it clear that it makes no difference whether the allegation is that the powers given by Parliament have been exceeded or the procedure for creating the delegated legislation has not been followed correctly. Either argument can be raised as a defence to a criminal charge.

R v Secretary of State for Education and Employment, ex parte National Union of Teachers (2000)
Under the powers within the Education Act 1996, the Secretary of State devised a new structure for teachers' pay, including a system of appraisal and promotion. This was brought in quickly with only four days for views to be obtained from interested parties. It was held by the court that the procedure was unfair and therefore beyond the powers given under the statute.

Summary

Nature • The need to delegate (time, practicality, etc.); how delegated legislation operates; (parent Act with powers given to another body); give examples, such as local government, railways; advantages and disadvantages; conflict with the separation of powers.

Types • Statutory instruments – negative resolution procedure and affirmative resolution procedure, with examples of when used, by-laws, orders in council.

Control • The need for control; methods of control.

   • Parliamentary control – with examples.

   • Control by the courts – with cases.

Tasks

1 Write a brief explanation of the following words and phrases. Use the glossary to check your answers.

electorate   void
policy   scrutinise
annulled   severance
ultra vires   separation of powers

2 Make a list of the advantages and disadvantages of delegated legislation. Expand on each point in your list, so that it becomes an argument for or against the use of delegated legislation. Try to illustrate each point in your argument with an example.

3 Describe how use of delegated legislation is controlled, both

(a) by Parliament, and

(b) by the courts.

How effective is each type of control?

4   Influences upon Parliament and law reform

What causes Parliament to change the law? There are many different influences upon Parliament. Some come from bodies created for the purpose of addressing the need for law reform, such as the Law Commission and Royal Commissions. Others come from bodies formed to press for change in the law on a particular issue or with respect to a particular group of people, such as pressure groups and interest groups. The judiciary influences the development of the law, particularly in speeches made by judges who have a high profile and reputation. Finally, there are the more subtle pressures that are brought to bear on the individuals who are the members of both Houses of Parliament.

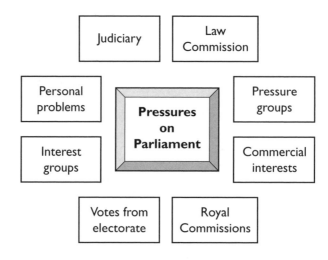

Figure 4.1

The Law Commission

Composition and function

The Law Commission was established by the Law Commissions Act 1965. There are, in fact, two Law Commissions, one for England and Wales and one for Scotland. Here, when we refer to 'The Law Commission' we mean the one for England and Wales, because that is the legal system with which this book is concerned. The Law Commission is important as it is the only full-time, permanent, publicly-funded body established for the purpose of reforming the law. It consists of five Commissioners, who are appointed to work full-time, one of them being a High Court judge to chair proceedings. The other four Commissioners may consist of solicitors, barristers and academic lawyers, thus obtaining a spread of backgrounds and views on the state of the law. Each of them is appointed for a term of five years (and may serve two terms) except for the judge, whose term is for three years. They have a staff of lawyers and administrators, and good law graduates are recruited to work for a year as research assistants.

The Law Commission has a duty under the 1965 Act to :

> keep under review all the law … with a view to its systematic development and reform, including in particular the codification of such law, the elimination of anomalies, the repeal of obsolete and unnecessary enactments, the reduction of the number of separate enactments and generally the simplification and modernisation of the law.

The Law Commission may be requested by the Lord Chancellor or other minister to consider a particular area of law in need of reform (this was the case with the recent report which led to legislation abolishing the 'year and a day' rule from the definition of murder). Equally it may select a range of projects after consulting with bodies such as the Bar, the Law Society and representatives of academic lawyers, and then produce a programme of projects. A new programme is produced every four to five years. The current one is the Seventh Programme, published in June 1999 and designed to run into 2001/2002 (see Figure 4.2).

**The Seventh Programme
of the Law Commission**

Includes the following subjects, among others:

- damages for personal injury
- limitation periods
- capacity to consent
- bail
- partnership
- assisting and encouraging crime
- easements.

Figure 4.2

The criteria by which the Law Commission decides what to put into its programme are:

- the importance of the issues;
- availability of resources – expertise and funding;
- suitability of the issues to be dealt with by the Commission.

Examples of recent projects cover a wide range of diverse subjects including: gene therapy, fraud, tobacco advertising, data protection, sentencing and stalking.

Projects can take much longer than the period of one programme, so topics 'roll over' from one programme to the next. In addition, the Law Commission may, during the course of a programme, have to deal with an issue of law that becomes very important either because the issue has come before courts or through the pressure of other events. The Computer Misuse Act 1990, introducing new criminal offences relating to the misuse of computers, is an example of legislation that was created following a report of the Law Commission, which arose because of fast development in technology in society. It is quite likely over the next few years that the Law Commission will research and report on issues arising when a court makes a declaration of incompatibility under the Human Rights Act 1998 (see Chapter 2, page 31).

The Law Commission has a budget of about £4 million each year. About two-thirds of its reports from the period 1966–99 have been implemented subsequently in full or in part. However, the record has not been consistent. In the early days of the Commission, most of its reports resulted in legislation. Then the rate slowed down, reaching a low point in 1990 when not a single report resulted in a change in the law. There has since been a backlog of reports awaiting implementation by Parliament, mainly due to government unwillingness to find parliamentary time. At the end of 2000 the Law Commission reported that 21 of its reports were currently awaiting implementation. Reports awaiting a response cover a wide range of topics, from liability for psychiatric illness (published in March 1998) to the recent report on the double jeopardy rule in criminal law. The wide range of current issues under discussion can be found on the Commission's web site (http://www.lawcom.gov.uk/), and covers both civil and criminal law.

The work of considering the reform needed is done by teams of lawyers and research assistants, each headed by a Law Commissioner. The first job is to research the existing law. Then a consultation paper is published, with recommendations for change. The Law Commission invites anyone who is interested to respond to the consultation paper and then prepares its report. If a change to the law is proposed, a draft Bill is added to the report. The drafting is done by Parliamentary Counsel working with the Law Commission. Law Commission consultation papers and reports are very thorough and written in a style that makes them easy to understand, even when the issues are complex. This is because many of the interested parties will not be lawyers but people whose work or lives would be changed by the proposals if they should become law.

These authors are aware that they are not writing only for lawyers. Within the Law Commission's reports are excellent accounts of the law, suggestions for change and arguments for and against the proposed changes.

Practical task

1 Read the following extract from the Law Commission's report 2000.

The Commission's recommendations for law reform will have a profound practical effect on the legal rights, duties and liabilities of a large number of people – but only if they are implemented by Parliament. We can make recommendations, but only Parliament can change the law. So far, however, more than two-thirds of the Commission's law reform reports have been implemented, and a number await the Government's reactions, or parliamentary time. As a result of the Commission's ongoing work, large areas of the law have been the subject of systematic investigation and improvement. Antiquated laws have been abolished, and new remedies devised appropriate for the times in which we live. Much has already been done, but there is still much more to do.

   (a) Explain in your own words the role of the Law Commission.

   (b) Consider some of the problems of reforming the law which are referred to in the report.

2 Use the Internet to find the Law Commission website at:

   http://www.lawcom.gov.uk/

   You will find a range of reports. Choose one from the current programme and summarise part of it.

Codification

In addition to this work on reform in particular areas, the Law Commission is proceeding with its long-term objective of codifying the criminal law. The *Draft Criminal Code* was published in 1985. It still makes good reading for students of criminal law and was an attempt to put the whole of the criminal law into one document. Where there were doubts about the meaning of the law, a rule was laid down by the code – but the main objective of a code is simply to put all the law on a topic in one document.

The *Draft Criminal Code* did not become law, mainly because parliamentary time was not allocated to it. The Law Commission has attempted to overcome this problem by splitting the work into smaller 'parcels', which are more likely to be given the time needed.

Consolidation and revision

The work on consolidation and statute law revision is less controversial. This is the 'elimination of anomalies, the repeal of obsolete and unnecessary enactments, the reduction of the number of separate enactments and generally the simplification and modernisation of the law' referred to in the Law Commissions Act 1965. The reports in these areas have generally been implemented. The Jellicoe procedure is used to implement these Bills. This is a shortened parliamentary procedure used for Bills that are not controversial.

Difficulties do occur, however, in areas where the law is developing more quickly. For example, the Powers of the Criminal Courts (Sentencing) Act was passed as a consolidating Act in 2000, only to be changed by the Criminal Justice and Courts Services Act 2000 within a matter of months (see Chapter 11 on sentencing).

Other aspects of law reform

The judges both influence the development of the law and act as reformers to a limited extent. Whenever a judge makes a decision which overrides a decision in a lower court, or using the Practice Statement powers in the House of Lords (see Chapter 6), the law is being reformed in some way. There are obvious difficulties here as the need for reform may be great, but the chance of a suitable case passing through the court at an appropriate level is slim. So, although case law is a useful method of reforming the law on some occasions, it is not consistent.

Judges, however, clearly make considerable use of Law Commission publications. When a judge has to decide on issues of law, considerable research is undertaken. It is very helpful to have the law and the arguments set out in one document, written in the spirit of research by someone totally independent from the case the judge is hearing. The following case gives a good example of this situation.

Kleinwort Benson Ltd v Lincoln City Council (1998)
The House of Lords was considering a well-established rule of the law of contract, that a payment made under a mistake of law would not be recoverable. The House decided to overturn that rule, making rather controversial use of their power under the Practice Statement of 1966 (see Chapter 6), and acknowledged studying the Law Commission's consultation paper *Restitution of Payments made under a Mistake of Law* in coming to their decision.

There have been other bodies set up to consider law reform. The Law Reform Committee was formed in 1952 to consider references from the Lord Chancellor on matters of civil law needing reform. The Law Reform Committee has been responsible for important pieces of legislation such as the Occupiers' Liability Act 1957 and the Latent Damage Act 1986, but its members only sit part-time and it has been rather overshadowed by the work of the Law Commission. The Criminal Law Revision Committee, formed in 1957 and last active in 1986, is a similar part-time body, working in the area of criminal law. It was responsible for the Theft Act 1968.

Royal Commissions

The Law Commission is a permanent body, given the duty of keeping the whole of the law under review. Having reported on one issue, it moves on to the next: indeed, it is constantly working on several projects at any one time. In contrast, Royal Commissions are set up to consider one area of law. When they have reported their job is finished and the Royal Commission is at an end. They are often referred to by the name of their chairman – for example, the Pearson Commission, the Phillips Commission.

The members of a Royal Commission are appointed from a range of people with expertise in the subject under consideration. They work part-time, continuing with their other jobs, so that a Royal Commission can take months or years to investigate and to report. Royal Commissions may have research done on their behalf by universities. For example, the Runciman Commission (the Royal Commission on Criminal Justice that reported in 1993) commissioned 22 research projects on various topics connected with the criminal justice system from academic lawyers.

Royal Commissions produce thoughtful and thorough reports but, just as is the case with the Law Commission, Parliament is under no obligation to do anything once the Royal Commission has reported. Some Royal Commissions have led to extensive legislation, such as the Phillips Commission's report in 1981 which led to the Police and Criminal Evidence Act 1984, providing a codification of the law on police powers.

At other times, a Royal Commission's report has been almost totally ignored. For example, there were few changes to the law following the report of the Royal Commission on Civil Liability and Compensation for Personal Injury (the Pearson Commission) in 1978. Also, Parliament may choose to implement some proposals of a Royal Commission, while rejecting others. The Runciman Commission's report was followed by some substantial legislation implementing many of its proposals, but Parliament restricted the defendant's right to remain silent, even though the Runciman Commission had recommended that no change in the law should be made.

Figure 4.3

Of course, a Royal Commission may also decide that the law is not in need of much change. This was the case with the Benson Commission (the Royal Commission on Legal Services) which reported in 1979.

The Civil Service

Government departments are staffed by civil servants. Each department has a minister as its political head. If there is seen to be a need for a change in the law in respect of the department's activities it is the civil servants who prepare either a Green Paper or a White Paper.

Green Papers

A Green Paper is a consultative document. It says, in effect, 'We think this is a collection of good ideas – what do you think?' Anyone who is interested can respond. For example, the Law Society and the Bar Council might both respond to a Green Paper that proposed changes to the law that affects the way the legal profession operates or is financed. Similarly, a Green Paper issued by the Department for Education and Employment might trigger responses from the teaching unions and employers' organisations.

White Papers

A White Paper is a statement of policy. The department is saying, 'This is how we propose to change the law'. Sometimes it follows a Green Paper and may reflect responses to the Green Paper. Sometimes only a White Paper is issued.

The Civil Service is very influential because its members stay in their jobs regardless of who is in government, developing expertise and a sense of what is achievable by way of reform and what is not, or, perhaps more accurately, what is not possible within the limits of a budget.

The people who produce policy documents are powerful because they set the scene for the new law. A Green Paper or, to a lesser extent, a White Paper, will tend to generate responses that are limited to approval or disapproval of the ideas put forward. It is unlikely that a response will provide a whole new framework for the law.

Political considerations

The House of Commons, by far the more powerful of the two Houses, is composed of politicians. They do not make decisions solely on the basis of what the best solution to a legal problem will be; they consider other factors, not least among which is the wish to stay in power. As was noted in Chapter 2, power really rests with the senior members of the political party which has a majority in the House of Commons. They decide their legislative programme with the primary aim of winning the next election.

This means that:

- The government may feel able to do necessary but unpopular things shortly after an election (when the need to win votes is at its lowest).
- As the next election draws nearer the government will be more careful to court public opinion, only creating law that is likely to be popular among voters.

The most noticeable example of this trend is the annual budget, which sets out the way in which the government plans to collect money and spend it on behalf of the country. Tax increases tend to be made early in a government's five-year life, tax cuts towards the end.

At the start of an election campaign each political party produces a manifesto, which outlines what they plan to do if they are elected to form the next government. Some of these promises to the electorate are fulfilled, but it is noticeable that ministers and governments come to see things in a different light once they are in power. To be fair, this may be because they have better quality information than they did while in opposition, but it is also true to say that the party in government has responsibility for the consequences of its actions, whereas the party in opposition can afford to criticise and make suggestions that are not particularly practical.

An example of a manifesto proposal for change that did not survive was the Labour party proposal for a Judicial Appointments and Training Commission, made in its 1997 manifesto but abandoned soon after its election success.

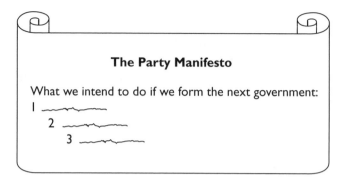

Figure 4.4

Public opinion

The politicians in the House of Commons need to be aware of what voters are thinking. In theory, the government represents the population, and any changes brought about need the general support of the country. So, how can the politicians find out the will of the people? Political parties commission opinion polls from time-to-time and each party has its local organisation, whose members can feed ideas and opinions to the national party. The problem is that party members are a small minority of the electorate as a whole and the other major sources of public opinion also tend to be formed and reflected by very small groups of people.

Practical task

Try to attend a local 'clinic' – a question session – run by your Member of Parliament, and ask how they ensure as far as possible that the views of the people in their constituency are heard.

The news media

Newspapers make a considerable impact on what ordinary people think because they are a major source of information and will often provide a very partisan view of an issue. The danger is that a single wealthy newspaper proprietor can use a newspaper to put their own views to a very large readership. There is less danger of this happening through the media of radio and television because the major companies have an obligation to present balanced argument.

Practical task

Buy, or read in your library, four newspapers for the same day. Find a story that is covered by all four newspapers and compare the coverage. Do some accounts give more details than others? Do the papers all distinguish clearly between fact and opinion? Is there any attempt to produce a balanced argument?

Pressure groups

If a group of people share a view about how the law should be changed they can work together to convince Parliament (which, for practical purposes, means convincing the government of the day) to change the law. Sometimes a pressure group will be formed to deal with one issue. It is quite common, for example, for local residents to form a pressure group to campaign for a by-pass to be built around their town. Once the by-pass is built or every avenue has been explored and a by-pass is refused, the group disbands.

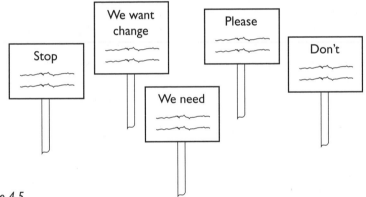

Figure 4.5

Sometimes a pressure group is a more permanent body with a wider agenda in a particular area. Such permanent groups tend to pursue a high profile campaign on a particular issue but remain in existence and continue working between major campaigns. A group wishing to pursue a particular issue may find it very useful to attach themselves to such a permanent body as it will have structures and resources in place and considerable expertise in running campaigns.

During the debate on fox hunting, those who support hunting have seen the advantage of working through the Countryside Alliance which has wider interests within country matters.

Pressure groups collect information and formulate arguments. They may wish to seek public support by raising public awareness of the issues, and this is the major reason for holding public meetings and demonstrations.

They may also advertise in newspapers and magazines and mail pamphlets to people who may be interested in their ideas.

Practical task

Look in local and national newspapers for an example of a pressure group. Identify:

(a) what it wants to achieve

(b) how it pursues its objectives.

The real targets for pressure groups are politicians and civil servants or local government officers. The purpose of rousing widespread public interest is to convince these people that there is a considerable body of opinion on the side of the pressure group. Large pressure groups will have formal or informal links with politicians and civil servants. Smaller groups may use a public relations organisation to make those contacts for them. The purpose of these activities is to get the pressure group's aim on to the political agenda so that politicians believe that the change being proposed is what a significant number of people want.

Pressure groups which are well organised can be very successful. The poll tax was abolished because it became unworkable as a result of concerted campaigns against it. Greenpeace and Friends of the Earth have raised public awareness on environmental issues to the extent that no government can afford to ignore the environmental consequences of its policies. Professional organisations operate as pressure groups and are, therefore, often consulted by governments before changes are made.

Summary

Law Commission	• Origins, composition and role (only permanent, full-time, government-funded body involved in law reform); duties under Law Commissions Act 1965; criteria for including issues in programme; current issues for reform programme; procedures for reform; examples of reform by this method; codification, consolidation; measure of success of Law Commission (many reports not implemented).
Other methods of law reform	• Reform via case law (difficult because of reliance on a suitable case) and via statute (difficult because of (a) lack of parliamentary time and (b) areas of reform often concern issues which are not high on the government's political agenda).

Royal Commissions	• Individual groups set up on a one-off basis to investigate a specific issue, e.g. Runciman Commission (on criminal justice) and Pearson Commission (on compensation for personal injury).
Civil Service	• Its role in preparing consultative documents – Green Papers and White Papers.
Politics	• The political issue of whether a proposal is debated, lack of willingness to legislate near to an election, budget matters, etc.
Public opinion	• The effect of the media and pressure groups on law reform.

Tasks

1   Write a brief explanation of the following words.

enactment	codify
incompatibility	consolidate
criteria	academic lawyer

Use the glossary to check your answers.

2   Use the Internet to find a Law Commission report on some aspect of an area of law that you will be studying. List the recommendations and keep your notes. You can use them as an example of reform, and they will also be useful when you study the area of law concerned.

3   When you study the criminal justice system you will be concerned with many issues that were discussed by the Runciman Commission. Then do one of the following:

(a) If you have already studied this topic, find what recommendations were made and which were implemented.

(b) If you have yet to study this topic, make a list of five of the issues covered by the Runciman Commission.

4   Consider how much influence the Law Commission, Royal Commissions, the news media and pressure groups exercise over Parliament.

(a) Which do you think exercises the most influence?

(b) Would your answer be the same whatever the issue, or do you think Parliament pays different amounts of attention to different bodies depending on the issue?

5   Statutory interpretation

Civil cases come before the courts because there is a disagreement between the parties either:

- as to what has happened (a matter of fact); or
- as to what rules apply to the situation (a matter of law).

Often, the parties disagree about both. Criminal cases are usually about questions of fact, but the more important cases legally are those concerning the meaning of the law. Courts have two roles, therefore: to decide issues of fact and to decide points of law.

In criminal cases the issues of fact are sometimes decided by a jury, but points of law are always decided by a judge or, in magistrates' courts, by magistrates. In civil cases, where use of a jury is very rare, a judge decides both issues. The judge will have the benefit of argument from both sides as to what the law is and will have had the opportunity to do some research.

Two major sources of English Law – European Law and Acts of Parliament – and the considerable quantities of delegated legislation, all consist of attempts to express the law accurately and concisely in a binding form.

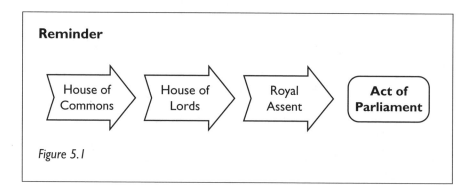

Reminder

House of Commons → House of Lords → Royal Assent → **Act of Parliament**

Figure 5.1

Once a Bill has passed through Parliament and has received the Royal Assent, it expresses the will of Parliament and becomes law. It is then the role of the judges sitting in courts to apply that law to situations arising in everyday life, so when a dispute arises over the meaning of a statute, it is up to the judges, not Parliament, to decide how the statute applies. This is what we mean by the interpretation of statutes. It is saying exactly what the language of a statute means.

The problems of interpreting statutes

It seems fair to assume that if the legislation has been carefully drafted by lawyers, other lawyers should be able both to understand what the legislation means and to apply the law to the facts before the court in order to come to a decision. Yet, if it was that easy, very few cases would ever come to court except on arguments about the facts.

Thinking point

What do you think makes the written law so unclear that the parties to a dispute can each have a valid but different view of what the law is?

Many explanations may be suggested for the problems in understanding exactly what Parliament intended to state in its statutes. Here are some suggestions, but you may think of other ideas of your own to add to the list.

- Language is not a precise tool. Although there are rules on grammar and punctuation, writing tends to be more of an art than a science. Words often take their meaning from their context, so that there are shades of meaning and sometimes quite different meanings for the same word. Take a word such as 'park'. Does it bring to mind an expanse of grass, or tarmac, or water, or forest? The answer depends on the context in which the word is used. If Parliament were to prohibit vehicles from entering parks, would we expect a vehicle for a disabled person to be banned, or a child's bicycle, or a skateboard? These are all open to debate, depending on our interpretation of the word 'vehicle'. This did arise, in fact, in the case of *Twining v Myers* (1982), where the court had to decide whether roller skates amounted to a 'vehicle'.

Twining v Myers (1982) – did roller skates amount to a 'vehicle'?

Figure 5.2

- The meaning of words changes over time – and many statutes remain in force for decades or even centuries. The Offences Against the Person Act 1861, for example, uses words such as 'maliciously' and 'grievous' which would either not be used today or, if they were, would be understood to mean something different from the meaning they would have been understood to have in 1861. When the Telegraph Act 1869 was passed the telephone had not been invented, so in subsequent cases it was necessary to extend certain provisions of the Act to cover telephone messages.

- The drafting of the legislation may have been hurried, and consideration by the legislature may have been incomplete. This is particularly likely to cause problems if the provision is not a controversial one – nobody challenges the wording because everyone is happy with the purpose of the legislation and this makes them much less inclined to look for problems with the language used. The Dangerous Dogs Act 1991 was passed quickly to deal with a perceived danger from pitbull terriers. In practice, however, it is a difficult Act for courts to apply because its wording is unclear.

Figure 5.3

- Legislation may come to be applied in situations not envisaged by the legislators. This can happen simply because it is not possible to foresee everything that might happen in the future, perhaps because of social or technological change. In *Royal College of Nursing v DHSS* (1981) (see page 67) the issue was whether a method of abortion was illegal. When the Abortion Act 1967 was passed it had been envisaged that there would be a doctor carrying out surgery, whereas by 1981 nurses were able to bring about the same result through drugs.

- In an Act, Parliament is communicating its intention to lawyers and the public generally, just as one person would in a letter to another, or as the manufacturer of a game would in a set of rules. So Acts of Parliament, apart from merely stating the law, are essentially a form of communication. In an ordinary conversation between two people, ambiguities may arise, and these problems increase in proportion to the importance and complexity of the topic being discussed. This is all the more likely to arise in interpreting something as important and wide-reaching as an Act of Parliament.

- Unlike a conversation between two people, there is no recourse to the original speaker when problems arise – no opportunity to say, 'Excuse me, but I didn't quite follow. What exactly did you mean by that?' If confusion arises in a written letter from a friend, it is not very difficult to write back and ask for more information. It is slightly more difficult with the rules of a game, and unless it is possible to contact the manufacturer and enquire about the unforeseen problem, the players would be forced to make up their own extensions to the rules. This takes us a little closer to the problems of interpreting statutes. No immediate opportunity exists for the courts to request an explanation from Parliament, as:

(a) it is a matter of practical policy not to put direct questions to Parliament;

(b) it is unlikely that, when a problem arises, exactly the same members within Parliament would be available to be questioned.

We therefore have a problem of *communication*, similar to that of normal communication in everyday life, but with a few added difficulties.

- The way in which we interpret, or understand the meaning of, any communication depends on who we are and what our past experiences have been. Professor Michael Zander once said in a lecture that we are all 'programmed by a million pre-conceptions', and it is these previous experiences and ideas which determine how we understand words that we hear. The judge and the two parties involved in a dispute in court may all have had different experiences, and therefore will interpret the statute in a different way.

Figure 5.4

Problems can arise, therefore, when a judge has to decide whether a particular piece of legislation applies to the situation before the court. How should the judge deal with the problem?

Presumptions

A judge begins by assuming certain things. These will be taken to be true unless a good argument is given to demonstrate that the presumption should not apply. The presumptions are:

- that the common law has not been changed – unless the Act shows a clear intention to change it;
- that *mens rea* is required in criminal cases (see Chapter 14);
- that Parliament has not changed the law retrospectively (that is, that the statute does not affect past acts, to make illegal something that was legal at the time it was done).

Rules of language

The judge will also apply certain rules of language:

- *Ejusdem generis* (of the same kind). If a list is followed by general words, the general words are interpreted in the context of the list.

Powell v Kempton Park Racecourse (1899)
The words 'other place' were held to mean 'other indoor place' because the list referred to a 'house, office, room or other place' and 'house', 'office' and 'room' are all indoors.

- *Expressio unius exclusio alterius* (the expression of one excludes others). If there are no general words at the end of a list, only things in the list are covered by the legislation.
- *Noscitur a sociis* (known by the company it keeps). Words are generally interpreted in the context of the Section and the Act as a whole.

The technical rules – a reminder

Presumptions

(Remember that these are only a starting point)	• No change to the common law
	• *Mens rea* required in criminal law
	• Statutes are not retrospective

Rules of language

Ejusdem generis	• General words following a list are interpreted in the context of the list
Expressio unius	• Where particular words are expressed, others are excluded
Noscitur a sociis	• Words are interpreted in context

Figure 5.5

Approaches to interpretation and the Human Rights Act

Even by applying the presumptions and the rules of language just explained, judges may still take different approaches when trying to decide what the words of a statute mean. Traditionally, there have been three 'rules' of interpretation (see below), known as the literal rule, the golden rule and the mischief rule – but they are not strictly rules, as a judge may decide which one to adopt.

Thinking point

The choice of approach is partly governed by the judge's view of the role and the process of interpretation. Should it be the task of the judge to decide in a mechanical way what any particular words mean, regardless of the consequences, or should there be an obligation to make sense of the words or even to reach a just decision in the case?

Many judges would agree that they begin with the literal rule and move on to the others if this would give a result which is unsatisfactory in some way, but there is now a new approach which all judges are obliged to take and which overrides the traditional approaches insofar as it is laid down by Parliament.

The Human Rights Act 1998 will have an increasingly important impact on how judges interpret statutes. It says in Section 3 that judges must read all primary and secondary legislation in a way that is compatible with the European Convention on Human Rights (ECHR). This means that if a section of an Act or a piece of delegated legislation has more than one possible meaning, the judge *must* choose a meaning that makes English law compatible with the Convention. If the piece of legislation is not compatible with the ECHR the judge will point out the incompatibility and the appropriate government minister can then choose whether to change the legislation so as to make it compatible.

Although Section 3 takes priority over the common law approaches, as it is laid down by Parliament as an instruction to the judges, it does not make them redundant because:

- it may be that there are several possible interpretations that are compatible with the ECHR;
- it may be that the piece of legislation in question has no human rights implications at all.

Practical task

Watch out for examples in the newspapers of judges referring to Section 3 of the Human Rights Act 1998 and giving it as their reason for a particular interpretation of a Section of an Act or a piece of delegated legislation.

The 'rules' of interpretation

As suggested above, the use of the word 'rules' is perhaps misleading, since there is some element of choice by judges as to which one to use. The so-called rules are more in the nature of approaches, or methods of interpretation.

The literal rule

In recent times this has been regarded as the traditional approach, although we will see that there was, in fact, an older rule. It was clearly stated in the *Sussex Peerage Case* (1844) that where the words of a statute are clear and

Judge

Figure 5.6

unambiguous, they should be given their literal and grammatical meaning. In old statutes the words should be taken to carry the meaning in keeping with the language of the period of time in which they were passed.

This rule seemed perfectly reasonable at the time of its formulation, but was soon extended to cover situations where the result was not at all reasonable. The unsatisfactory extent to which the courts would go was shown in the following statement from *Abley v Dale* (1951):

Abley v Dale (1951)
'If the precise words are clear and unambiguous, in our judgment, we are bound to construe them in their ordinary sense, even though it do lead, in our view of the case, to an absurdity or manifest injustice.'

We should remember that this rule was at its height of popularity in Victorian times, when most aspects of life were strict and rigid (think of the Victorian way of life, particularly clothes fashion – long sleeves, high necks, black coats and dresses, hats for men, etc.). The rule itself reflected the Victorian approach, and the courts would not be flexible, even when the rule led to absurdity. In *R v Judge of the City of London Court* (1892) it was even said that 'the court has nothing to do with whether the legislature has committed an absurdity'. Examples of absurdity produced as result of this approach abound, and can be seen in the following cases.

London and North Eastern Railway v Berriman (1946)
The Fatal Accidents Act, which was specifically designed to give a railway worker's dependant family compensation in the event of an accident, was interpreted in a literal way which denied Mr Berriman's wife any money. This was because the Act referred to repairing or relaying lines, and Mr Berriman was maintaining the line, by topping up the oil boxes at the points when the accident occurred.

Fisher v Bell (1960)
In this case the aim of the Restriction of Offensive Weapons Act was defeated, because of very literal interpretation. Some flick-knives were displayed in a shop window and the defendant was charged with 'offering for sale' flick knives contrary to the Act. He was acquitted, as he had not technically 'offered' the knives for sale, because under contract law his display was an invitation to treat and it was the customers who were making the offers. So the Act, which was intended to reduce the number of dangerous weapons available, was rendered ineffective in this case.

Here, the court looked at the common law and applied the presumption that Parliament did not intend to change the common law – in other words, the court assumed that Parliament knows the legal technical meaning of the word 'offer'. It could, of course, also have been argued that Parliament intended to prevent the sale of flick-knives and the court's decision flew in the face of Parliament's intention. The classic response to this is that if the courts have uncovered an error in the way the Act was worded, it is for Parliament to correct the error. In fact this was achieved by passing an amending Act very soon afterwards.

R v Harris (1836)
It was a statutory offence 'unlawfully and maliciously ... to stab, cut or wound any person'. Harris was held not to have committed this offence by biting off the end of a person's nose, because the words, read literally, indicated the use of an instrument.

Whiteley v Chappell (1868)
The defendant pretended to be someone who had died in order to use that person's vote. It was a statutory offence to 'personate any person entitled to vote'. As dead people cannot vote, the defendant was held not to have committed an offence.

No nose – not
a malicious wound

Figure 5.7

The judge's job is to apply what Parliament has said to the facts of the case. It is not generally for the judge to say whether the law is good or bad, although there is an increasing tendency for judges to make recommendations where they feel that the law is unsatisfactory. The traditional role of the judge is to apply the law, not to make it. Following this literal approach, the only difficulty then is to decide what it is that Parliament has said (see Aids to Interpretation, page 68).

The golden rule

It was logical and reasonable that another 'rule' should evolve, as judges generally do not aim to bring about absurd results! An alternative approach is to support the idea that it is the court's job to give effect to the clear words used by Parliament but to adapt the meaning of the words just enough to stop short of arriving at an absurd decision. That is the golden rule. Lord Blackburn explained this rule in the following case.

> *The River Wear Commissioners v Anderson* (1877)
> 'We are to take the whole of the statute together and construe it altogether, giving the words their ordinary signification, unless when so applied they produce an inconsistency, or an absurdity, or inconvenience, so great as to convince the court that the intention could not have been to use them in their ordinary signification, and to justify the court in putting on them some other signification, which, though less proper, is one which the court thinks the words will bear.'

So, under the golden rule, the court takes the literal approach unless it results in great absurdity, inconvenience, or inconsistency, and then it modifies the meaning, within the context of the statute, just as far as is necessary to avoid the absurdity.

Re Sigsworth (1935)

A person who had murdered his mother was not allowed to benefit from the proceeds of her estate, when she died without leaving a will. If statutory law had been interpreted literally, the son would have formed the 'issue' of the dead woman, and have been able to claim her money. The court felt able to modify this, within the context of the statute, on grounds of public policy, to prevent the murderer benefiting from the fruits of his crime.

Judge

Figure 5.8

It would clearly be absurd for a court to insist on applying a literal interpretation to the wording of an Act, without giving any thought to the consequences. One difficulty, however, with the golden rule lies in deciding when there is an absurdity and when there is simply a logical conclusion that the judge does not like. This point was made by Lord Diplock in the following case.

Duport Steels Ltd v Sirs (1980)

The House of Lords needed to interpret a section of the Trades Union and Labour Relations Act 1974 which gave immunity to union members committing torts in contemplation or furtherance of a trade dispute. Having established that this is clearly what Parliament was saying, since the phrase had been used in statutes since 1906 and its meaning was well settled, Lord Diplock pointed out that no matter how repugnant the judges might find the consequences of this interpretation, it was their duty to apply it as intended by Parliament. He said:

> Where the meaning of the statutory words is plain and unambiguous it is not for the judges to invent fancied ambiguities as an excuse for failing to give effect to its plain meaning because they themselves consider that the consequences of doing so would be inexpedient, or even unjust or immoral. In controversial matters such as are involved in industrial relations there is room for differences of opinion as to what is expedient, what is just and what is morally justifiable. Under our Constitution it is Parliament's opinion on these matters that is paramount.

The case of Duport Steels shows the importance of the role of the judge in interpreting statutes; steering clear of any political tendency or any wish to show empathy with one party. The following case is an example of an uncontroversial use of the golden rule, nevertheless it illustrate the importance of reasonable interpretation within the 'rules'.

> *R v Allen* (1872)
> Allen had been through a marriage ceremony with two women, and was accused of bigamy. The Offences Against the Person Act (1861) provided that anyone who 'being married shall marry any other person during the life of the former husband or wife … shall be guilty of bigamy'. A person who is married cannot technically 'marry', as the second ceremony would be void and of no effect. If this Act was interpreted literally, therefore, it would be impossible for anyone ever to commit bigamy. It is clearly absurd to imagine that Parliament intended to create an offence that could not be committed, so the court therefore decided that what Parliament meant was not 'shall marry' but 'shall go through a ceremony of marriage'. Applying the golden rule, therefore, Allen was guilty of bigamy.

The mischief rule

The literal and golden rules are concerned with finding out what Parliament *said*. The mischief rule is applied to find out what Parliament *meant*. It is a contextual method of interpreting statutes, and looks for the wrong, or mischief, which the statute was trying to correct. The statute is then interpreted in the light of this. The rule is an old one, based on *Heydon's Case* (1584), in which certain steps were identified as a way to interpretation. It was said that judges should:

- consider what the law was before the Act was passed;
- identify what was wrong with that law;
- decide how Parliament intended to improve the law through the statute in question;
- apply that finding to the case before the court.

This was a sincere sixteenth-century attempt to discover the intention of Parliament and to apply it to the cases before the courts. As this approach gave the judges a fair amount of scope, however, and because of a change in society's attitude towards freedom in general – particularly during strict Victorian times – the trend moved away from the mischief rule approach, with the literal rule becoming the norm. Later the need was seen again for some flexibility, and the golden rule was developed. There has been a further move, however, and today the pendulum seems to have swung to somewhere quite near to the mischief rule again, moving toward discovering the purpose of the statute and making it work if reasonably possible.

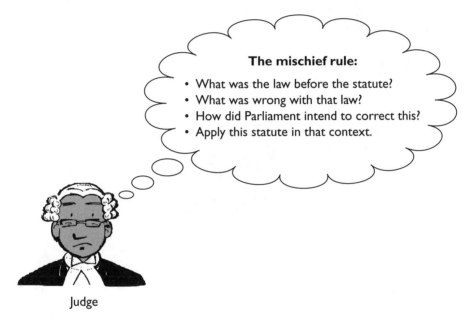

The mischief rule:

- What was the law before the statute?
- What was wrong with that law?
- How did Parliament intend to correct this?
- Apply this statute in that context.

Judge

Figure 5.9

Lord Denning said in a dissenting speech in the case of *Magor and St Mellons RDC v Newport Corporation* (1950): 'We sit here to find out the intention of Parliament and of ministers and carry it out, and we do this better by filling in the gaps and making sense of the enactment than by opening it up to destructive analysis'. By this he meant that it was better to interpret statutes in a way which carries out Parliament's intention than to be so restricted by the exact wording that this is not achieved. In contrast to *Fisher and Bell* (see page 61), where the purpose of the legislation to prevent the sale of offensive weapons was defeated, the courts have been seen on occasions to go out of their way to enable a statute to work.

Many judges and leading academic lawyers today favour this approach to interpreting statutes. Professor Zander has suggested that for the courts to jump straight in with a literal interpretation is actually wrong, and that the purpose of the statute should *always* be considered if they are to carry out their task in a reasonable way.

Smith v Hughes (1960)

Some prostitutes were accused of soliciting, contrary to the Street Offences Act 1958 which made it an offence to 'solicit in a street ... for the purpose of prostitution'. The defendant, along with other prostitutes, sat on a balcony, or inside a building tapping on the window, to attract the attention of men in the street. Interpreted literally, there would therefore be no offence. Applying the mischief rule, it did not matter that the women were not themselves in the street, as they were still soliciting men in the street, which was what the Act was designed to prevent. They were therefore found guilty. Lord Parker said, 'Everybody knows that this was an Act intended to clean up the streets ... I am content to base my decision on that ground and that ground alone'.

Figure 5.10

The purposive approach

A modern descendant of the mischief approach is the purposive approach, where the court considers what Parliament intended to be the purpose of the statute, and applies it to the present case. When Lord Denning suggested this in *Magor and St Mellons RDC v Newport Corporation* (above), he was reprimanded by Lord Simonds in the House of Lords, who, still used to the traditional literal approach, referred to Lord Denning's proposition as 'a naked usurpation of the legislative function, under the thin disguise of interpretation'. The approach has eventually found favour, however, and Lord Simon suggested a modern version, loosely calling it the purposive approach, in the case of *Maunsell v Olins* (1975). He said: 'The first task of a court of construction is to put itself in the shoes of the draftsman – to consider what knowledge he had and, importantly, what statutory objective he had .... being thus placed .... the court proceeds to ascertain the meaning of the statutory language'. The draftsman, of course, is the person who takes the material proposed by Parliament, and turns it into a statute. Lord Simon was saying that in exactly the same way, the judges should endeavour to interpret Parliament's words to bring about the effect which was intended.

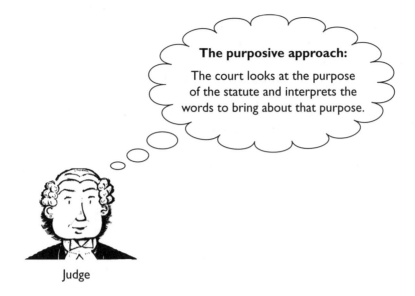

The purposive approach:

The court looks at the purpose of the statute and interprets the words to bring about that purpose.

Judge

Figure 5.11

Lord Diplock's warning, in Duport Steels (see page 63), that judges' views on expedience and morality should not be allowed to cloud their judgment when interpreting statutes, gives an indication of the difficulties that arose in the following case.

Royal College of Nursing v DHSS (1981)
The Abortion Act 1967 envisaged legal abortions being performed only by doctors, but by the 1970s it was common for abortion to be induced by using a drug – a job which could be performed by nurses. Using a literal approach, such abortions would be illegal. Alternatively, the court could look at the 'mischief' Parliament intended to address. It was clearly Parliament's intention to make abortion legal in certain controlled circumstances and to prevent 'back-street abortions' performed by unqualified people. Drug-induced abortions were performed in hospital under the supervision of doctors and the House of Lords decided that such abortions were, therefore, legal. It would be tempting for a judge who regarded abortion as morally wrong to adopt a literal approach and take the view that Parliament had expressed itself clearly. Consideration of the purpose of the act, however, and the 'mischief' which was being avoided, makes it clear that Parliament intended that properly supervised abortions in hospitals should be legal.

R v Kensington and Chelsea London Borough Council ex parte *Lawrie Plantation Services Ltd* (1999)
The word 'consideration', which has a limited, technical meaning within the law of contract, was given a wider meaning for the purposes of interpreting the Greater London Council (General Powers) Act 1973. The court looked at the purpose of the statute they were interpreting, which was to control the use of properties as temporary accommodation, and gave the word 'consideration' a wider meaning in order to give effect to that purpose.

Time-line of statutory interpretation	We can see that statutory interpretation has been passed through a series of approaches, to now reach a modernised version of the original 'rule'.
Sixteenth century	• A common-sense approach to law-making resulting in the **mischief rule**.
Victorian times	• A strict approach to life in general and to law-making, resulting in the **literal rule**.
Early twentieth century	• Some relaxation in approach, resulting in a slight freedom to modify wording in the **golden rule**.
Present day	• An attempt to discover the meaning behind statutes and apply it using a modern version of the mischief rule – the **purposive approach**.

Figure 5.12

In *Fisher v Bell* the court used the common law meaning of 'offer' and so by applying a literal interpretation defeated Parliament's purpose. The House of Lords used a much more liberal, purposive, interpretation of a legal word in the following case.

Aids to interpretation

So, how do judges find out what Parliament's purpose was? The rule in *Heydon's Case* relied on each Act having a preamble, which was a statement of purpose at the beginning of each Act. Preambles ceased to be used in Public Acts during the nineteenth century, although they are still used in Private Acts, which are Acts of Parliament passed to change the law relating to an individual or organisation rather than the community as a whole. There was for many years a reluctance to allow judges to use anything other than the exact words of the statute in order to find its meaning. This meant that the judge would be limited to his own experience of the words before him (*remember*: 'programmed by a million preconceptions', see page 56) and the arguments of the parties.

The tools, or aids, which could be of help to a judge in interpreting statutes fall into two groups:

- those found within the statute itself – known as intrinsic aids;
- those that exist outside the statute – known as extrinsic aids.

Thinking point

Imagine that you have a section of a book to read for homework, and it contains some words which you do not completely understand. Where might you obtain help?

Now consider what the courts may wish to use to help them understand words within a statute which are not clear.

Intrinsic aids

Intrinsic aids are part of the body of the statute. The examination of the statute as a whole gives a general idea to the reader of its purpose, and a judge may make use of any of the wording found within the statute, such as the long title. Lord Simon said in *Black Clawson International* (1975) that the long title provided the 'plainest of all guides to the general objectives of a statute'. This is helpful to the court as it often acts as a useful summary of Parliament's intention. The long title of the Access to Justice Act 1999 is:

> An Act to establish the Legal Services Commission, the Community Legal Service and the Criminal Defence Service; to amend the law of legal aid in Scotland; to make further provision about legal services; to make provision about appeals, courts, judges and court proceedings, to amend the law about magistrates and magistrates' courts; and to make provision about immunity from action and costs and indemnities for certain officials exercising judicial functions.

The judge may also look at interpretations given within the Act itself, either in an interpretation section towards the end of the Act or within sections themselves. An example is found in the Breeding and Sale of Dogs (Welfare) Act 1999, which provides:

Section 8(1) The keeper of a licensed breeding establishment is guilty of an offence if he sells a dog otherwise than at a licensed breeding establishment, a licensed pet shop or a licensed Scottish breeding establishment.

Section 8(5) then defines 'licensed breeding establishment', 'licensed pet shop' and 'licensed Scottish breeding establishment'.

Punctuation, although absent from older statutes, is an integral part of modern statutes. It has taken a surprisingly long time for punctuation to be allowed as an aid to interpreting statutes, but it was suggested in *DPP v Schildkamp* (1971) that reference could be made to punctuation in cases of ambiguity. It does seem particularly absurd to ignore such a basic tool, as was pointed out in the case of *Hanlon v The Law Society* (1981), where Lord Lowry said that to ignore punctuation disregards the reality that literate people, such as parliamentary draftsmen, do punctuate what they write.

The side-notes, in the margins of a statute are put there to help, but as they are not discussed in Parliament they are not officially part of the statute. It was said in *Schildkamp* that there was no sensible reason why they should be ignored, but their use in interpretation is in any case of limited value, as they indicate the subject matter of a section, rather than its scope.

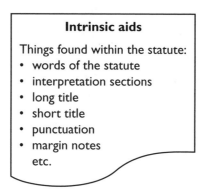

Intrinsic aids

Things found within the statute:
- words of the statute
- interpretation sections
- long title
- short title
- punctuation
- margin notes
  etc.

Figure 5.13

Extrinsic aids

A dictionary is an extrinsic aid because it is outside the statute itself, the *Oxford English Dictionary* being the standard work of reference. Judges may use dictionaries, for example if the statute is old the judge can look at the meaning of the word at the time the statute was passed, rather than at its modern meaning. When a judge is following the literal approach, a dictionary is the most common extrinsic aid he will use. It would also be appropriate for a judge, following the literal approach, to refer to other statutes that have used the same word and to cases that have been decided on the meaning of the word in those statutes.

**Extrinsic aids which
have generally been allowed**

Things found outside the statute:
* the *Oxford English Dictionary*
* other statutes
* cases
* Law Commission reports.

Figure 5.14

Over the years, the courts have been reluctant to allow external material
to be used in court to help to interpret statutes. Gradually, however, it
became acceptable and then commonplace, following *Black Clawson
International* (1975), to use Law Commission reports and similar documents to ascertain what 'mischief', or problem, Parliament may have
intended to address in creating a statute.

There was much more resistance to the idea of judges looking at the
record of debates in Parliament, known as *Hansard*. We said at the beginning of this chapter that it is impossible to question Parliament in person.
Reading *Hansard*, which is a verbatim account of the debate which leads
to a statute being passed, would seem to be the nearest anyone could get
to finding out why a statute was passed, and the purpose behind it. Until
as recently as 1992 there was a rule that *Hansard* could not be admitted
as evidence in courts. For some time Lord Denning had campaigned for
it to be allowed, as seen in the following judgment.

Davis v Johnson (1978)
This case concerned the Domestic Violence and Matrimonial
Proceedings Act 1976, and Lord Denning believed that if an answer
to the question of what Parliament intended was clearly available
in *Hansard*, the Court of Appeal should be able to use it, to
prevent further delay to obtaining justice for the parties concerned.
He said:

> Some may say ... that judges should not pay any attention to what
> is said in Parliament. They should grope about in the dark for the
> meaning of an Act without switching on the light. I do not accede to
> this view.

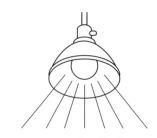

Now we can see .... what Parliament intended

Figure 5.15

On appeal to the House of Lords, while agreeing with the outcome of the case, all five Law Lords disagreed with Lord Denning's reference to *Hansard*. The matter may then have seemed to be resolved, but not for Lord Denning! He later managed to bring the contents of *Hansard* into court by quoting an extract from his own book which just happened to contain a relevant section of *Hansard*. Eventually the House of Lords themselves had need to refer to *Hansard*, and did so in *Pickstone v Freemans* (1988) to find out why an amendment to the Equal Pay Act 1970 had been made. Finally, the House of Lords decided that it was appropriate for a court to look at *Hansard* if the wording of the Act was ambiguous. This decision came about in the following case.

Pepper v Hart (1993)
The case concerned an interpretation of the Finance Act 1976. Some teachers' sons had been given the opportunity to take up surplus places at concessionary fees and the question arose as to the basis on which tax should be paid for this benefit. The words of the statute could have been interpreted in two ways, one resulting in a much higher tax payment than the other.

It was established that reference to *Hansard* would provide the exact answer to the question, by showing what was intended in creating the statute. This information was eventually allowed as evidence to show that Parliament had intended the section of the Act to be interpreted in favour of the taxpayer.

Hansard

What was said in Parliament *might* help the judges

Figure 5.16

So, reference to *Hansard* is now allowed in certain circumstances. These are:

- where the legislation is ambiguous or obscure, or leads to an absurdity;
- where a statement has been made in Parliament by a minister or the promoter of the Bill;
- where the statement to be used is clear in its meaning.

These restrictions arose out of genuine reluctance of the House of Lords to allow open access to *Hansard* in court. Their reluctance arose from various legitimate concerns.

- They felt that in some circumstances the debates recorded in *Hansard* could be just as unclear as the statute, and could contain biased views of members of political parties.
- They feared that many hours would be spent by lawyers in preparation and by courts in examining the speeches of long debates.
- The debate in court of what is said in Parliament seemed contrary to the idea of parliamentary privilege (under which action cannot be taken against a Member of Parliament for statements made in debate).

The use of *Hansard* by courts in interpreting statutes was confirmed, however, in the case of *Three Rivers District Council v Bank of England* (1996) where the importance of using a purposive approach in interpreting law of a European or international nature was stressed. A further recent example of the use of *Hansard* is found in the following case.

Tuppen v Microsoft (2000)
The plaintiffs, who were originally accused of producing pirate software, claimed that the defendant company had initiated police raids and litigation amounting to harassment. As harassment is not defined in the Protection from Harassment Act 1997 the court referred to

speeches, recorded in *Hansard*, where the Home Secretary and the Lord Chancellor had given examples of the kind of behaviour that the statute was aimed at preventing. This did not include the circumstances of the plaintiffs, and their claim failed.

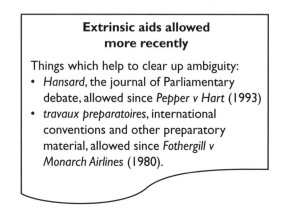

Extrinsic aids allowed more recently

Things which help to clear up ambiguity:
- *Hansard*, the journal of Parliamentary debate, allowed since *Pepper v Hart* (1993)
- *travaux preparatoires*, international conventions and other preparatory material, allowed since *Fothergill v Monarch Airlines* (1980).

Figure 5.17

This has all taken us a long way from the previous position, and shows a greatly relaxed attitude on the part of the courts, which is certainly in keeping with the UK's membership of the European Union. In line with the broadly purposive approach of other European countries, courts can now also make use of original international conventions and preparatory materials (*travaux preparatoires*), following the case of *Fothergill v Monarch Airlines* (1980).

European legislation is different in character from English statutes. It is, therefore, considered appropriate to make more use of extrinsic aids, including a more detailed look at what was said in Parliament, when interpreting European materials or English provisions designed to give effect to European directives. From 1999 a set of explanatory notes is issued with each statute. They are designed to assist the understanding of the Act but do not form part of it or have legal authority. The explanatory notes to the Access to Justice Act 1999 begin:

> These explanatory notes relate to the Access to Justice Act 1999. They have been prepared by the Lord Chancellor's Department in order to assist the reader in understanding the Act. They do not form part of the Act and have not been endorsed by Parliament.

Later in the notes, the following is given as an explanation of Sections 29–31 of the Act:

The Act reforms the law relating to conditional fees and 'after the event' legal expenses insurance ... It will enable the court to order a losing party to pay any uplift on the successful party's lawyers' normal fees and any premium paid by the successful party for insurance against being ordered to pay the other side's costs. The intention is to:

- ensure that the compensation awarded to a successful party is not eroded by any uplift or premium – the party in the wrong will bear the full burden of the costs;

- make conditional fees more attractive, in particular to defendants and to plaintiffs seeking non-monetary redress – these litigants can rarely use conditional fees now, because they cannot rely on the prospect of recovering damages to meet the cost of the uplift and premium;

- discourage weak cases and encourage settlements; and

- provide a mechanism for regulating the uplifts that solicitors charge – in future, unsuccessful litigants will be able to challenge unreasonably high uplifts when the court comes to assess costs.

These explanatory notes are a very recent development, so it is uncertain as to whether they are admissible in court, but a judge taking a purposive approach may feel that they are very helpful in interpreting ambiguous wording.

The present day approach

The way in which judges interpret statutes today has already arisen in discussing the 'rules' of interpretation and in considering the aids to interpretation which may be used. A purposive approach is generally taken, and, in line with other European member states, a much broader approach than was previously the case is taken when allowing the use of extrinsic aids. There are few absolute rules on methods of interpretation, however.

For example, when interpreting a statute and applying it to a case, should a judge have regard to the consequences of the court's decision? Clearly, the judges in the following case believed they had to do so.

R v Registrar General ex parte *Smith* (1991)
Under the Adoption Act 1976, a birth certificate may be obtained by any person who has been adopted. Smith applied for a copy of his birth certificate but the Registrar General refused to supply one because Smith, who was detained in Broadmoor Hospital, had committed two murders and it seemed likely that, if he found out who

his natural mother was, he would attempt to kill her. The Court of Appeal upheld the Registrar General's decision, saying, 'Clearly, in this case, it would be absurd for a court to insist on implementing the clear words used by Parliament without having any thought to the consequences'.

The decision here seems sensible in the circumstances, even though it effectively ignored Parliament's words and, instead, asked the question: 'What would Parliament have intended if it had directed its mind to this particular situation?' It could be dangerous to ask the question. What does the 'intention of Parliament' mean? Does it mean the Parliament that passed the Act, or those members who were present during the debates, or those members who voted with the majority? Can a body with as many members as the House of Commons and the House of Lords be said to have an 'intention'? Judges have to be very careful once they move away from a literal interpretation of the words of the statute. On the other hand we are likely (hopefully) to see far fewer absurd results using a purposive approach than was the case when the literal approach was commonly used, and we are certainly witnessing a genuine intent to bring about justice. A problem which arises, however, is knowing which approach is likely to be taken, as can be seen from the following cases.

Cheeseman v DPP (1990)
Two policemen waited in a public toilet to arrest a man who was accused of willfully and indecently exposing his person in a street to the annoyance of passengers. Were the policemen 'passengers'? The court applied the dictionary meaning from the time when the statute was passed, which was someone passing by or through a street. As the policemen did not fall within that meaning no offence had been committed.

Cutter v Eagle Star (1998)
The defendant's insurance company would be liable to pay damages to Cutter if the car in which he was injured was on a road when he was injured. The car was in a car park. The Court of Appeal decided that the car park was a 'road' for the purposes of the Road Traffic Act 1988 because it had been Parliament's intention to provide compensation for those injured in car accidents.
    The House of Lords reversed this decision. Lord Clyde explained:

It may be perfectly proper to adopt even a strained construction to enable the object and purpose of legislation to be fulfilled. But it cannot be taken to the length of applying unnatural meanings to familiar words or of so stretching the language that its former shape is transformed into something which is not only significantly different but has a name of its own. This must particularly be so where the language has no evident ambiguity or uncertainty about it.

He added towards the end of the speech, with which all the other judges agreed:

One cannot but feel sympathy for [the victim of the accident] but it must be for the legislature to decide as a matter of policy whether a remedy should be provided in such cases as these, and more particularly it must be for the legislature to decide, if an alteration of the law is to be made, precisely how that alteration ought to be achieved.

This lack of clarity as to whether the courts will approach cases of statutory interpretation using a purposive or literal approach is bound to cause the legal system to retain an element of uncertainty and therefore inconsistency, albeit in a general attempt to bring about just results.

Summary

Problems of interpretation	• Changing society and language patterns; unforeseen events and developments; communication difficulties; drafting problems; the need to find the intention of Parliament; the role of the courts.
Presumptions	• Statute makes no change to common law; *mens rea* is normally required in criminal law; statutes are not retrospective.
Language rules	• *Ejusdem generis, Expressio unius, Noscitur a socius* – or English equivalent – and how they apply.
Human rights	• The need to interpret in the light of the Human Rights Act 1998; changing approach.
Rules of interpretation	• The literal rule – the reason for its strictness of operation and examples of absurd results produced. • The golden rule – the need for it, examples of its operation and limitations.

- The mischief rule – principles from *Heydon's Case*, operation and examples from cases; the need to find the intention of Parliament.
- The purposive approach – current debate over use, with case examples.

Aids to interpretation

- Intrinsic (internal) aids – wording, punctuation, short and long headings, margin notes, etc.
- Extrinsic (external) aids – dictionaries, legal writing, use of *Hansard* (daily journal of Parliamentary debate): *Pepper v Hart* (1993) and its limitations; preparatory materials (*travaux preparatoires*) and European conventions.

Present approach   The European model – purposive and liberal use of aids. Recent case examples.

Tasks

1   Write a brief explanation of the following words. Use the glossary to check your answers.

context   repugnant
legislature   expedient
envisaged   ambiguous
compatible   litigant

2   Explain why it is sometimes not clear what a section of an Act of Parliament means.

3   Describe each of the three traditional approaches to statutory interpretation, using cases to explain these approaches.

4   (a)   What is the 'purposive approach'?
    (b)   List the advantages and disadvantages of the literal approach *and* the purposive approach.

5   Look out for reports in newspapers of cases which involve the interpretation of statutes, and consider which approach the judges may have used in coming to their decision.

6   Explain what 'intrinsic' and 'extrinsic' aids are, giving examples of each.

7   (a)   Why was the use of *Hansard* forbidden and in what circumstances may it now be used?
    (b)   What other extrinsic aids may a judge wish to use in interpreting statutes?

8   Imagine that a statute has been passed with the aim of promoting dental health, containing the following provision:

'It shall be an offence to eat confectionery in any school, playground or similar public place.'

Pat visits a chocolate museum as part of a school group outing and is given various miniature chocolate bars to taste. Explain whether an offence has been committed using (a) the literal rule, or (b) the purposive approach?

6 The doctrine of judicial precedent

Following precedent means being consistent, and therefore being fair. The idea of precedent does not just apply to the legal system. If the headmaster of a school was known to let pupils eat lollipops in lessons, it would be seen as unfair to suddenly punish Fred one day for eating a lollipop during his History lesson. This would be seen as inconsistent and unfair. The headmaster could be said to have set a precedent in allowing lollipop eating in the first place.

One of the most fundamental requirements of any system of rules is consistency. It is seen as fairness by those who have to obey the rules, and this is also true of legal systems. Like cases should be treated alike. It is important because it is just, but also because it means people can decide on a course of conduct knowing what the legal consequences of that conduct will be. We need a system, then, which is consistent, objective and rational.

Another general principle within organisations is that the people at the head of the organisation usually lay down the rules for those below. Again, this is mirrored in the English legal system in the idea of lower courts being bound by the decisions of higher courts.

These two rules together form a doctrine that is known as *stare decisis* – which can be translated literally as standing by the decisions. It means that courts are bound in two ways: higher courts bind lower courts, and like cases are decided alike.

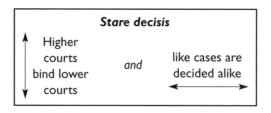

Figure 6.1

If the rules are laid down in statute or regulations of some kind there is still the problem of deciding precisely what they mean and how they apply in different circumstances, as we have seen in Chapter 5. Much of English law is not in the form of written rules but comes from judicial decisions.

It used to be said that any situation not mentioned in a statute was covered by the common law (rules already in existence to be discovered by looking at past cases). If a case that fitted the situation exactly could not be found, the writings of long-dead legal scholars could be used. This view sits very well with the notion that the law should be consistent, but it is now recognised as being something of a myth to say that the common law has a rule for *every* situation.

The modern reality is that when a point of common law (in this context, any law not governed by statute) arises, the lawyers on each side of the argument try to find similar cases that have been decided by the courts in the past. They then try to persuade the court to choose between different lines of authority. The judge has to decide which cases provide the closest 'fit'. This may be a matter of looking at the facts of the cases and choosing the case or cases most similar in a factual sense, but it may also involve looking at the legal principles involved and applying a principle established in an apparently very different set of circumstances from the facts of the case before the court.

Terminology of judicial precedent

There are lots of new words in studying judicial precedent. To understand how case law operates you will need to be familiar with some of these, as they will help in reading and explaining cases. Do not try to learn them all in one go as a list, but use this section as a point of reference. You will need to review expressions again at the end of this chapter.

- **Follow** – *when a decision is based on the outcome of another case which is binding, e.g. a Court of Appeal decision which is based on a previous House of Lords decision.*

- **Overrule** – *when a court goes against a decision in another case which is not binding, e.g. a House of Lords decision which goes against a previous Court of Appeal decision.*

- **Reverse** – *when a court overturns a decision made by a lower court in the same case.*

- **Disapprove** – *when a court expresses disapproval of a decision but is nevertheless bound to follow it in the present case.*

- **Dissent** – *when a judge does not agree with the majority, e.g. if one judge out of three does not hold the same views as the other two, the judgment is a dissenting one.*

- **Distinguish** – *when certain important facts of a case (referred to as material facts) are found to be different from another case which would normally be binding.*

To see how precedent operates we will now examine the following very famous case.

> *Donoghue v Stevenson* (1932)
> The claimant visited a café with a friend, who bought her a bottle of ginger beer. The drink came in an opaque bottle. She poured some of the ginger beer into a glass and drank it. When she poured the remainder into the glass from the bottle, along with the ginger beer came the decomposing remains of a dead snail. The claimant was unwell as a result of this and she sued the manufacturer of the ginger beer, claiming that her illness was his fault. Her claim was in the tort of negligence and at the time this was a new idea.

Donoghue v Stevenson ... with the ginger beer came the decomposing remains of a dead snail ...

Figure 6.2

Usually, the first stage in a legal action is to establish the facts, but when there is a new point of law at issue this can be argued out first. That is what happened in *Donoghue v Stevenson* and the issue came before the House of Lords Judicial Committee (the highest court in the system). They decided that it was possible to sue successfully in these circumstances because a manufacturer of goods that cannot be examined before they are used owes a duty to the consumer. The duty is to take reasonable care that the goods are safe.

This ruling was all that was required to deal with the question before the House of Lords. The case could then go back to the court of first instance (that is, the court in which the case was started) to decide the following:

- whether there was a snail in the bottle;
- whether its presence was caused by the manufacturer's negligence;
- whether it was her consumption of contaminated ginger beer that made the claimant ill.

The House of Lords had more to say, however, regarding the law. They said that there was a general principle that each of us owes a duty to other people.

That duty is to take reasonable care when we are doing something that may affect other people. Lord Atkin thought about it in terms of a general duty to others and compared it with the Christian duty towards our neighbour. We have a legal duty, therefore, not to harm our neighbour. He said:

> The rule that you are to love your neighbour becomes in law, you must not injure your neighbour ... You must take reasonable care to avoid acts or omissions which you can reasonably foresee would be likely to injure your neighbour. Who then is my neighbour? The answer seems to be – persons who are so directly affected by my act that I ought reasonably to have them in contemplation as being so affected when I am directing my mind to the acts or omissions which are called in question.

This principle was new to the courts, but once the case had been decided, it formed a precedent – that is, it formed a new rule to be followed in later cases. It was highly unlikely that anyone else would become ill from drinking a snail found in their ginger beer, but cases would arise which involved similar *legal* circumstances. *Donoghue v Stevenson* was heard in 1932. There soon followed others with similar claims.

Daniels v White (1938)
A bottle of lemonade was bought, but on drinking it the plaintiff felt a burning sensation. The lemonade was found to contain a chemical, and compensation was available based on *Donoghue v Stevenson.*

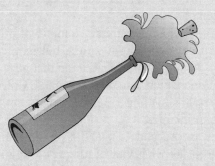

Daniels v White ... the plaintiff felt a burning sensation ...

Figure 6.3

This widened the precedent beyond ginger beer, applying Lord Atkin's neighbour principle to a person selling a consumable item.

Grant v Australian Knitting Mills (1936)
Some underwear was bought which was found to be made from material containing a chemical which had a harmful itchy effect on the skin.

Grant v Australian Knitting Mills ... a chemical had a harmful itchy effect on the skin ...

Figure 6.4

Compensation was given, again based on the precedent set by *Donoghue v Stevenson*, widening the principle and applying it to an item to be used by a consumer.

This general principle has now been applied to very different circumstances. It covers, for example, doctors treating patients, drivers of motor vehicles, people such as lawyers and accountants giving advice and employers organising their employees' working conditions. The House of Lords has since decided that the principle is rather too wide and has adopted narrower rules to decide cases in negligence where there is no well-established precedent.

Donoghue v Stevenson is an extreme example of a case giving rise to a general principle of very wide application, but in any legal decision it is important to look beyond the factual situation that gave rise to a case and to consider the legal issue which is to be determined. Consistency requires not only that similar factual situations receive similar treatment but also that the law follows general principles.

These principles, or precedents, make it possible for lawyers to look at previous cases and to say what view a judge is likely to take, even though the precise factual situation has never come before a court. The important questions to ask about precedent are:

1 How do judges know about previous decisions?
2 What makes a case important?
3 To what extent is a judge bound to follow any previous decision?
4 How do judges make the choice between the different lines of authority that *could* govern the case before the court?

Note that when a case does form a new precedent, this becomes the law immediately. In the case *Re Schweppes Ltd's Agreement* (1965) the issue arose as to whether certain documents should be produced at the order of the court. When the decision was made, one judge dissented (did not agree with the other two). There then followed, on the same day, in the same court, with the same bench of judges, the case of *Re Automatic Telephone and Electronic Co Ltd's Agreement* (1965), which concerned exactly the same issue of producing documents in court. The dissenting judge still held the same view, but in this second case he agreed with the decision of the other two, considering himself now bound by the precedent of the first case.

Law reporting

Law reports contain full accounts of cases which are considered important. Each report consists of an account of the facts of the case and a summary of the decision. This is followed by the judgments, reported exactly as they were delivered because the precise words used by a judge can be very important in determining the significance of the case.

For the doctrine of precedent to operate and expand at all there must be an efficient system of law reporting on which it can depend. Prior to 1865 reports had been scanty and widely varying in their standard and approach, the earliest dating from the thirteenth century. In 1865 the Council of Law Reporting was established to publish reports of cases heard in superior courts, and overseen by trained barristers. In addition a private firm, Butterworths, publishes the series known as the *All England Law Reports*. Among the general series of reports, The *Law Reports* and the *All England Law Reports* are the most significant, but in addition there are many series of specialist reports covering particular areas of law, such as employment law.

Surprisingly, the decisions as to which cases should be reported are made by employees of the commercial organisations who publish the reports. These companies employ barristers to authenticate the reports for them – every law report has to bear the name of a barrister who was in court when the judgment was given and can confirm that the case has been accurately reported.

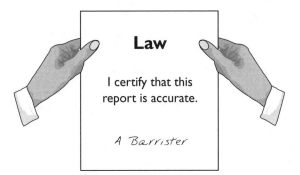

Law

I certify that this
report is accurate.

A Barrister

Figure 6.5

One problem is that there are so many reports that it is difficult for lawyers to find the relevant ones. It is somewhat easier now that most reports can be searched electronically on a computer system. In *Copeland v Smith* (1999) the Court of Appeal held that a barrister is expected to be aware of any relevant case reported in the more general reports, but not the specialist reports.

All advocates have an obligation to bring relevant cases to the attention of the court, even those which do not support their argument. Law reports are available in libraries, on the Internet and through specialist databases. The following is an example of a case. There is a headnote, summarising the key points raised by the case, the facts of the case and the decision reached. The report is the *All England Report* of *Reeves v Commissioner of Police of the Metropolis* (1999) 3 All ER 897.

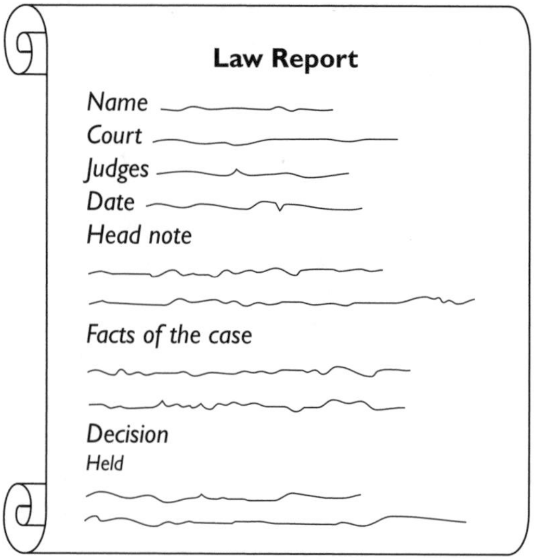

Law Report

Name _____
Court _____
Judges _____
Date _____
Head note

Facts of the case

Decision
Held

Figure 6.6

Reeves v Commissioner of Police of the Metropolis
HOUSE OF LORDS
LORD HOFFMANN, LORD MACKAY OF CLASHFERN, LORD JAUNCEY OF TULLICHETTLE, LORD HOPE OF CRAIGHEAD AND LORD HOBHOUSE OF WOODBOROUGH
10, 11 MARCH, 15 JULY 1999

Police – Negligence – Duty to take care – Person in custody – Suicide risk – Police taking person with suicidal tendencies into custody – Police having knowledge of prisoner's suicidal tendencies – Prisoner committing suicide by hanging himself using shirt tied through spyhole on outside of cell door – Administratrix on behalf of prisoner's estate bringing action for negligence against police – Whether police failing to take reasonable steps to prevent prisoner committing suicide – Whether defences of volenti non fit injuria *and* novus actus interveniens *available – Whether prisoner contributorily negligent.*

The plaintiff sued as administratrix of L, who had committed suicide while in police custody. The police had known that L was a suicide risk because of incidents on earlier occasions when he had been in custody; and because the police surgeon who had examined L on the day in question had considered that he was a suicide risk and that he should be kept under observation, although she had found no evidence of specific mental disturbance. L had hanged himself shortly after the examination, by tying his shirt through the spyhole on the outside of his cell door; he had been able to do that because the flap in the cell door had been left down. The plaintiff claimed damages against the commissioner of police for negligence. The judge found that L was of sound mind at the time of his suicide; that the officers owed L a particular duty to take care to prevent him from committing suicide because they knew he was a suicide risk and that they were negligent in failing to shut the door flap after putting L in the cell. The judge held, however, that the defendant could rely on the defences of *volenti non fit injuria* and *novus actus interveniens*, and on the question of contributory negligence assessed L's responsibility in accordance with s.1(1)a of the Law Reform (Contributory Negligence) Act 1945 at 100 per cent. He accordingly dismissed the plaintiff's claim. The plaintiff appealed to the Court of Appeal which, by a majority, allowed the appeal and awarded her damages in the full amount of £8,690. The defendant appealed to the House of Lords.

Held – (Lord Hobhouse dissenting)

(1) Where the law imposed a duty on a person to guard against loss by the deliberate and informed act of another, the occurrence of the very act which ought to have been prevented could not negative causation between the breach of duty and the loss. That was so not only where the deliberate act was that of a third party, but also when it was the act of the plaintiff himself, and whether or not he was of sound mind. It followed in the instant case, bearing in mind the police's admission that they had breached their duty of care towards L, that the defences of *novus actus interveniens* and *volenti non fit injuria* were not available to the commissioner; *Kirkham v Chief Constable of the Greater Manchester Police* [1990] 3 All ER 246 considered.

(2) For the purposes of s.1(1) of the 1945 Act, a plaintiff's deliberate and intentional act in causing injury to himself constituted 'fault',

as defined in s.4 b of the Act. Thus, since the fact that L's suicide did not prevent the police's breach of duty from being a cause of his death did not mean that his suicide was not also a cause of his death, both causes contributed to his death and the 1945 Act applied and provided the means of reflecting that division of responsibility in the award of damages. In all the circumstances, the appropriate division was to apportion responsibility equally. Accordingly, the appeal would be allowed and the damages reduced to £4,345.

Decision of the Court of Appeal [1998] 2 All ER 381 reversed in part.

Practical task

Read the *All England Report* of *Reeves v Commissioner of Police of the Metropolis* (1999) and answer the following questions.

1 Who is the plaintiff? Who is the defendant?

2 From which court is the case being reported?

3 In which two other courts had the case already been heard?

4 Name two of the judges sitting on the case.

5 Over how many days was the case heard in this court?

6 From the headnotes identify some of the issues involved.

7 In your own words, very briefly summarise the facts of the case.

8 Use a dictionary to find out the meaning of the word administratrix.

9 In your own words, very briefly summarise the decision(s) of the court.

10 You do not have to be a qualified lawyer to have an opinion. Having read these facts, do you think that the police should pay damages to L's family? Give reasons for your answer.

The hierarchy of courts

The place of each court within the system is important in both civil and criminal cases. To avoid confusion, what follows concentrates on the *civil* courts (see page 104 for precedent in the *criminal* courts).

Each year, thousands of cases come before the courts. They all begin with a dispute between parties which may be settled at an early stage or may continue to the point at which one party issues a formal claim. It is still quite likely that the parties will come to an agreement because litigation is very expensive and time consuming and it is usually more sensible to reach a compromise than to take a case to court (see Chapter 8).

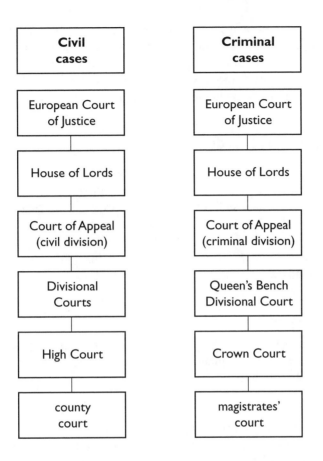

Figure 6.7

If the parties to a dispute decide that the case is worth bringing to court they begin in either the county court or the High Court (see Chapter 7). Cases in these courts are almost always largely concerned with determining arguments about the facts. If there is an argument about the law and one side does not agree with the judge's ruling on the law there can be an appeal (again, provided the party considering an appeal decides it is worth the money and inconvenience to continue with the action). Appeals in such cases are heard by the Court of Appeal (Civil Division) and it is possible in certain circumstances to appeal once more, to the Judicial Committee of the House of Lords.

It is worth noting at this point that it is thus often a matter of chance as to whether a legal issue comes to be decided by the courts and thus to form the basis for precedent. There has to be:

- a dispute over a legal issue between two parties;
- parties who are in a position to fund litigation, if necessary, to the Court of Appeal or the House of Lords before there is much chance of any impact being made on the law.

The European Court of Justice (ECJ), of course, is now in theory the court of highest authority in the UK legal system. A case does not necessarily have to go through the system to the House of Lords before being referred to the European Court of Justice, however. If a case involves a point of European Community law, reference can be made to the European Court of Justice from a court at any level, and its decision will be binding on all courts in the English legal system (see Chapter 1).

The House of Lords

Decisions made by the House of Lords are binding on all other courts through-out the system, so the Court of Appeal, the High Court and county courts all have to apply rules made in this way just as if they were applying a statute.

The House of Lords was at one time totally free to decide cases without being bound by previous cases, but in the case of *London Street Tramways v London County Council* (1898) it decided that from then onwards it *would* be bound by its own previous decisions.

Thinking point

This decision seems a strange one to have taken, in some ways. Before read-ing on, pause for a few minutes to consider why a court with such high authority might wish to be bound.

The law developed greatly during the nineteenth century, and as so many cases were going to court, the law was becoming inconsistent and therefore uncertain. The *London Street Tramways* case is a product of the Victorian era (see Chapter 5) when it was very important to be consistent with rules, and therefore the law needed to be certain. Both lawyers and the general public needed a set of rules to follow that were clear. So the decision in this case was reasonable at the time.

In the twentieth century, however, both society and the law developed even faster, and a point was soon reached where decisions made in much earlier cases were now inappropriate.

Thinking point

Imagine some of the differences between society as it was at the time of *London Street Tramways* in 1898 and as it was in the swinging sixties. The case itself gives one clue – trams had given way to cars, buses, etc. Think about fashion, culture, etc.

The law needed a new way of operating, so that it could change to be relevant to the society which it served. On the other hand, total freedom from prece-dent would not be good, either, as the idea of consistency was still a good one. The way in which some flexibility was achieved was for the House of Lords to give itself the power to change a legal rule if the point came before it again. This power, was taken by the House of Lords making a Practice Statement in 1966. The Practice Statement is not a case, nor is it a new statute law, it is merely the court issuing a statement of what it intends to do. Since, however, it was read by the Lord Chancellor with the unanimous approval of the rest of the Law Lords, it was as authoritative as any official law.

The new power to change the law is used cautiously because of the need for consistency in legal rules, and also to deter people from making appeals on the slight hope that the House of Lords will change the law in their favour.

Text of 1966 Practice Statement
Their Lordships regard the use of precedent as an indispensable foundation upon which to decide what is the law and its application to individual cases. It provides at least some degree of certainty upon which individuals can rely in the conduct of their affairs, as well as a basis for orderly development of legal rules. Their Lordships nevertheless recognise that the rigid adherence to precedent may lead to injustice in a particular case and also unduly restrict the proper development of the law. They propose, therefore, to modify their present practice and while treating former decisions of this House as normally binding, to depart from a previous decision when it appears right to do so. In this connection they will bear in mind the danger of disturbing retrospectively the basis on which contracts, settlement of property and fiscal arrangements have been entered into and also the especial need for certainty as to the criminal law. This announcement is not intended to affect the use of precedent elsewhere than in this House.

Only applies
to the House
of Lords

Figure 6.8

So this statement said that the House of Lords could now change the law by giving themselves power to 'depart from a previous decision' – or overrule it – 'when it appears right to do so'. This is obviously a point of difficulty, because in order for a change in law to arise, it has to be 'right' in the eyes of those who make up the House of Lords – some would say a group of elderly gentlemen, albeit very respected and experienced. Note that their Lordships actually say that, on the one hand, they will bear in mind the need for certainty, but, on the other, that the new powers give them a way of avoiding injustice in a particular case and undue restriction in developing the law.

In fact the new powers were used extremely sparingly in the period following the statement. The House of Lords did overrule a previous decision in *Conway v Rimmer* (1968), but only on a technicality. The first real occasion that the Practice Statement was used was not until six years later, in the following landmark case.

British Railways Board v Herrington (1972)
A child was badly injured after going on to an electric railway line via a gap in a broken fence. The railway was near to some open ground and a play area, and the station master knew that the fence was broken.

A previous case, *Addie v Dumbreck* (1929), had involved a similar situation, but on this occasion a child was killed while trespassing in a privately owned colliery. The decision was that there was no liability towards the child, and this probably reflected the view of society in 1929 that the safety of the child was the responsibility of the child or the parents, not the colliery owners.

By 1972, society had come to expect some responsibility by authorities, including British Rail, to provide as safe an environment as possible. This was reflected in the decision of the House of Lords to overrule *Addie v Dumbreck*, using the powers of the Practice Statement, and hold British Rail liable for compensation. The court said that British Rail were aware of the environment in which the railway line was sited, knew of the damaged fence and knew of the power of 'their own lethal weapon' – meaning the trains and railway track.

In a similar way, the case of *The Joanna Oldendorf* (1974) overruled the case of *The Aello* (1960) reflecting political and economic change in attitudes within society.

The Aello (1960)
In the first case the ship, *The Aello*, had been unable to anchor in the harbour because of industrial dispute, and the captain was told to wait just outside. The court held that the ship had not therefore 'arrived', creating liability for non-delivery (see Figure 6.8 overleaf).

The Joanna Oldendorf (1974)
The Joanna Oldendorf was similarly unable to dock because of industrial dispute, and was told to anchor at a recognised waiting place well outside the mouth of the river Mersey, in order to unload later at Liverpool. By then the views of the House of Lords on liability for such situations had changed, and it was held that the ship had 'arrived', overruling *The Aello*.

Figure 6.9 The Aello

Other, more recent, changes to the civil law can be found in:

- *Murphy v Brentwood District Council* (1990) where the House of Lords overruled the decision in *Anns v London Borough of Merton* (1977) concerning duty of care to the purchaser of a house.

- *Pepper Hart* (1993) (see Chapter 5) overruling the ban on allowing reference to *Hansard* in interpreting statutes.

- *Hall v Simons* (2000) where the tradition that a barrister can neither be sued for advocacy work nor, in turn, sue a client for fees was abolished, overruling *Rondel v Worsley* (1969). In *Hall v Simons* (2000) the House of Lords felt that although immunity from being sued had been right in its time, it could no longer be justified. They therefore used the Practice Statement powers to enable the development of the law to keep in step with modern society.

Cases which change the law at House of Lords level have been few on the ground, however, probably reflecting the need to ensure certainty in the law. There was a spate of cases involving criminal law, which seemed to disregard the declared caution in the Practice Statement regarding such changes, but apart from these there have only been about a dozen civil cases in over thirty years.

A problem arises if the House of Lords changes the law because, as mentioned previously, there is a theory (called the declaratory theory) that the common law has always existed and the judges merely find it. It can be argued that the judges do not change the law only for the future but also for the past. In other words, when the judges change the common law the change is retrospective. This problem arose in the following case.

> *Kleinwort Benson Ltd v Lincoln City Council* (1998)
> There was a very old established rule of contract law that if the parties to a contract made their agreement based on a mistake about what the law was they were still bound by the contract. A mistake as to the law was of no effect. If the parties made a mistake about the facts then in some circumstances the contract would not be binding. This distinction had been recognised as rather illogical and the judges decided, by a majority of 3–2, to abolish the rule about mistakes in law.

If this change to the law had been made by Parliament it would have come into effect some time after an Act was passed but because the change was made by the judges it was regarded as having always been the law. This meant that it would become possible for parties to contracts made years before to allege that there had been a mistake as to the law and they should not be bound by the contract – even though, at the time of contract and for years afterwards, it was clearly the law that a mistake as to the law was of no effect.

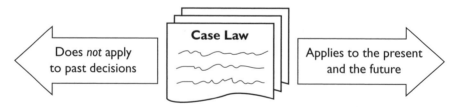

Figure 6.10

This problem of retrospective effect arises in criminal cases too. The House of Lords would not want to create offences (which is seen as the role of Parliament) because it would make conduct, which was legal when it happened, illegal at a later date. That would clearly be unjust. The judges in the House of Lords are usually careful not to overstep their constitutional role, which is to apply the law rather than to make it. They are prepared to be a little more innovative in traditional common law areas – where the judges have always made the rules – but do not like to intervene in matters which are usually dealt with by Parliament. An example is shown in the following case.

Southwark London Borough Council v Mills (1999)
In this case tenants of council flats claimed that the ordinary use of surrounding flats amounted to a nuisance because the sound insulation in the flats was so poor. The House of Lords refused to extend the tort of nuisance, which is made up of common law rules, because they considered that such an important decision, which would have meant councils all over the country having to spend huge sums of money on sound insulation, was a matter for Parliament. Lord Hoffman said:

> I think that in a field such as housing law, which is very much a matter for the allocation of resources in accordance with democratically determined priorities, the development of the common law should not get out of step with legislative policy.

The Court of Appeal

Next down in the hierarchy of courts is the Court of Appeal. It is usually bound by its own decisions and always bound by those of the House of Lords. For this reason, if an important point of law arises in a civil action it is possible for the parties to agree to the 'leap-frog procedure' laid down by the Administration of Justice Act 1969. The permission of the House of Lords is needed but, provided this is given, the case can go straight from the High Court to the House of Lords. This makes sense if the Court of Appeal would have been bound by an existing House of Lords or Court of Appeal decision.

The Court of Appeal and its own decisions

The Court of Appeal is generally bound by its own decisions. The authority for this principle is laid down firmly, in legal terms, as it was the outcome of a case, and so forms its own precedent.

Young v Bristol Aeroplane Co (1944)
In this case the Court of Appeal declared that it *would* generally be bound by its own decisions, it also laid down the grounds on which it would *not* be bound by them:

- Where two previous decisions of the Court of Appeal conflicted the Court of Appeal could choose which decision to follow. The other would then be overruled.

- Where there was a later decision of the House of Lords which conflicted with a Court of Appeal decision, the Court of Appeal would follow the House of Lords decision.
- Where a Court of Appeal decision had been made *per incuriam*, that is, without taking into account a relevant case or statute, then the decision made in error can be overruled.

Rules for
the Court of
Appeal

Figure 6.11

In addition, a further exception must be present now, in that if a case exists which conflicts with a decision of the European Court of Justice, the Court of Appeal will be obliged to follow the decision of the European court rather than its own.

This seems clear enough, and there are good reasons for the Court of Appeal being bound – in particular the argument of consistency and therefore certainty. The Court of Appeal hears a lot more cases than the House of Lords (several hundred per year compared with less than one hundred), and if these did not follow precedent the law could be in a position of obtaining flexibility and instant justice, but lacking a stable system.

There have been arguments voiced in favour of giving more power to the Court of Appeal, however, notably by Lord Denning when he was Master of the Rolls (and therefore in the position of head of the Court of Appeal). He argued in the case of *Gallie v Lee* (1969) that the rule binding the Court of Appeal was made in a case decided in that court, and could therefore be changed in the same way. He said: 'It was a self-imposed limitation, and we who imposed it can also remove it.'

Lord Denning was in the unique position of having previously sat in the House of Lords, and so he knew how it operated, and understood well the need for changes to the law in some circumstances. He therefore saw no reason why the Court of Appeal could not make those changes on occasion to bring about justice, rather than causing delay and expense by sending cases on further appeal to House of Lords. A classic example follows from a case seen previously in Chapter 5.

Davis v Johnson (1978)

Apart from taking the liberty of referring to *Hansard*, Lord Denning wished to provide relief and justice as quickly as possible for a spouse in a matrimonial dispute. He claimed that it was only a rule of practice that the Court of Appeal was bound, and that it should be able to overrule a previous decision if convinced that the decision was wrong.

The House of Lords, while agreeing with the decision and the need to bring about justice, 'unequivocally and unanimously reaffirmed' the rules of precedent in *Young*.

Figure 6.12 Young v Bristol Aeroplane Co. (1944)

Where a case is not recent, it could be argued, on the one hand, that it has not been challenged because it is accepted and respected. On the other hand it could also be argued that it is time for change. In this respect, therefore, it is useful that in *Rickards v Rickards* (1989) the issue of the Court of Appeal being generally bound by its own previous decisions was confirmed. The court added a new exception to the rule, to accompany those listed in *Young*, which is when a previous court has acted outside its jurisdiction (that is, outside its normal powers or field of work). Of course, Lord Denning is no longer with us, but the law on the Court of Appeal does appear to be more settled now than some years ago.

The Court of Appeal in relation to the House of Lords

The doctrine of *stare decisis* imposes a binding precedent on the Court of Appeal, in that it must follow the decisions of the House of Lords. On occasion, however, it has gone against this doctrine, as the following cases show.

Broome v Cassell (1971)

The Court of Appeal, under Lord Denning, did not follow a previous decision of the House of Lords concerning aspects of payment of damages. The court claimed that the decision of the House of Lords was *per incuriam* (remember that if its *own* decision was felt to be *per incuriam* the Court of Appeal need not be bound – see *Young*). When the case went the House of Lords on further appeal, however – *Cassell v Broome* (1972) – the House of Lords reprimanded the Court of Appeal, Lord Hailsham stated that it was not open to the Court of Appeal to lead courts to think that they can choose not to follow House of Lords decisions.

Undeterred, the Court of Appeal (again under Lord Denning) thought it right to change the law, feeling that the decision of the House of Lords was wrong in an older case, *Havana Railways* (1961), concerning the currency in which compensation should be paid. In the cases of both *Schorsch Meier v Henning* (1975) and *Miliangos v George Frank (Textiles)* (1976) the Court of Appeal went against the House of Lords' *Havana* decision. On further appeal, the House of Lords clearly agreed with the outcome of *Miliangos*, but once more reprimanded the Court of Appeal for ignoring the rules of precedent.

Apart from the cost and time involved to make a further appeal, there is the also the problem that very few cases do actually go to the House of Lords. This, it could be argued, leaves the law in an unsatisfactory state, and individuals without a just remedy. Perhaps there should be a compromise where the Court of Appeal is bound to follow precedent, but has the right to recommend that certain cases be heard urgently by the House of Lords with costs met from public funds.

Practical task

It would be a good idea now to go back to the terminology on page 78 and check that you understand all the expressions.

What makes a case important?

It is not very precise to speak of a court being bound by a decision made in a previous case. The part of the decision which is binding is called the *ratio decidendi* – the reason for the decision. So, in the example of *Donoghue v Stevenson* given on page 82, the rule that emerged to bind judges in future cases was the rule that a manufacturer of goods owed a duty of care to the ultimate consumer of those goods. That was the *reason* why the claimant could sue the manufacturer of the ginger beer.

The interesting thing about the *ratio* is that it is not identified by the judge who makes the decision. It is identified by lawyers looking at the judgment later, perhaps because they have a similar case in which they have been asked to advise or because they are academic lawyers trying to work out what the law is. So it is possible for two lawyers to disagree as to precisely what the principle of law taken from an earlier case is.

- One lawyer may take a narrow view: 'manufacturers of ginger beer owe a duty to the person who drinks their ginger beer to keep snails out of their bottles'.

- Another lawyer may take a wider view: 'anyone who ought to appreciate that he might cause harm to another person owes a duty to people generally to take care in what he does'.

These two views are very different and there is scope for several different versions in the middle.

The *ratio* is only a tiny part of any judgment. Anything else a judge says is called the *obiter dicta* – words by the way. Things said *obiter* are very important because they may include the judge's reasoning, his explanation of why he came to the decision he did about the law and its application in the case before him. The neighbour principle in *Donoghue v Stevenson* is considered to be *obiter*, but it is one of the most important statements in English law made during the twentieth century.

Reminder

Terminology time again:

- ratio decidendi – *the reason for the decision – is the central 'core' of a judgment.*
- obiter dicta – *words said by the way – includes the rest of the judgment.*

Sometimes, senior judges do not agree as to what the law is. In the Court of Appeal there are usually three judges and very occasionally five. In the House of Lords there are five and very occasionally seven. When the judges do not agree the majority view prevails, but the minority judgments are often important because things said by dissenting judges may, some years later, be adopted by a higher court and become the law. The whole of a dissenting judgment is *obiter*.

For law students and practising lawyers it is not just a matter of knowing what the law is but also of understanding the reasons for the decision and the dissenting views because they will govern how the law develops in the future. For example, in the Court of Appeal Lord Denning gave a dissenting judgment in the case of *Candler v Crane, Christmas & Co* (1951). He considered that a person who negligently makes a statement should be responsible for the consequences if another person relies on the statement and they know that the person is relying on the statement. The other members of the Court of Appeal did not agree with him but later, in the case of *Hedley Byrne v Heller & Partners Ltd* (1964), the House of Lords decided that Lord Denning had been right. His *obiter dictum* in *Candler* became the basis of the *ratio* in *Hedley Byrne* and therefore the law. This is then a binding precedent whenever the issue before a court concerns liability for a negligent statement.

Statements which are *obiter* but which explain the *ratio* are also very important because they will influence the way in which later courts interpret and apply the *ratio*.

Avoiding an awkward precedent – how far is a judge bound?

Practical task

Imagine that you are a judge

Figure 6.13

- You sit in the Court of Appeal.
- You are to hear an appeal in a civil case.
- You will have an account of the facts and the outline arguments for the two sides.
- Advocates are not allowed to 'ambush' the other side by producing precedents like rabbits from a hat during argument – they have to give notice of the precedents on which they will be relying and to supply a summary of their argument. This gives the judges and the other side a chance to think about the arguments and read the authorities. As litigation is an expensive business and because permission has to be given before an appeal is allowed there must be a sound argument on each side, supported by statutes and/or cases.

How do you decide between the two arguments?

The advocate for each side (probably a barrister) will present arguments and the judges will be able to ask questions and discuss the issues with both barristers. The judges then take time to think about what they have heard and to discuss the case amongst themselves. They draft judgments and read each other's drafts. If they are in agreement, one judge gives a judgment; if they disagree either about the outcome or the reasons for their decision, each judge who does not agree with the leading judgment will give a judgment.

It is possible that one line of authority is clearly binding on the court. In that case, it must be *followed*.

It might be that another authority is perceived to be wrong. In that case that other authority will be *overruled*. This means it ceases to be good law. For example, the House of Lords decision in *Hedley Byrne* overruled the Court of Appeal decision in *Candler*.

It is much more likely that the judges have to consider what appear to be two valid lines of authority. In this case what they do is to *distinguish* between them, pointing out why one case is binding on the court and the other is not. Distinguishing is a question of finding material differences between the facts of the case before the court and the case said to be binding on the court.

If, for example, the case concerned illness caused by a dead worm in a bottle of ginger beer, the fact that the case involved a worm rather than a snail would not be a material difference. If, however, the case involved a dead snail in a clear bottle (the bottle in *Donoghue v Stevenson* was opaque) the court might well regard this as a material difference because it would be possible to see that there was something wrong with the ginger beer before drinking any of it.

So, how do judges make the choice between the different lines of authority?

The process of making a decision in a case is clearly not a mechanical process. It is not a matter of simply deciding the facts, finding a rule to fit and declaring a result.

The facts have to be based on evidence. Sometimes it is not possible to produce evidence that can be used in court – so courts have to work on a partial view of what happened, or, occasionally, an inaccurate view.

The law, as we have seen, depends on judges' interpretations of what Parliament has laid down and what other judges have decided. There may also be a dispute as to which rules apply to the particular case.

Judges in county courts and the High Court have very little room for discretion. They are strictly bound by precedents set by higher courts and it is unlikely that they will declare that a precedent was decided *per incuriam*.

There is some limited scope for developing the law in the Court of Appeal. Very few cases progress to the House of Lords – they can do so only with permission, and an appeal to the House of Lords is very expensive. Lord Denning, who sat in the Court of Appeal for many years, believed that he exercised more power in the Court of Appeal as one judge among three than in the Lords as one among five. He also believed, of course, that the Court of

Appeal should have the same power that the House of Lords gave to itself in 1966 to overrule its own previous decisions. There are limited occasions for the Court of Appeal to develop law in the *Young* exceptions, but the only real scope for the Court of Appeal to be creative arises if there appears to be no case previously decided on the issue either by itself or the House of Lords.

New law –
mostly for the
House of Lords

Figure 6.14

Only the judges from the House of Lords have the power to declare a change in the law. As we have seen, they are usually cautious in using the Practice Statement. If it is possible to deal with an issue by distinguishing, rather than by overruling a previous decision, the House of Lords will take that approach. This has been particularly noticeable in development of the law of negligence. Looking at cases decided decades apart there are major changes to the law but these have usually been made in small steps, case by case.

Sometimes, of course, judges do come across situations which are totally new to the law. This is especially likely to arise in cases concerning medical treatment, for example:

- *Gillick v West Norfolk & Wisbech Health Authority* (1985) – whether a doctor would be acting illegally in giving a child under 16 contraceptive treatment.
- *Airedale HA v Bland* (1993) – whether it was lawful for a doctor to end treatment which sustained life artificially for a victim of the Hillsborough disaster.
- *Marks & Spencer v One In A Million* (1998) – whether a person or business should be able to 'bag' the names of well known companies or other organisations and register them for later sale at high prices. Further cases are likely to follow in future concerning e-commerce.
- *Re A (children)* (2000) – whether doctors should be authorised to separate conjoined twins, when it was likely that the helping of one would lead to the death of the other, but no operation at all would lead to the death of both.

Judges are influenced by the law in other countries, particularly the common law countries such as Australia, Canada and New Zealand which share English legal history. Some appeals from overseas are still made to the Privy Council, the membership of which is very similar to that of the House of Lords. Although Privy Council decisions are not binding on English courts they are considered to be persuasive precedents.

It seems likely that most judges, most of the time, choose to follow the authority which appears to be the 'closest fit' to the case before them. Sometimes a judge will engage in fairly sophisticated distinguishing to avoid a precedent which gives what the judge perceives to be an unjust result. The danger of this approach is that the law becomes difficult to ascertain because the distinctions drawn are so fine. This problem is particularly noticeable in criminal cases.

Judges at the very highest level do consider the implications of their decisions for the development of the law. Over the past thirty years or so they have gradually begun to discuss these issues in their judgments. It was uncommon among judges in the 1970s but is seen fairly frequently today. It is quite common for judges to comment that they are not entirely happy with the rules they are having to apply under the common law but that they have an obligation to follow precedent, and that any change to the law is a matter for Parliament.

One consideration that is certain to become of increasing importance to judicial precedent is the implication of the Human Rights Act 1998. Judges will not be able to rely on precedent if it contravenes this statute, and the statute is very wide-reaching in its implication. See, for example, the case of *Douglas and others v Hello! Ltd* (2001) in which Michael Douglas and Catherine Zeta-Jones were denied an injunction preventing *Hello! Magazine* from publishing photographs of their wedding. In interpreting this wide-reaching statute the judges will be involved in both setting new precedents and modifying previous decisions.

Advantages and disadvantages of judicial precedent

The English system of binding precedent followed by judges carries both advantages and disadvantages. Sometimes one feature is both an advantage and a disadvantage. For example, until 1966 its rigidity was seen as an advantage in creating certainty in the law, and allowing people to make out of court settlements and other decisions easily. The same rigidity was, however, a disadvantage in not allowing the law to change, or be flexible, in an ever changing society.

The following are some suggested benefits and problems of the doctrine of precedent, but you should think about them carefully and perhaps add your own views to these.

Thinking point

Advantages:

* *Certainty* – slightly less since 1966. We need a firm foundation on which out of court settlements can be made.

* *Flexibility and aptitude for growth* – more since 1966. It is important for the law to be able to change with society.

- *Greater detail* than is possible in a purely enacted system of law.
- *Practicality* – meets the individual needs of those who take cases to court.

Disadvantages:

- *Rigidity* – judges' discretion is limited to some extent by the obligation to follow decisions of predecessors.
- *Over-subtlety* – sometimes arises from the need to find a logical 'excuse' for not following an existing precedent where it would cause hardship to do so.
- *Bulk and complexity* – most English case law can be found in some 1,000 volumes of reports containing 400,000 cases, dating back to Middle Ages. Electronic retrieval makes research much easier, however.

Precedent in the lower courts

Each division of the High Court has its own Divisional Court in which two or three judges sit to hear appeals from inferior courts. The Divisional Courts are governed by the same rules as the Court of Appeal, their decisions being binding on themselves subject to the exceptions in *Young v Bristol Aeroplane Co* (1944). Judges sitting alone in the High Court and county courts do not create binding precedents and are bound by decisions of all the courts above them.

Precedent in the criminal courts

This chapter on judicial precedent has been written in terms of the civil courts, but the system of precedent applies in almost exactly the same way to the criminal courts. At the top of the hierarchy is the House of Lords (subject, of course, to the European Court of Justice), its decisions binding every court below and being subject to change only if it decides to invoke the 1966 Practice Statement. The House is cautious about changing the criminal law because of the problem of retrospection but it did so in *R v Shivpuri* (1987), acknowledging that its decision in *Anderton v Ryan* (1985) had been wrong. Rather less dramatically, the House of Lords has gradually adjusted the law with regard to intention in criminal law in *R v Moloney* (1985), *R v Hancock and Shankland* (1986), *R v Nedrick* (1987) and *R v Woollin* (1998). The House of Lords deals only with points of law of general public importance, so as criminal cases tend to turn on their own facts, its decisions in this area are few but important.

The Court of Appeal (Criminal Division) is bound by decisions of the House of Lords and generally regards itself as bound by its own previous decisions. It will, however, take a slightly more flexible approach than the Civil Division if following its own previous decision would result in an injustice. The Divisional Court of Queen's Bench Division is governed by the same rules as the Court of Appeal (Criminal Division) when hearing appeals by way of case stated from magistrates' courts and the Crown Court. The Crown Court and magistrates' courts are bound by the decisions of the Divisional Court of Queen's Bench, the Court of Appeal (Criminal Division) and the House of Lords and do not ever make precedents themselves.

Summary

Concepts	• Binding nature – based on fairness, recognising the need for consistency and flexibility; the doctrine of *stare decisis* – higher courts bind lower, like cases decided alike. • Terminology – following, reversing, overruling, dissenting, distinguishing. • The *ratio decidendi* and the *obiter dictum* – its binding nature.
Law reporting	• The importance of reporting and retrieval in precedent.
Hierarchy	• European Court of Justice, House of Lords, Court of Appeal and other courts.
House of Lords	• Freedom reversed in *London Street Tramways v London County Council* (1898). • Significance of Practice Statement 1966 and its operation – not bound, therefore freedom to overrule and develop the law. • Cases arising either side of 1966, e.g. *Addie v Dumbreck* (1929) and *British Railways Board v Herrington* (1972). Still subject to European Court of Justice if conflict arises.
Court of Appeal	• Bound by own previous decisions apart from exceptions in *Young v Bristol Aeroplane Co.* (1944). • The 'Denning' years – *Davis v Johnson* (1978) – the need for individual justice. • Bound by House of Lords decisions – but see *Broome v Cassell* (1971) and *Miliangos v George Frank Textiles* (1976). • Need for futher flexibility balanced against the need for certainty.
Case law	• *Ratio decidendi* and *obiter dictum*; difficulty of defining; persuasiveness of cases.
Limits of precedent	• Avoiding an awkward precedent; exceptions in *Young*, distinguishing, re-defining a *ratio*; the creative role of the judge.

Arguments • Advantages and disadvantages of precedent – the balancing of certainty and flexibility.

Other courts • Precedent in the criminal courts and lower courts.

Tasks

1 There is a lot of new terminology in this chapter. Write a brief explanation of the following words and phrases.

   (a) precedent
       hierarchy
       authority
   (b) follow
       overrule
       reverse
   (c) *stare decisis*
       ratio decidendi

   opaque
   litigation
   retrospective
   disapprove
   dissent
   distinguish
   obiter dicta

   Use a dictionary and the glossary to check your answers.

2 The question on page 101 is answered in the text that follows.
   Read the piece of text relating to this question and then try to answer in your own words. Remember to use cases as examples to illustrate your answer.

3 Think about the case of *Donoghue v Stevenson*.

   • What were: the facts; the decision; the *ratio decidendi*?
   • What was said *obiter*?

4 Why are *obiter dicta* important?

5 Explain how judicial precedent operates in:

   (a) the House of Lords;
   (b) the Court of Appeal.

6 Make a list of the advantages and disadvantages of the system of precedent in English law.

7 Consider whether the current system maintains a satisfactory balance between the certainty of knowing what the law is, and flexibility to develop the law to meet the needs of a changing society.

Part 2

Dispute solving (1): the machinery of justice

How do we make the law work for us? How can we be sure of its protection? We have considered where law comes from, and how rules of law are formed, but all of this would be of little value if we could not enforce these rules. It would not be of much use, for example, to say that the law states that a person can claim compensation for damage to property, if it was not possible to enforce the payment.

This is, of course, why we need courts. A judge takes the role of an independent person who can settle a dispute between two parties (people or organisations) and enforce any settlement agreed by the court. Wearing a wig and gown means that a judge is not acting in the role of his individual personality enforcing his own views, but on behalf of the state, representing the views of the law.

Figure P2.1

As law has grown more complex over the centuries, so have the courts, and the levels of courts, or hierarchy, play an increasingly important part in law enforcement, as we have seen in the study of judicial precedent. This section of the book examines:

- the role of the courts;
- the relationship between the different courts;
- alternatives to courts in solving disputes;
- the part played by the police in law enforcement.

7 The court structure and appeal routes

In studying the court system, it is important to think about other related issues, such as:

- funding of litigation
- the legal profession
- judges
- magistrates

- the jury
- the role of the police
- the operation of the doctrine of judicial precedent.

You should also keep up to date with recent, current and proposed changes to the procedures, financial limits and jurisdiction (or power to hear a case) of each of the courts, as they do change from time to time.

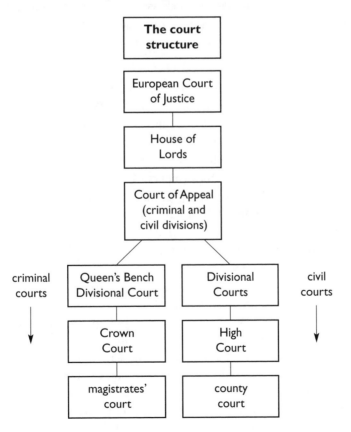

Figure 7.1

Original jurisdiction of civil and criminal courts

'Original jurisdiction' means when courts hear cases for the first time, as opposed to *appellate* jurisdiction which is when courts hear appeals from a previous decision. Remember, from work on judicial precedent, that in theory any new issue raised before a court, even at the lowest level, may form a new legal rule, but the higher the court, the more likely it is to carry authority and form a stable legal rule. Note that higher courts bind lower courts.

The criminal courts

The criminal court structure is progressive – all cases start in the magistrates' court, then the more serious ones go on for trial at the Crown Court.

Table 7.1

Type of offence	Example
Indictable	More serious offences, e.g. murder, manslaughter, rape.
Offences triable either way	Those which may be committed in a serious or minor manner, e.g. theft, assault causing actual bodily harm.
Summary	Minor offences, e.g. many motoring offences, not paying television licence, minor criminal damage.

- A *summary offence* is one where the maximum penalty is less than a £5,000 fine and/or six months' imprisonment. Where the court is required to deal with two or more offences, the most severe penalty available is 12 months and/or a £10,000 fine. Minor offences come within this category, including most driving offences, non-payment of council tax and licence fees, and some criminal damage and assault cases.

- An *indictable offence* is a more serious one and carries a more serious penalty. It is begun by a bill of indictment (a charge which is read out at the beginning of the case), and must be tried in the Crown Court by a judge and jury. Offences within this category include murder, manslaughter and rape.

- The third category of offence is known as *offences triable either way*, where the accused may select trial by magistrates or by a judge and jury. In these cases, even when the accused opts for trial in the magistrates' court, the magistrates may decide that their powers of sentencing are insufficient, and refer the case to the Crown Court just for the sentencing stage of the trial. The most common offence in this category is theft, as this could cover all kinds of situations, from stealing a bar of chocolate to raiding a bank or the Great Train Robbery.

Table 7.2

Type of offence	Mode of trial
Indictable	Crown Court
Triable either way	Magistrates' court or Crown Court
Summary	Magistrates' court

Practical task

Make a list of common criminal offences, using reports of cases in local newspapers for ideas if you need to. Divide your list into what you consider to be 'more serious' and 'less serious' offences. Compare your list with those made by other people. What do you consider makes some offences more serious than others?

The magistrates' court

The magistrates' courts have existed for hundreds of years. Their jurisdiction has been amended over the centuries so that they now have very wide powers in both civil and criminal matters. There are over 700 courts in towns around the United Kingdom. These are really seen as local courts, with each court being responsible for the trial of criminal offences within the area surrounding it. Cases are heard by magistrates, who are mostly lay people – people who are not legally qualified and who do this work voluntarily, not receiving a salary (see Chapter 13). There will normally be a 'bench' of three lay magistrates, one of them acting as chairperson. In some courts there may be a district judge (formerly known as a stipendiary magistrate) who is paid and legally qualified and who sits alone to hear cases. There will always be a clerk to the court, who advises the magistrates on the law and generally administers the court proceedings.

The criminal jurisdiction of the magistrates' court revolves around trying relatively minor (or summary) offences. More serious matters (indictable offences) are referred to the Crown Court for trial by a judge and jury. It is a very busy court, trying over 95 per cent of criminal cases, and in reality the role of the magistrates is very wide. The court is responsible for the following.

- The initial hearing of *all* criminal cases.
- Trial of summary offences.
- Trial of those offences which are triable either way but where it has been decided to try the case in the magistrates' court.

- Referral of more serious offences to the Crown Court, either:

    (a) immediately, by transfer proceedings, for indictable offences; or

    (b) following committal proceedings (where the court considers written evidence and commits the case to the Crown Court) for offences triable either way.

- Dealing with applications for bail and for the granting of legal aid.
- Issuing search and arrest warrants, although dealing with warrants can be carried out by a single magistrate and need not take place at the court itself.

There are proposals to downgrade the standing of some offences, so that they may be tried more quickly and efficiently, and with less expense, in the magistrates' courts. This suggests that despite the problems which exist, the overall picture of magistrates' courts is one of efficiency and success.

Practical task

1   Using your local newspaper reports of cases heard in the magistrates' court, make a note of:

    (a) the offence;

    (b) the sentence given (if reported).

2   Visit your local magistrates' court and observe a day's activities – you are allowed to sit in the public gallery, which is an area reserved for the public at the back of the court.

Youth courts

Magistrates who have been specially trained may also sit as a youth court, dealing with young offenders, and with special powers of sentencing. These courts sit at a different place or time from the full court in order to protect the young people being tried. This ensures that they do not come into contact with adult offenders, and press reporting is restricted so that the young offenders' reputations are not adversely affected. These courts are staffed by a panel of three lay magistrates, with both men and women sitting in order to attain a balance.

There are several experiments being carried out in the North of England where magistrates' courts are setting aside one day, or part of a day each week, to deal with specific issues, such as drug-related offences or crimes of domestic violence. The magistrates who sit in these courts may receive special training at some point in the future, although it is felt by the Lord Chancellor's department that, at least for the moment, there is no need.

The reason behind the scheme is to allow all the experts involved in these cases to be assembled together in one place at one time, rather than having to attend at different times throughout the week; thereby dealing with cases more effectively and more efficiently. The probation service, social workers and drugs counsellors may meet and coordinate their efforts to attempt to deal with the problems before the court. Should the experiments prove effective, it is likely that the scheme will be extended across the country.

The Crown Court

The Crown Court is where trials of the more serious offences are held. There are approximately 90 of these courts throughout the United Kingdom. They were introduced by the Courts Act 1971 to replace the Assizes. The Assizes were originally set up by Henry II at the end of the twelfth century to tour the country taking the King's justice to the provinces. The Crown Courts similarly operate on a circuit system, where judges travel around the courts in one of the six circuits in England and Wales, hearing cases. Crown Courts are divided into three categories or 'tiers', according to how they are staffed and the kind of cases which they may hear. These tiers are: First, Second and Third.

Indictable offences are also placed into different categories depending on their severity:

- class 1 offences are the most serious, such as murder and treason;
- class 2 offences are second in 'seriousness' – manslaughter, sedition and mutiny;
- class 3 offences are defined as all those indictable offences not in classes 1, 2 or 4;
- class 4 offences are the least serious, such as offences triable either way, causing death by dangerous driving, causing grievous bodily harm, and robbery.

Offences in class 1 may only be tried by a High Court judge in a First-tier Crown Court, but offences class 4 may be tried by a circuit judge or recorder in a Third-tier Court. The object is to ensure that the more serious offences are tried by the more senior, experienced judges. This also saves money, as trying a minor theft using a High Court judge would be unnecessarily expensive. As a rough guide: the higher the tier, the higher the judge, the higher the class of offence.

Table 7.3

Type of judge	Level	Class of offence
High Court judge	First-tier	I
Circuit judge	Second-tier	2 and 3
Recorder	Third-tier	4

The importance of the Crown Court lies in the fact that it involves trial by judge and jury, unlike the magistrates' court where the magistrates are the judges of both fact and law.

Crown Court =  +

Judge   Jury

Figure 7.2

In the Crown Court, the role of the jury is to listen to the facts, and bring about a verdict based on those facts. It is the role of the judge to decide any points of law, and then to sentence. The judge has sentencing powers which are only limited by the relevant statute.

Thinking point

Why choose trial at the Crown Court?

- The verdict is decided by a jury (the public has confidence in this mode of trial).
- The defendant may be a regular offender who is known by local magistrates.
- Defendants believe that there is a greater chance of acquittal.

But

- It is possible that a defendant found guilty at Crown Court will be given a higher sentence.
- There is a long wait for Crown Court trial, and the trial itself will take longer.
- The costs are much greater (but many defendants will obtain legal aid).
- Representation must be by a barrister (or a solicitor who is a certified advocate).

Reform of the criminal courts

In 1998 a consultation document called 'Determining Mode of Trial in Either-way Cases' was issued proposing a reduction in the number of people who could choose jury trial (Home Office, July 1998). In May 1999 the Home Secretary announced that he intended to implement suggestions put forward by the Runciman Committee, the Royal Commission on Criminal Justice 1993, relating to the restriction of the right to trial by jury. The proposal was that 'middling' offences, in other words the less serious hybrid offences such as theft and assault, would no longer be triable at the Crown Court, but only by magistrates. The justification for such a change is that about 79 per cent of such offenders plead guilty anyway, and that the savings in time and cost will more than compensate for the reduction in the rights of the individual. It was also proposed that, of the remaining offences that will still be triable either way, the choice of mode of trial would be made by the magistrates rather than the accused.

Some commentators, such as the writer John Mortimer, are concerned that such moves are likely to seriously undermine civil liberties by taking away the historic right to trial by one's peers set out in the Magna Carta. Others, such as Michael Zander, a leading academic lawyer, believe that the practical differences will be minimal. The House of Lords have twice rejected Bills proposing changes aimed at abolishing the right to choose jury trial.

More recently, Sir Robin Auld, in his review, has recommended that there should be an intermediate level of trial, with initial allocation to the right level, rather than election by defendants. The Auld Review, said by the Lord Chancellor to be 'a wide-ranging, independent review of the criminal courts', was set up to review how the criminal courts work at every level. The task (referred to as 'terms of reference') is set out below:

A review into the practices and procedures of, and the rules of evidence applied by, the criminal courts at every level, with a view to ensuring that they deliver justice fairly, by streamlining all their processes, increasing their efficiency and strengthening the effectiveness of their relationships with others across the whole of the criminal justice system, and having regard to the interests of all parties including victims and witnesses, thereby promoting public confidence in the rule of law.

The review includes, but is not limited to, the following matters:

- the structure and organisation of, and distribution of work between, courts;
- their composition, including the use of juries and of lay and stipendiary magistrates;
- case management, procedure and evidence (including the use of information technology);
- service to and treatment of all those who use or have to attend courts or who are the subject of their proceedings;
- liaison between the courts and agencies involved in the criminal justice system;
- management and funding of the system.

Among the 328 recommendations, one of the most fundamental was the proposal to have a unified criminal court with three divisions. These would be:

- *Crown Division* – this would be similar to the current Crown Court, dealing with indictable offences and the more serious 'either-way' offences allocated to it.
- *District Division* – this would be made up of a judge (normally a District judge or Recorder) and at least two lay magistrates. It would be a middle court, trying 'either-way' offences for which a sentence may be up to two years' custody.
- *Magistrates' Division* – this would be much as the current courts, with lay magistrates or District judges, trying summary offences and the simpler 'either-way' offences.

The review also recommended a single line of appeal and changes to jury selection (see Chapter 13).

The report was published in 2001. In the meantime the government produced a Criminal Justice Plan as part of its manifesto. This was seen by many as a highly political manoeuvre to attract public support prior to an election, and many are critical of a political body attempting to have such an input into criminal justice, especially with a major review headed by a leading judge already in progress

Practical task

Visit the following web site to read more about the Auld review, and to find out what changes are recommended to the criminal process:

http://www.criminal-courts-review.org.uk

The civil courts

Although this section is entitled 'The civil courts', it is more appropriate to say 'courts with civil jurisdiction', as some courts deal with both civil and criminal cases. Unlike the criminal courts, the civil system is not progressive. Cases enter the system at different levels depending on the seriousness of the case and the amount of money involved.

Reform of the civil courts

The whole civil process was reviewed via an enquiry led by Lord Woolf. His view was that the civil justice system should ensure access to justice, and he listed a number of aims, for example:

- It should be just in the results it delivers.
- It should be fair and be seen to be so by:
  - ensuring that litigants have an equal opportunity, regardless of their resources, to assert or defend their legal rights;
  - providing every litigant with an adequate opportunity to state his or her own case and answer his or her opponent's;
  - treating like cases alike.
- Procedures and cost should be proportionate to the nature of the issues involved.
- It should deal with cases with reasonable speed.
- It should be understandable to those who use it.
- It should provide as much certainty as the nature of particular cases allows.
- It should be effective: adequately resourced and organised.

Lord Woolf went on to identify a number of problems with the existing process, such as the expense and delay of taking a case to court, the complexity of the procedures, and the adversarial system (see below) which reduces the likelihood of a settlement being made out of court. The Woolf Report, called 'Access to Justice', was published in 1996 and contains 303 recommendations. It made suggestions for reform, including extending the small claims procedure, a new fast track, and more use of alternative dispute resolution.

A second report, the Middleton Report, was commissioned in 1997 by the newly elected Labour government, the combined result of both of these reports being the new Civil Procedure Rules which came into force in April 1999.

The Civil Procedure Rules aim to enable the courts to deal with cases justly, as quickly and inexpensively as possible. An appropriate share of the court's time should be allocated to cases, and the court should deal with cases in a way which is proportionate to:

- the amount involved
- the importance of the case
- the complexity of the issues.

In addition, the use of information technology was encouraged, and the use of old or unintelligible language, especially Latin words, was disapproved. A person beginning a case now, for example, would not be a *plaintiff*, but a *claimant* (as most of the cases in this book refer to previous case-law, the word plaintiff has been retained within the book).

A report issued in March 2001 by the Lord Chancellor called: *Emerging Findings: An Early Evaluation of the Civil Justice Reforms* states as its key findings that:

- Overall there has been a drop in the number of claims issued, in particular in the types of claim where the new Civil Procedure Rules have been introduced.

- Anecdotal evidence suggests pre-action protocols are working well to promote settlement before issue and to reduce the number of ill-founded claims.

- There is evidence to show that settlements at the door of the court are now fewer and that settlements before the hearing day have increased.

The magistrates' court

Although primarily a court dealing with criminal matters, this court also has some civil jurisdiction. It has some administrative duties, being responsible for granting licences for the sale of alcohol and provision of entertainment, as well as dealing with 'civil debts' – such as money owed for council taxes, gas and electricity bills and television licences, although these debts may be treated as criminal offences as well as civil liabilities.

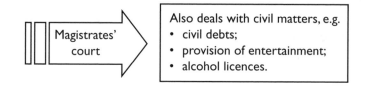

Magistrates' court

Also deals with civil matters, e.g.
- civil debts;
- provision of entertainment;
- alcohol licences.

Figure 7.3

The largest area of civil business dealt with by magistrates is matrimonial, and when dealing with such cases the court sits as the family court. Magistrates require special training before undertaking this work, and rarely make absolute decisions. So, for example, they can grant a judicial separation but not a divorce, periodic payment orders but not a property settlement.

The county court

The county courts were originally created in 1864 to provide a system of inexpensive, local dispute resolution. There are over 220 courts in the United Kingdom in most major towns, which deal with a range of civil matters, ranging from contract and tort, through to probate, landlord and tenant disputes, credit issues, uncontested divorces and other ancillary (associated) family matters such as children and property.

Following the new Civil Procedure Rules a three-track system was introduced.

1   The *small claims track* deals with relatively minor claims (a system which was previously known as Small Claims Arbitration). The system was set up because it would not be worth the expense, time and effort for a person to make a small claim via the normal court procedure. The financial limit for small claims was originally £75 in 1973, but this has now risen to £5,000 for most claims and £1,000 for personal injury claims.

    Costs are kept to a minimum as winning parties are not allowed to claim costs for solicitors, and are encouraged to represent themselves or use lay helpers. Although the case is heard in a normal court room, the atmosphere is more relaxed and the court operates on an inquisitorial rather than an adversarial basis. This 'inquisitorial' approach means that the judge (usually a district judge), will enquire into what has gone on between the parties and will take an active role to establish the truth, as opposed to the more formal 'adversarial' court process which requires each side to 'win' by presenting their own side of the case.

    According to research, the court has a reputation of success, with most users, even those who lose, feeling that the process was fair. Nearly 90 per cent of all civil claims not immediately admitted or set-tled are dealt with by the small claims track. A report from the National Audit Office shows that 94 per cent of claimants won their case. About 75 per cent of these are business or public authorities, however, and most of their claims are for unpaid bills.

2   The *fast-track system* deals with cases up to £15,000. The district judge sets out a timetable to ensure that cases are dealt with within 30 weeks of allocation and giving directions concerning exchange of witness statements and disclosure of documents. The other side is allowed to see witness statements and all relevant documents unless there is a good legal reason why they should not do so. This saves time by avoid-ing parties producing unexpected evidence on the day. The track is designed for cases not expected to last for more than one day, and is a way of providing affordable justice in the majority of cases outside small claims.

3   The *multi-track system* is for claims which involve large sums of money or which raise difficult points of law. It also allows for transfer of cases between courts depending on complexity.

Following the new Civil Procedure Rules the financial limits have been raised. Almost any case except defamation *may* begin in the county court, and any claim worth under £15,000, or personal injuries or contract claim under £50,000, *must* use the county court. Generally matters between £25,000 and £50,000 may be heard in a county court or the High Court.

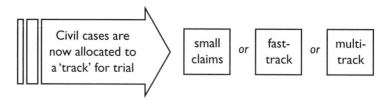

Figure 7.4

Since April 1999, when the Woolf report was implemented in part by the Civil Procedure Act 1997, the hearing of cases is now determined according to complexity as well as amount, so that simple cases involving more than the specified amount *may* still be tried in the county court, whereas more complex cases involving lesser amounts *may* be transferred to the High Court. A case manager, who may be the judge, is responsible for ensuring that cases are dealt with as quickly as possible. The case manager supervises the system and ensures that cases are correctly allocated and remain within the time constraints imposed for hearings.

Practical task

Look in local and national newspapers over a period of time for reports on civil cases (you will find that there are not many of these compared with reports on criminal cases). Make a note of:

- what the case concerned;
- the court in which the case was heard;
- the remedy that was awarded.

The High Court

The High Court is divided into three divisions, each of which has some original jurisdiction:

- the Queen's Bench Division (QBD)
- the Chancery Division
- the Family Division.

The High Court was created in its original form by the Judicature Acts of 1873–75 to combine the courts of common law and equity, but has since been reorganised to reflect modern social trends. It generally operates in London, but judges also sit as the High Court in various towns around the country. The court is staffed by High Court or *puisne* judges, but each division is headed by a senior law officer, and each division has its own specialised area of responsibility.

- The QBD deals mostly with contract and tort disputes and is headed by the Lord Chief Justice. Cases are usually tried by a single judge, but there is sometimes a jury for actions in defamation, fraud, malicious prosecution and false imprisonment. It also has an important role in judicial review (review of whether a decision taken by a public body has been made via the correct procedure). About 70 judges hear about 700 cases each year.
- The Family Division deals with matrimonial matters and is headed by the President. It has a staff of about 17 judges and hears family matters, such as complex matrimonial cases and issues connected with the Children Act 1989.
- The Chancery Division deals with equitable issues such as mortgages and trusts and is headed by the Lord Chancellor, although in practice the work is undertaken by the Vice-Chancellor. Other work undertaken by its staff of about 17 judges includes financial issues, such as bankruptcy, liquidation and copyright.

Again, since the introduction of case managers, the cases that are referred to the High Court are those involving the more complex legal issues rather than just those involving the most money.

Courts with appellate jurisdiction

It is important to understand the routes of appeal as well as the grounds on which those appeals can be based. In criminal cases the defendant could appeal against conviction or against sentence, whereas the prosecution can only appeal against the sentence imposed. In a civil case, either party can appeal against the decision or the award. In either case, the appeal can be based on a point of law or a question of fact.

There are several courts which deal purely with appeals, however, as mentioned previously, some of the courts detailed above also hear appeals, that is, they have a dual jurisdiction – largely original but with some appellate authority. Here we consider the courts which have purely appellate jurisdiction:

1   the Divisional Courts of the High Court;
2   the Court of Appeal (Criminal Division);
3   the Court of Appeal (Civil Division).

The Divisional Courts of the High Court

Each of the divisions of the High Court (QBD, Chancery and Family) has a corresponding Divisional Court which has appellate jurisdiction. The Divisional Court hears appeals from the lower courts, but not from the divisions. One of the most important aspects of the work of the Divisional Court of the QBD is the hearing of applications for judicial review, which, although not an appeal, may deal with cases initially heard by the lower courts.

The Court of Appeal (Criminal Division)

This court deals exclusively with appeals from the Crown Court, and is staffed by Lord Justices of Appeal. The court is headed by the Lord Chief Justice, who is the head of the criminal justice system.

Criminal courts word search

Find the words below; they are all connected with criminal courts.

```
H  B  H  T  K  G  E  T  I  Y  I  W  F  I  W  Q  H  U  Y  N
E  T  E  R  K  G  U  V  N  L  D  M  F  I  Q  X  G  S  T  V
O  L  A  D  A  O  S  S  I  A  N  O  T  U  E  B  F  H  L  M
Y  Q  G  O  I  P  A  B  P  D  D  N  T  E  R  I  L  E  I  T
P  B  L  W  F  T  Y  B  R  Y  E  N  X  S  V  M  I  R  U  M
D  Z  Z  H  X  J  C  X  O  S  O  N  E  L  U  Y  A  U  G  O
T  C  I  D  R  E  V  L  S  T  K  R  C  F  H  C  B  R  P  L
C  O  U  R  T  E  Q  W  E  K  C  O  D  E  E  K  I  M  S  I
S  H  Q  S  V  H  O  G  C  R  I  N  W  O  C  D  A  Q  U  S
Y  N  R  X  S  N  H  Q  U  D  K  Q  A  E  R  G  R  E  M  P
D  B  D  Z  H  H  W  B  T  T  Z  R  E  O  I  T  E  X  M  F
F  D  S  C  Z  V  S  A  I  N  H  D  T  S  I  K  T  P  A  W
J  H  R  Q  J  Q  T  D  O  V  O  I  T  U  J  J  S  D  R  W
S  E  N  T  E  N  C  E  N  E  C  R  Q  W  W  W  I  Z  Y  W
E  L  B  A  T  C  I  D  N  I  A  C  J  J  X  B  R  F  R  Q
G  Q  P  S  Q  R  E  I  L  T  A  D  F  U  I  F  R  R  P  R
D  I  R  L  J  W  F  O  E  J  G  U  O  S  Z  G  A  S  D  J
I  X  L  W  T  U  S  L  U  H  J  V  B  I  X  L  B  U  Q  Q
S  Y  U  T  T  O  U  R  J  I  C  S  I  M  Y  O  U  N  P  H
S  N  Q  M  Q  O  Y  H  R  W  P  D  M  S  O  A  P  B  N  I
```

ACQUIT	BAIL	BARRISTER
CLERK	COURT	CUSTODY
DEFENDANT	DOCK	EVIDENCE
FINE	GUILTY	INDICTABLE
JURY	MAGISTRATE	OATH
PROSECUTION	SENTENCE	SOLICITOR
SUMMARY	USHER	VERDICT
WITNESS		

Figure 7.5

The Court of Appeal (Civil Division)

This court deals with appeals from the High Court, although cases can be 'leap-frogged' directly to the House of Lords where a case is subject to an existing precedent or involves a matter of statutory interpretation, as a result of the provisions of the 1969 Administration of Justice Act. It is staffed by 35 Lord Justices of Appeal and is headed by the Master of the Rolls, who has primary responsibility for the civil justice system. It is a very busy court, with a great problem of delay and a backlog of cases.

Proposed reforms

In 1997, the Lord Chancellor, dealing with the incorporation of the European Convention on Human Rights into the British constitution, identified the central role of the appeal courts in its implementation. As a result of the increased number of cases expected following the Human Rights Act, Lord Irvine suggested that many of the proposals put forward by the Bowman Report, including reforming the civil division's jurisdiction, constitution and requirements of leave to appeal, should be implemented.

Lord Woolf, the Master of the Rolls, also reviewed the work of the Court of Appeal (Civil Division) in 1997. He, too, emphasised the importance of implementing the Bowman recommendations. He discussed the establishment of a management committee to oversee the court's work, and to attempt to clear the backlog of cases, speeding the process for applying for leave to appeal, aided by the introduction of judicial assistants and a Deputy Registrar for case management. He also announced the setting up of a pilot ADR (Alternative Dispute Resolution) scheme for the Court of Appeal.

The aim of recent changes is to ensure that the civil system is 'accessible, fair and efficient'. The number of judges was increased to help deal with the backlog and working hours were increased. The Civil Procedure Rules have provided that, since May 2000, appeals from the county court (even from the small claims track) go to the next judge up in hierarchy, e.g. appeal from a District judge will be with a Circuit judge. There is still, however, a delay if appeal is sought. Surely an 'efficient' system is one which includes a right to appeal within a reasonable time scale?

The House of Lords

This is the highest court of appeal in the United Kingdom, and has the authority to hear appeals from the lower courts which involve a point of law of public importance, although either the House of Lords or Court of Appeal must give permission for a case to advance here (previously called 'leave to appeal'). This permission is difficult to obtain, the House of Lords hearing less than 100 cases each year.

Occasionally a 'leap-frog' procedure is used, where permission is given to appeal and the trial judge grants a certificate, the case then goes directly from the High Court to the House of Lords. This rarely happens, and it

The 'leap-frog' appeal procedure for civil cases

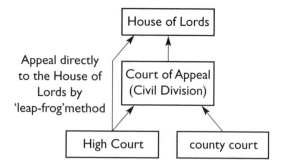

Figure 7.6

arises in cases of general importance concerning interpretation of a statute or where a court is bound by the precedent of the Court of Appeal or the House of Lords.

The House of Lords sits in an ante-room at the Palace of Westminster as a court of five – although occasionally there are seven judges in a particularly important case. The Law Lords (or Lords of Appeal in Ordinary) wear ordinary suits rather than formal judicial clothing. The court is headed by the Lord Chancellor, and hears evidence by written summaries of the previous hearings, and submissions from barristers. The Lords then present their findings in written form at a later date. Recent criticisms of this have included the difficulty of obtaining a referral to the court, and the delay in receiving a decision.

Appeals in criminal cases

Appeals from the magistrates' courts can be made by the defendant to the Crown Court. From the Crown Court, appeals are made to the Court of Appeal (Criminal Division) and from there to the House of Lords – but only with leave to appeal and on a matter of law of general public importance. Following a plea of not guilty, a defendant who is found guilty can appeal over conviction or sentence. Following a guilty plea, a defendant can appeal only over sentence.

A case may be referred by the magistrates to the Divisional Court of the Queen's Bench Division of the High Court, by way of case stated, for clarification of a point of law or procedure. An appeal by this route can only concern an appeal against conviction or acquittal – not against sentence. A written record of the case is sent to the Divisional Court (a statement of the finding in the case), and no witnesses are called. Further appeal is possible to the House of Lords on a point of general public importance. Either the prosecution or the defence can ask for a case to be sent to the Divisional Court where the judges will conduct a judicial review to decide whether the case has been heard according to the rules of natural justice ('let both sides be heard' or *audi alterem partem*, and no one can be a judge in their own case, or *nemo judex in causa sua*). Judicial review will also be concerned to ensure that a court has not exceeded its jurisdiction (called acting *ultra vires*, or beyond one's powers). Such a hearing may result in the case being sent back for a re-trial.

Appeals to the Court of Appeal (Criminal Division)

Defendant

The defendant can appeal to the Court of Appeal (Criminal Division) in the following instances:

- *Appeal against conviction.* The Criminal Appeal Act 1995 states that a defendant must either have a certificate from the trial judge that the case is fit for an appeal or permission from the Court of Appeal (Criminal Division) in order to appeal. The Court will allow the appeal if they think that the conviction is 'unsafe'. They may hear evidence that was not called at the original trial, provided that:
    - it seems capable of belief;
    - it may afford a ground of appeal;
    - there is a reasonable explanation as to why it was not called at the original trial.
- *Appeal against sentence.* A defendant may appeal against sentence but the Court of Appeal will cut a sentence only if it was wrong in principle.

Prosecution

Under the Criminal Justice Act 1982, appeal is not strictly a right of the prosecution, but the Attorney-General may be asked to refer a point of law to the Court of Appeal if the prosecution believes that the trial court made an error of law. This has no effect on the defendant but helps to prevent mistakes being perpetuated.

Similarly, the Attorney-General may be asked to appeal against a sentence which is regarded as too lenient, under the Criminal Justice Act of 1988.

Criminal Cases Review Commission

This body was set up in Birmingham as an independent organisation under the Criminal Appeal Act 1995. The Criminal Cases Review Commission says of itself that it is:

an independent, thorough, investigative, impartial, open and accountable body responsible for investigating suspected miscarriages of criminal justice in England, Wales and Northern Ireland.

Appeal routes in criminal cases

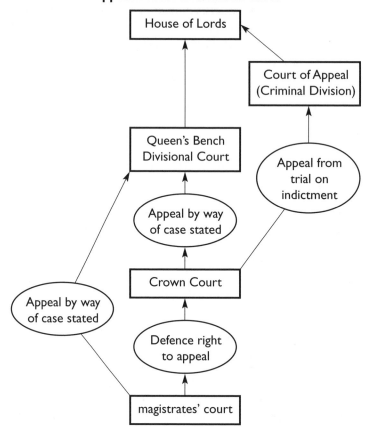

Figure 7.7

It was created on the recommendation of the Runciman Commission to investigate suspected miscarriages of criminal justice, which had previously been dealt with by the office of the Home Secretary. When the Criminal Cases Review Commission (CCRC) took over the responsibility for investigating such cases in March 1997 over 250 were transferred from the Home Office to the Commission. It now consists of a staff of nearly 100, including 15 members drawn from a wide variety of backgrounds and over 40 case-workers.

In order to refer a criminal case to the relevant court of appeal, whether Court of Appeal (Criminal Division) or Crown Court, a majority of at least three members sitting as a committee must agree, taking into account whether or not there is a real possibility that the conviction, finding, verdict or sentence would be overturned. This requires:

• presentation of an argument or evidence not raised during the original trial or appeal; or
• exceptional circumstances.

The first of these requirements needs a legal argument or information about the individual or the offence not raised at the trial or appeal. The second relies on very unusual circumstances, such as those surrounding the conviction and execution of Derek Bentley in 1953. (For further details of this case, see the film *Let Him Have It*, or any of the true crime books dealing with twentieth-century crimes.) The CCRC determined that this case should be referred back to the Court of Appeal, which determined 45 years after the execution that Bentley should not have been convicted. The Queen then exercised the royal prerogative of mercy and granted a posthumous pardon.

Having referred the case back to the appropriate court of appeal, the CCRC has no further involvement in dealing with the issue. Only about 5 per cent of new cases received by the CCRC since 1997 have been against summary convictions.

In the March 2001 CCRC statistics update it is noted that 124 cases had been referred to the Court of Appeal (Criminal Division), of which 65 had been heard, 48 of which had resulted in sentences or convictions being quashed by the end of March 1999. A total of 3994 applications for review had been received by the CCRC, of these 2926 had been dealt with.

It is difficult to assess how effective the CCRC has been, except to say that 48 people are now free of conviction who would otherwise still be suffering from a miscarriage of justice. Each working day generates at least three further cases to review, and each case has, on average, about 2500 pages of material to be considered. Despite more staff being taken on, the workload is still great.

Practical task

- Look at the CCRC Internet site: www.ccrc.gov.uk to read more about the CCRC.

- Find out the latest statistics.

- Look at some of the cases listed. Choose one which interests you and make brief notes on it (e.g. the original offence with which the person was charged, the circumstances, the sentence given, the length of time served (if custodial) and the findings of the CCRC).

Appeals in civil cases

Certain appeals from magistrates' courts may be made to a county court, but more usually they are dealt with by the appropriate divisional court of the High Court. From there, cases are appealed to the Court of Appeal (Civil Division) and then to the House of Lords on the same basis as criminal cases. Appeals from the High Court go to the Court of Appeal (Civil Division).

Having heard an appeal, the court may uphold the original decision or award, or may set it aside. An appeal court may then decide to uphold the lower court's decision, and either maintain the award or vary it according to the evidence presented and points of law discussed.

The Civil Procedure Rules have replaced separate sets of rules for the High Court and county courts and it is now necessary to have permission to appeal in a civil case. Further, only in exceptional circumstances is a litigant allowed to appeal more than once.

The Privy Council

This court remains rather an anomaly (a peculiar and unusual thing). It is part of the House of Lords, but it only deals with appeals from the supreme courts of Commonwealth countries. The judges are Law Lords, and they hear both civil and criminal appeals. The court has achieved a degree of importance recently in hearing appeals from countries which still have the death penalty, in that the decision of the Privy Council will determine whether or not the convicted appellant should hang.

While the Privy Council is composed of members of the House of Lords, its decisions do not technically form a binding precedent. Some of its decisions have formed important persuasive precedents in our legal system, however, due to the seniority of the judges making the decision.

Civil and criminal processes

The procedures of the courts are both complex and highly specialised, so this section will only provide a general outline of the processes involved.

Civil process

There have been several recent changes to the civil process, which were introduced after the publication of the Woolf Committee Report in 1996. The report was concerned with improving the court system, and formed the basis of the Civil Procedure Act 1997. The resulting procedural changes related to terminology (the 'plaintiff' is now known as the 'claimant') and to process (the terms 'writ' and 'summons' or 'plaint' are now known as 'claims'). As a result of these changes, a case will be allocated to the small claims track, the fast-track procedure or the multi-track system. This allocation depends on the amount of the claim involved and its complexity, with matters being governed by a case manager who is responsible for ensuring that the case proceeds as quickly and simply as possible (see page 119 earlier in this chapter).

The primary obligation of all qualified advocates has been extended, so that both barrister and solicitor advocates have an overall duty to the civil justice system rather than the client.

Practical task

Read the material in this chapter on Civil Courts again. Then investigate the Woolf Report called 'Access to Justice'. Use the library, CD-Roms for newspaper reports and the Internet.

- How far have the recommendations been implemented by the Lord Chancellor and the government?
- How far will they improve 'access to justice'?

In general terms, however, the civil process remains broadly similar whether at a lower or higher level. A case is begun by issuing a claim (formerly a summons or a writ), which the claimant serves to the defendant, who has a limited time in which to respond. The defendant can respond in one of the following ways:

- they can admit liability and offer to settle;
- they can deny any liability at all;
- they can accept some liability but dispute the amount claimed; or
- they can make a counter-claim.

In a contentious matter (one which is contested), a questionnaire will be issued by the case manager (usually the judge) and the case will be listed for a suitable 'track' for trial. The parties will provide any documents required, agree witness statements and evidence in advance, so that by the time the case is listed for trial, only the disputed areas will be contested. Many cases are 'settled at the door of the court' when the parties agree to settle at the last minute rather than face the ordeal of a trial.

If a case does go to trial then the claimant puts their case first, calling witnesses and introducing evidence in support of the claim. The defendant may challenge or cross-examine witnesses throughout this presentation. The defence then presents their side of the argument in the same way, before each side sums up to the judge. (It is rare to find a jury in civil cases – see Chapter 13 on lay people). The judge will then determine liability (whether the defendant is responsible as claimed) 'on the balance of probabilities' –

the standard in civil cases. The judge will also assess and award damages to the claimant if successful, and determine who will bear the costs of the case (usually the loser).

The small claims provision is much less formal. The parties meet in court with the district judge, but with less formality. Note that there is no need for strict rules of evidence or an award of costs, as each party pays their own.

Thinking point

(You may also like to make brief notes.)

Think of the problems that seem to be part of the civil court system, such as cost, delay, formality, loss of commercial or domestic goodwill.

Now think of the benefits, such as enforcement of awards and decisions, formality, independence of decision.

Consider:

- why some cases are settled 'at the door of the court';
- how far this goes against the effectiveness of the civil justice system.

Criminal process

When an offence has been committed, it is the task of the police to investigate the crime, question witnesses and suspects, and arrest and charge the person they feel is the culprit. Once all the evidence has been assembled, the file is sent to the Crown Prosecution Service (CPS), where it is assessed by a legally qualified assistant.

The CPS was established under the Prosecution of Offences Act 1985. It is the role of the CPS to manage the prosecution procedure. It is led by the Director of Public Prosecutions (the DPP) and it carries out work which was formerly undertaken by the police. The idea was that the formation of the CPS would leave the police free to detect and investigate crime, and enable cases to be presented to the court be trained specialists.

The tasks which fall within the responsibility of the CPS are:

- advising police on whether to charge;
- reviewing cases passed to them to see if there is enough evidence to proceed with a trial;
- deciding whether it is in the public interest to proceed with a trial;
- taking responsibility for the management of the prosecution in a case;
- presenting cases for the prosecution in the magistrates' court – usually carried out by Crown Prosecutors who are lawyers;

- presenting cases for the prosecution in the Crown Court – this can be done by instructing a barrister, or, under the power given in the Access to Justice Act 1999, Crown Prosecutors with advocacy rights may present the case.

Once a file has been received from the police, the CPS must then decide whether or not there is a case to answer, and to determine what charges, if any, will be brought, depending on their chances of success. There has been criticism, especially in the Glidewell Report (1998), that the CPS drops too many cases. This has resulted in some reorganisation of the service and local Chief Crown Prosecutors being appointed.

There are certain guidelines set down to help in making the decision whether to prosecute, such as the public interest, the chances of success, and the age and vulnerability of both the accused and the victim. In minor offences, the police may decide that it would be better to caution the accused, if the individual admits to the offence and accepts the caution. It is estimated that about one in nine recorded crimes lead to a charge, and about two-thirds of those cautioned are found not to have committed a further offence within two years.

The Crime and Disorder Act 1998 abolished cautions for children and young people (they were thought by many to be particularly effective with this group, especially for first offenders) and put in its place the power to reprimand and warn. There is a limit to how many times a person may be reprimanded or warned before a more severe sentence is given.

The way in which a case progresses through the criminal courts depends upon whether the offence is classed as a summary, triable either way or indictable offence.

Summary offences

A summary offence is begun by the laying of an information. A summons is served on the accused telling them when and where to attend the magistrates' court for the hearing. If the accused pleads guilty, as most do, then a summary of the facts is read to the court, a plea in mitigation may be made, and then the magistrates pass sentence, up to a maximum of six months' imprisonment and/or £5,000 for one offence, or double that for more than one, subject to the statutory limits for the particular offence.

Indictable offences and offences triable either way

The first stage is to appear before the magistrates where the defendant is asked how they intend to plead. For an either way offence it is then determined whether or not there is sufficient evidence to warrant a full trial before a judge and jury at the Crown Court. These are known as committal proceedings, where the prosecution is required to prove that a *prima facie* case exists. This is done by producing the written statements of prosecution witnesses. The defence may claim there is no case to answer and the magistrates make a decision.

The Crime and Disorder Act 1998 provides for indictable offences to go straight to Crown Court under transfer proceedings, and any claim of 'no case to answer' will be heard there once the provision is in force. With offences which are triable either way the decision as to whether the case is dealt with by magistrates or at the Crown Court is made by the accused, although the magistrates can refuse to hear a case if they feel that the case is too serious or that their sentencing powers are likely to be insufficient.

It is proposed that the categories of offences classed as triable either way be extended, and the choice of whether or not trial by jury is available will be left with the magistrates rather than the accused, although there will be a right of appeal against their decision. There has been much debate about the effect on civil liberties caused by this change to the law (see Reform of the Criminal Courts, earlier in this chapter) and the House of Lords, in particular, has been unwilling to pass the legislation.

Committal proceedings are dealt with in the form of 'paper committals', also known as Section 6 committals, which means that all of the evidence does not need to be presented just for a preliminary hearing. This allows the magistrates' court to read the prosecution file and decide quickly whether or not there is sufficient evidence. When the court decides that there is insufficient evidence to proceed, the accused is released but is not acquitted – the prosecution may bring the same case again at a later date if more evidence comes to light. If there is enough evidence to permit a committal, the accused is sent to the Crown Court for trial by a judge and jury.

At the Crown Court, the procedure is as follows.

- The prosecution outlines its case.
- The prosecution calls witnesses and produces evidence in support of its case – the defence is permitted to challenge the evidence and cross-examine the prosecution witnesses.
- The defence then presents its own case in the same way, with the prosecution similarly challenging and cross-examining.
- Each side sums up its case, followed by a judge's summing up.
- The jury is sent out to determine their verdict, which should be 'beyond reasonable doubt' and unanimous, although the judge will accept a majority verdict of at least 10 to 2 after two hours and ten minutes have elapsed without a unanimous verdict having been reached.
- Following a guilty verdict, a plea in mitigation is made by the defence (generally asking the judge to be lenient for various reasons) and sentence is given by the judge. Following a not guilty plea, of course, the defendant is free to leave the court.

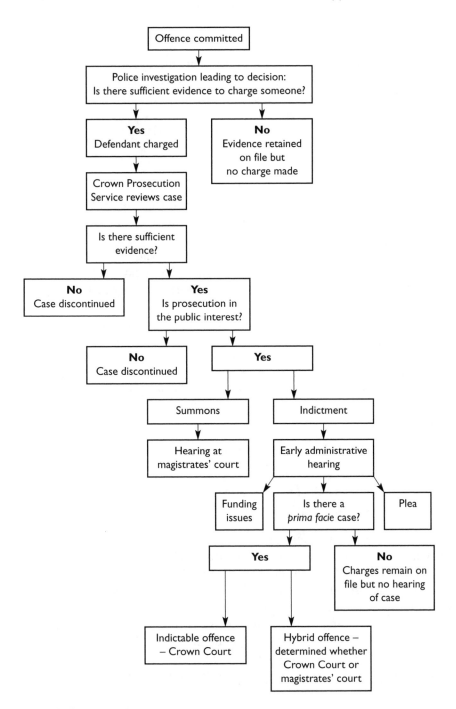

Figure 7.8 The criminal process

Bail

When a person is asked to return to the court for a hearing on another day, the decision has to be made as to whether it is reasonable for that person to be at liberty and on trust to return, or whether they should be kept in custody. We say that they are either:

- remanded in custody; or
- remanded on bail.

Bail can be given by the police and by the court.

Bail may be granted by the police custody officer, under the Police and Criminal Evidence Act 1984, while further enquiries are made, or after a charge has been made. Bail may be refused, for example, if the police cannot establish the person's name and address. The Criminal Justice and Public Order Act 1994 gives the police the right to impose conditions on the bail, such as taking away the suspect's passport or asking them to report to the police station.

Under the Bail Act 1976 the court also has power to grant bail. In fact, for summary offences, there is a *presumption* that a person charged with a criminal offence will be given bail, unless the court believes that the defendant would, if released, not return to court, commit a further offence or interfere with witnesses. The court may also believe that the defendant needs to be kept in custody for protection. The court will take into account the following:

- the defendant's character and past record;
- the seriousness of the offence;
- whether the defendant has previously kept to the terms of bail;
- the evidence against the defendant.

For indictable offences and offences triable either way the presumption is not applied, but the court can still grant bail. There was once no freedom to grant bail for murder, manslaughter or rape, but this has been challenged as being against the Human Rights Act 1998. The court may now grant bail even for these offences, but only in exceptional circumstances.

Bail is clearly important as many people who await trial are later found not guilty – they should not, therefore, be in custody. This must be balanced by the need to keep people in custody who are a danger to the public, and who, if released on bail, may commit further offences.

Practical task

Look out for the progress of the proposed Criminal Justice Act 2003

Summary

Criminal courts	• Difference between summary (minor offences – £5,000 fine or six months' custody), indictable (serious offences) and triable either way offences (offences which could be either, e.g. theft). • Magistrates' court – role in initial hearing; trial of summary and either way offences; referral to Crown Court; bail applications; issue of warrants. • Youth courts – need for training and sensitivity; limits on press; new proposals. • Crown Court – trial of indictable and either way offences; tiers of courts; role of judge and jury; proposed reform. • The role of the Crown Prosecution Service.
Civil courts	• Civil wrongs (not crimes) increasing importance of county courts, local, accessible. • Magistrates' courts – small role in civil law, administrative matters, e.g. licences. • County court – where most civil cases begin. Cases allocated by trial manager (judge) to a track: small claims (convenient but limit on damages awarded), fast-track (fast but limited to £15,000 damages), multi-track (flexible and allows for transfer to other tracks). • High Court – three divisions, Queen's Bench, Chancery, Family.
Appeals	• Appeals in criminal and civil cases – draw a flow chart (see pages 124 and 126). • Need to obtain leave (permission) for House of Lords – slow therefore expensive. • The role of the Criminal Cases Review Commission.
Reform	• Woolf report on civil courts – importance; partly implemented, e.g. three 'tracks' introduced; also linked to access to justice in general, i.e. funding and ADR. • Auld review on criminal courts – importance; progress report published.

Tasks

1   Study the flow chart of the criminal process (Figure 7.8). Make your own copy and colour the path of a person who is eventually found guilty of murder (indictable offence, so Crown Court trial).

2   Construct a similar flow chart for the civil process.

3   Write a brief explanation of the following words and phrases. Use this chapter and the glossary to check your answers.

jurisdiction	ultra vires
summary offence	sentence
indictable offence	conviction
offence triable either way	posthumous
adversarial	persuasive precedent
inquisitorial	contentious
plea in mitigation	liability
committal proceedings	small claims track
prima facie	CPS

4   Using the flow charts (see question 1, above) as a guide, write an account of:

(a)   criminal procedure

(b)   civil procedure.

5   Explain the grounds and routes of appeal in:

(a)   criminal cases

(b)   civil cases.

8   Alternatives to the courts

In recent years, there has been a significant growth in the use of alternative methods of resolving civil disputes. The reasoning behind this has revolved around the cost of formal court processes, the legal formality, the loss of good will between parties, the length of time it can take to settle a case through the courts, and the fact that many disputes are of a highly technical nature which may be better determined by specialists in that field rather than by judges.

Tribunals

Tribunals may be either domestic or administrative. They are like court hearings, without all of the formality, and are an attempt to hear a case in an efficient way, treating the issues seriously, but conducting the proceedings more quickly and inexpensively than would be possible in a full court hearing.

Domestic tribunals

Domestic tribunals are used within professions to determine questions relating to the professional conduct of their members, and are usually of a disciplinary nature. The Bar Council has such a tribunal, as does the Law Society and the General Medical Council. They are staffed by senior members of the profession, and have powers to fine, suspend or disbar (prevent from practising) a member for misconduct.

Administrative tribunals

Administrative tribunals have a more general jurisdiction, although each tribunal is set up individually by the legislation creating the rights and duties for which the tribunal has responsibility. These tribunals are regarded as being part of the welfare state provision: as new rights and responsibilities are created, so a tribunal is also created to 'referee' in disputes arising from the application of that law.

Each tribunal is headed by a legally qualified chairperson who sits with two independent members, one representing the respective positions of each side of the dispute. Thus in an employment tribunal or an employment appeals tribunal, the legal chairperson sits with an employer and a trade unionist. Similarly, in inland revenue tribunals, the legal chairperson sits with a tax expert and an accountant.

Lay person Legally qualified Lay person
chairperson

Composition of a tribunal

Figure 8.1

Although none of the tribunal members are personally involved in the dispute being heard, the panel remains balanced with representatives from both sides of the relationship. The Lord Chancellor's department keeps lists of appropriately qualified people who have been selected to sit on tribunals, which are set up as and when the need arises. A tribunal does not need a formal setting, and can meet at any appropriate place, although most towns have designated accommodation.

Representation is allowed, but only legal advice is available, so many individuals take a trade union representative, or a lay person from the Citizens' Advice Bureau, rather than hiring a professional lawyer. Businesses or larger organisations may take their own lawyer for representation, which causes imbalance to the equality of the parties. This is countered to some extent, however, by the approach of the tribunal, as it is encouraged to take an inquisitorial rather than an adversarial approach. The panel will ask questions if needed, and will not be too strict over procedure when a person without legal representation is giving evidence.

Tribunals make an award rather than giving a judgment. They are not absolutely bound by previous decisions of the tribunal, although they may look at previous cases for assistance in making their decision, but they *are* bound by decisions of courts. Parties may appeal, usually to the High Court, on a point of law. Tribunals are also subject to the rules of natural justice, and may be subject to a judicial review on matters of procedure.

The Tribunals and Inquiries Act 1958 was created to implement the recommendations of the Franks Report, which said that tribunals should be characterised by 'openness, fairness and impartiality'. This could be achieved by the inclusion of a legal chairperson, taking account of previous decisions so as to achieve a degree of continuity, the introduction of rights of appeal and legal representation. There have been two successive pieces of legislation in 1971 and 1992 which have further controlled the operation of such bodies by the introduction of the Council on Tribunals, responsible for ensuring that tribunals operate effectively, although it has little power other than to report to Parliament. Tribunals are required to give reasons for their decisions, which may form the basis of an appeal under the provisions of the Tribunals and Inquiries Act 1992.

The Leggatt report on tribunals was issued in 2001. It recommended that there should be a single unified system of tribunals, divided into Divisions. This would help to ensure consistency and efficient management. A single route of appeal was also recommended, and a Tribunals Board to oversee the selection of members and management of the system.

Other alternative methods of dispute resolution

Inquiries

Inquiries are set up by the government to enquire into individual issues, such as planning proposals and road developments, or individual incidents such as the Hillsborough Stadium disaster in 1989. They are generally headed by a judge and make recommendations which can be implemented by legislation, or make findings which are directly applicable, but may lead to changes in the law or practice.

Arbitration

In many commercial or business contracts the parties insert a clause stating that, in the case of a dispute, the matter will be referred to arbitration rather than becoming the subject of litigation. This means that an independent adjudicator can be appointed by the parties to determine the issue. The arbitrator will be an expert in the appropriate technical field, trained to conduct arbitration in a judicial manner which means, for example, ensuring that both parties have the opportunity to put their case. This allows the parties to maintain a good relationship, set a convenient time and place for the hearing, keep costs to a minimum, and be sure that the arbitrator understands any specialised issues that may arise.

One of the best-known examples of arbitration is found in the work of ACAS (the Arbitration and Conciliation Advisory Service). This is an organisation which acts to help settle disputes between employers and trade unions in industrial and employment cases. More recently, many trade organisations have introduced their own arbitration schemes, where a dissatisfied customer can take their case to arbitration rather than going through the courts. Examples would include the travel business and laundering and dry-cleaning organisations.

Mediation

This is a modern form of dispute resolution, which is quite informal, and is an attempt to bring the parties together by finding common ground. As well as the service offered by ACAS (see above), mediation is becoming more important in matrimonial cases. The service is offered to spouses with matrimonial problems through an organisation called Relate, formerly known as the Marriage Guidance Council.

Legislation was introduced to make mediation a compulsory element of any divorce proceedings, so parties would have to undergo some form of mediation to deal with ancillary matters, such as arrangements for children and financial settlements. This legislation has never been implemented, however. Early responses to pilot schemes did not prove successful, as mediation depends on the willingness of the parties to take an active part in the mediation, and warring spouses are often not prepared to see it as a positive means of settling their disputes.

As the system is not adversarial, that is, the parties are not suing each other but working together to reach a solution, the process is less traumatic for the parties who can maintain a better relationship, whether commercial or personal.

Conciliation

This is another modern form of dispute resolution and, like mediation, an informal one which hopes to find common ground. Conciliation involves bringing the parties together, again in an informal setting, to try to find a way in which their dispute may be resolved. ACAS is involved in this aspect of dispute resolution, particularly in employment issues. These forms of *alternative dispute resolution* (ADR) are becoming increasingly widely used in disputes such as those between neighbours over matters such as noise, hedges and shared driveways.

Negotiation

As with the preceding forms of dispute resolution, negotiation is an informal method of dealing with problems between the parties. Similarly, the system is supposed to be non-adversarial, where the parties negotiate with each other, often through their respective solicitors, usually before litigation is begun. They try to agree on what each side wants so as to avoid going to court, or any other more formal method of dispute resolution, and to avoid the inconvenience, expense and loss of good relationship. It is only after negotiations have failed that proceedings are begun. Negotiations may also be undertaken after a claim form has been issued in order to avoid a full court hearing.

Ombudsmen

The word 'ombudsman' comes from Scandinavia, and the term relates to those individuals who are appointed to deal with certain types of disputes. An ombudsman is a person who is appointed to oversee particular aspects of legal application. The Local Government Act 1974 first established the Commissioner for Local Administration, known as the Local Government

Ombudsman, although the first to be created was the Parliamentary Commissioner for Administration in 1967. There is also an ombudsman responsible for the National Health Service. Each ombudsman has particular responsibility for their own area of concern, dealing with issues of maladministration rather than individual issues of unfairness or inequality.

Other ombudsmen include:

- a *Prison Ombudsman* created in 1994;
- the *Legal Services Ombudsman*, created under the Courts and Legal Services Act 1990, who deals with complaints handled by the Law Society and Bar Council;
- the *Ombudsman for Conveyancing*, who also deals with the Council for Licensed Conveyancers, and who can award compensation, although their main remit is to deal with complaints against these organisations;
- the *Pensions Ombudsman* (Pensions Schemes Act 1993);
- the *European Ombudsman* (Article 138 EEC Treaty).

These last two ombudsmen were created by legislation to deal with particular maladministration issues arising from the application of the relevant legislation.

Ombudsmen are not empowered to deal with individual complaints, and they cannot be approached directly by an individual with a particular grievance. Their role is to investigate the way in which such a complaint was originally dealt with, including such issues as delay, rudeness, bias, discrimination, misleading or inaccurate advice and failing to follow administrative rules and procedures. Referrals may only be made through an MP, local councillor or MEP. The ombudsmen have little real power, and they are only able to report on the issue rather than in any way interfere in the outcome of the particular case, but their reports do carry considerable weight and may lead to internal changes within the appropriate department.

In the *Sachenhausen* case, the Parliamentary Commissioner for Administration found that the Foreign Office procedures for distributing compensation to former Nazi concentration camp victims was subject to serious defects. The Foreign Secretary did not agree with the findings, but did pay out extra compensation to the 12 individuals who had complained. A similar result occurred after the *Barlow Clowes* affair, when the government was found to have committed maladministration, and, although rejecting the findings, did pay out *ex gratia* compensation to investors in the company. As the ombudsmen have no 'teeth' (they cannot enforce their decisions), they are sometimes referred to as the 'ombudsmice'.

Following strong recommendations in the Woolf report, the civil procedure rules require parties to litigation to pursue alternative methods of dispute resolution and judges have a duty to encourage the use of alternatives. Court action should be seen as far as possible as a last resort.

Practical task

Read these advantages and disadvantages of:

- the civil process;
- the criminal process;
- alternative methods of dispute resolution.

Notice how the advantages and disadvantages tend to be complementary – each advantage has a corresponding disadvantage.

1   Make your own lists based on these points. Try to think of other points to make (you may like to leave spaces to add in points which you think of later).

2   Try to expand on each of the points made by giving examples, or explaining how issues apply.

3   Notice how various parts of the legal process are involved, for example, the legal profession, the cost of legal advice and representation, the role of lay people in the law.

The civil process

Strengths of the courts	**Weaknesses of the courts**
Formality – strict time limits and procedures mean parties know what to expect and are prepared.	Formality – can destroy good relationships between parties and complicate simple disputes.
Legal representation – allows for professional assistance in preparing and presenting cases.	Legal representation – may be slow, formal and very expensive, causing imbalance between parties.
Use of precedent – provides certainty for making settlements.	Precedent – may be too rigid, leading to individual injustice.
Clear lines of appeal – satisfies need for justice.	Appeals – slow and expensive.
Effective methods of enforcement.	Delays in enforcement.

The criminal process

Strengths of the courts	**Weaknesses of the courts**
Magistrates – fast, efficient and inexpensive.	Lack of training, reliance on clerk, too rapid to be seen to be fair.
Juries – understanding of accused's plight, 12 heads better than 1, trial by peers popular.	No legal knowledge, too sympathetic, do not understand complex legal issues.
Availability of funding – protects the accused.	Changes in funding may reduce effectiveness.
Clear appeal routes – justice done and seen to be done.	Appeals may be slow, expensive, governed by precedent.

Alternative methods of dispute resolution (ADR)

Strengths of ADR	Weaknesses of ADR
Faster and less expensive than courts.	Lack of public funding may result in injustice to the individual.
No need for representation, staffed by lay and professional experts, good relationships can be retained.	Lack of representation may be daunting when facing a represented party, e.g. an employer.
Less formal procedure means increased flexibility.	Lack of formal precedent reduces certainty.
Choice of date, time and venue, retains privacy.	Restricted rights of appeal.
An efficient means of providing local justice.	Difficulty in enforcing awards.

Summary

The need for alternatives
- Court process slow, expensive, inconvenient – generally inaccessible.
- Alternative Dispute Resolution provides justice for many who would not otherwise have a remedy.

Tribunals
- Domestic and administrative.
- Fast, inexpensive, accessible.
- Staffed by a qualified chairperson and two lay people representing different fields, e.g. trade unions and management.
- Lack of formality, local, no need for representation.
- But – no right of appeal in general, and increasing use of representation by employers.
- Increased delays due to popularity – needs to be addressed by more tribunal venues.

Other methods
- Inquiries, arbitration, mediation, conciliation, negotiation – all methods of self-help settlement outside the court structure.

Ombudsmen
- Government appointed to deal with disputes outstanding in certain areas, e.g. Local Government Ombudsman, Prison Ombudsman, Legal Services Ombudsman.

Tasks

1   Write a brief explanation of the following words. Use the glossary to check your answers.

litigation   liability
tribunal   arbitration
conciliation   mediation

2   Using what you have read in the chapter, and in the practical task on pages 142–3 at the end, compare and contrast the formal court system with the informal methods used in ADR.

3   What are the benefits of settling a dispute by ADR rather than by litigation? How might parties be encouraged to make more use of ADR?

9   Police powers

What exactly *should* the police be doing? Do we want them to protect us? Or to keep out of our business? Sometimes we want it both ways – to be protected, but to have no intrusion into our private lives.

The balance of detection and protection

That is exactly the issue lying at the heart of problems over the powers of the police. Their task is to enforce the law, and to provide protection for society from crime and disorder. In order to do that, however, they have to investigate situations, question individuals, search property, etc. all of which goes against the grain of the British concept of privacy.

So how do we reach some kind of balance between protection and privacy? Mostly, the answer lies in careful legislating to give the police the powers that they need, with built-in codes of practice (or codes of behaviour) to ensure that they do not go too far with those powers. The majority of police powers are now found in the Police and Criminal Evidence Act 1984 (usually known as PACE). In addition, we now have an extra 'layer' of protection from the Human Rights Act 1998.

Under English law there has been a long-standing underlying freedom for individuals to go about their business without having to justify themselves or account for their movements. Under the Human Rights Act 1998, this will become a firmer right. The Human Rights Act introduces the European Convention on Human Rights and Fundamental Freedoms into English law. Parliament can choose to pass laws that do not comply with the Convention but it has to state at the beginning of the Bill that it is intending to do so. If English law does not comply with the Convention it can be made to do so through a piece of delegated legislation passed under powers given to Ministers by Section 10 of the Human Rights Act.

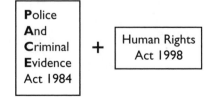

Figure 9.1

A feature of the Convention is that it does not give absolute rights – except for Article 3 which says:

> No one shall be subjected to torture or to inhuman or degrading treatment or punishment.

The other Articles all contain exceptions. So, for example, Article 5 says:

> Everyone has the right to liberty and security of person. No one shall be deprived of his liberty save in the following cases and in accordance with a procedure prescribed by law.

It then lists exceptions to the right to liberty, such as:

> (c) the lawful arrest or detention of a person effected for the purpose of bringing him before the competent legal authority on reasonable suspicion of having committed an offence or when it is reasonably considered necessary to prevent his committing an offence or fleeing after having done so.

When considering the traditional English approach of basic freedoms, or the Convention's approach of giving rights, there is a need to strike a balance between the freedom of the individual and the interests of other individuals and of society as a whole. So, freedom of speech must be exercised with due respect for those who are spoken of, and the right to privacy does not mean the right to download pornography from the Internet, even in the privacy of one's own home.

The interests of society as a whole require that we have a police force that is able to investigate crime effectively. Ideally, the role of the police should be preventative, making it difficult to commit offences or making

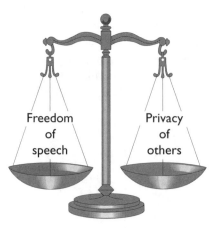

Figure 9.2

discovery and arrest so likely that few will think the risk is worth taking. We generally have to settle for second best, which is that once an offence has been committed it will be investigated and that a good proportion of offenders will be caught and brought to trial.

It would not be possible to do this job if the police were not given powers to arrest and detain people, to search premises and vehicles and other powers, all of which are an infringement of the basic rights of the individual concerned. The problem for the legal system is how one can regulate these powers so that they are effective, yet not open to abuse.

The Police and Criminal Evidence Act 1984 (PACE) was an attempt to provide a package of police powers, setting out the rules in a statute and providing, in addition, a series of codes and notes for guidance on how the powers are to be exercised. The codes and notes for guidance are not sources of law – only the statute itself is legally binding. If the codes are not followed, however, it may indicate some liability on the part of the police, if harm occurs as a result.

Thinking point

The status of the Codes of Practice under PACE can be likened to the Highway Code. Much of the Highway Code is not actually law, but recommended practice. If a driver does not obey it, and as a result causes an accident or some damage, then the breach of the Highway code may indicate liability on the part of the driver.

What might be the effect of a breach of the Codes found in PACE?

Powers of stop and search

The major power of stop and search is contained in Section 1 of PACE, though there are other statutes that give police officers powers to stop and search people in connection with particular offences. This Section is possibly one of the most important tools to the police in the detection of crime.

> Section 1 of PACE gives police officers a right to stop and search a person or a vehicle in a public place or a place to which the public have access, provided that the officer has reasonable grounds to suspect that they will find stolen or prohibited articles.

'Reasonable grounds' means that this is an objective test, based on what an ordinary person may think to be reasonable, and not the hunch of a policeman. Such tests occur in both the law of tort and in criminal law. The power to stop and search is legal only if a reasonable person would suspect that there are stolen or prohibited articles to find. This means that a stop cannot be a 'fishing expedition' – police officers are not entitled to stop people at random on the off-chance that something interesting will turn up.

> *Tomlinson v DPP* (1992)
> In this case, the court stated that the police did not have the power to stop and search a person for drugs who was 'walking aimlessly' in Soho, just because it was an area where drugs are often found.

The power of stop and search is governed by Code A (found in Section 66 of PACE). This acts as a check on the wide powers of Section 1. The code explains that 'reasonable grounds' involves an objective test and then says:

> For example, a person's colour, age, hairstyle or manner of dress, or the fact that he is known to have a previous conviction for possession of an unlawful article, cannot be used alone or in combination with each other as the sole basis on which to search that person.

There have been several recent complaints by high-profile black people, such as Neville Lawrence (father of Steven Lawrence who was murdered in a racist attack), that they have been stopped and searched because of their colour. There is considerable evidence to support the view that police officers are stopping people on the basis of colour, in contravention of the Code. A black peer, Lord Taylor, was stopped while out running, and the Bishop of Stepney has (at the time of writing) been stopped eight times.

It is reasonable to argue that it is something of a civic duty to bear the inconvenience of being stopped and searched because a police officer might have grounds to believe that someone has been involved in an offence, or is likely to be in possession of drugs. It is quite another thing to be regularly stopped, and the Bishop did comment on the change in police attitude whenever he identifies himself. It may well be that the attitude of

Figure 9.3

officers conducting a stop and search can make the difference between a minor inconvenience and an offensive denial of a basic human right. Perhaps that should be addressed through police training.

So, it is an offence to actually obstruct the police in the carrying out of their duties, but, on the other hand, they must act within their powers in detection of crime and interrogation, and nobody can be forced to accompany the police to a police station or to answer questions without reasonable grounds for suspicion.

Rice v Connolly (1966)
A person refused to give his name and address and to go to a police station for questioning. He was later convicted of obstructing the police in the execution of duty, but the decision was reversed, as although there may be a moral duty to cooperate with the police, there is not a legal duty to do so.

The police are obliged to keep a record of each stop and search and it is clear that more black people are stopped in many areas of the country than one would expect if the proportions of stop and searches mirrored the proportions of white and black people in society as a whole. In 1995 out of 160,000 people stopped in London under Section 1 of PACE 60 per cent of them were black. This is obviously much higher than the proportion of black people in London in general.

If a person is stopped under Section 1 of PACE, then Section 2 provides that the name and police station of the officer must be stated, along with an explanation of the object of the search and the grounds for believing stolen or prohibited articles will be found. The police officer must also make a written record of the search (Section 3 of PACE).

Must remember to state:
• my name
• police station
• reason for the search.

PC Plod

Figure 9.4

Section 5 of PACE provides that chief constables must include information about searches in their annual reports – which is where we can find the statistical information about use of stop and search powers.

If a search is voluntary (for example, if the suspect willingly agrees to 'help the police with their enquiries'), none of these safeguards and none of the other rules in PACE, the Code or the notes for guidance apply. It is probably fair to suppose that most people, if stopped by a police officer and asked if they would mind showing him or her what they have in their pockets would not appreciate that the search was voluntary and unprotected by PACE. The officer might feel the need to invoke PACE only if a person refused to 'volunteer'.

Thinking point

(You should also make notes on this.)

- Consider whether police powers of stop and search are within the provisions of the Human Rights Act 1998.

- How might a person who has been stopped and searched challenge the legality of the stop and search under the Human Rights Act?

Powers of arrest

Anyone may arrest a person who is reasonably suspected of committing an arrestable offence under Section 24 of PACE. An arrestable offence is generally one where the sentence is set by law (e.g. murder), or where the sentence could be at least five years in custody (e.g. theft or criminal damage). There are certain other 'arrestable offences', such as taking away a motor car or being equipped for stealing. Obviously, the power to arrest someone clearly equipped and about to steal is of no use to the police if they must wait for that person actually to steal something, in circumstances where there is a high risk of 'losing' the offender.

A person other than a police officer runs a substantial risk, however, when arresting someone. The arrest will not be lawful if either:

- an offence has been committed, but it is not an arrestable offence; or
- no offence has been committed.

Police officers may arrest for non-arrestable offences under Section 25 of PACE if they reasonably believe that an offence has been committed, and

- they cannot ascertain (or establish) the defendant's name or address; *or*
- they believe an arrest is necessary to protect the defendant or others from injury, or to protect property, or to prevent an offence against public decency or an obstruction of the highway; *or*
- to protect a child or other vulnerable person.

Figure 9.5

Once again, the power to arrest depends on having 'reasonable grounds for belief'. Arrests are governed by Code C.

The defendant must be told that they are under arrest and the grounds for their arrest (Section 28) but there is no need for the use of technical language. What is important is that the defendant must be aware of the arrest and the reason for it. As soon as practicable after arrest the defendant must be taken to a police station (Section 30).

The police retain a common law right to arrest a person for breach of the peace in addition to their statutory rights, which is governed by case law. These rights were reviewed in the following recent case.

Bibby v Chief Constable of Essex Police (2000)
There are four tests to be applied before arresting a person who has been causing a disturbance:

- Only a sufficiently real and present threat can justify depriving a person of their liberty.
- This threat must come from the person to be arrested.
- The conduct must interfere with the rights of others.
- The conduct of the person to be arrested must be unreasonable

Arrests are also governed by Article 5 of the European Convention on Human Rights and Fundamental Freedoms, which provides that no one shall be deprived of their liberty except in certain circumstances.

Powers of detention and the treatment of suspects at the police station

A person who is detained in a police station is the responsibility of the custody officer, who must ensure that the requirements of PACE have been complied with.

Section 41 of PACE provides that a person who has been arrested must be released within 24 hours of their arrival at a police station, unless they have been charged. This period of 24 hours can be extended by a further

12 hours under Section 42 of PACE, and a further extension can be granted by magistrates under Section 43. The maximum time a person can spend in police custody without charge is 96 hours.

The length of detention may change to 36 hours in all cases under the Criminal Justice Bill going through Parliament in 2003.

Responsibility of the custody officer

- A custody record must be kept for each defendant.
- The custody officer makes a record of the defendant's possessions and may seize items.
- The defendant may be searched.
- Fingerprints may be taken either with the defendant's consent or, if the defendant does not consent, with authorisation by an officer of the rank of Superintendent or above.

Figure 9.6

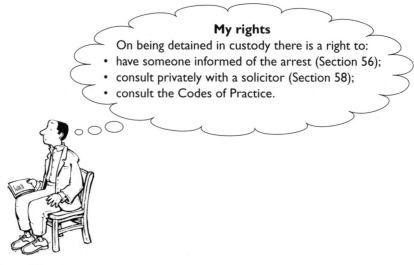

My rights
On being detained in custody there is a right to:
- have someone informed of the arrest (Section 56);
- consult privately with a solicitor (Section 58);
- consult the Codes of Practice.

Figure 9.7

Given that the concept of PACE is two-fold, i.e. to give the police the opportunity to investigate crime, and at the same time to protect the rights of the citizen, along with the right to detain a person there are also safeguards for the detainee.

These rights may be withheld, however, under Sections 56 and 58 if a senior officer has reasonable grounds for believing that the immediate exercise of the right would lead to interference with evidence of a serious offence or would alert other people. For example, if a series of arrests were to be made and it had not been possible to make them all at one time, the police would not want a defendant under arrest to be able to inform possible co-defendants that he or she had been arrested, and so warn them of their own impending arrest. These rights must, however, be granted within the first 36 hours of custody.

Code C covers treatment of suspects and provides that they must be given breaks for meals and to sleep.

The purpose of holding a person is to interview them. PACE provides that all interviews should take place at a police station and be recorded. Section 78 of PACE says that a court may exclude prosecution evidence if it would have 'such an adverse effect on the fairness of the proceedings that the court ought not to admit it'. This does not mean, however, that all evidence obtained by methods not allowed by PACE or the Codes is necessarily excluded. If the defendant claims that a confession was made under pressure, the prosecution has to prove beyond reasonable doubt that the confession was not improperly obtained (Section 76 of PACE).

The defendant should be cautioned (warned of the consequences of speaking or not speaking) on three separate occasions:

- when an officer suspects that the defendant is involved in a criminal offence;
- on arrest; and
- before interview.

The wording of the caution is as follows:

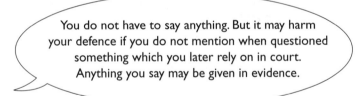

You do not have to say anything. But it may harm your defence if you do not mention when questioned something which you later rely on in court. Anything you say may be given in evidence.

Figure 9.8

The caution makes it clear that a defendant does not have to say anything – but that the defendant runs the risk, by keeping silent, that a later explanation of their behaviour might not be believed. Further, if a defendant chooses not to give evidence at their trial, the magistrates or jury can draw inferences from that lack of explanation. It is still for the prosecution to prove their case, but a defendant who remains silent now runs a greater risk, for example that by staying silent this may be interpreted as having something to hide.

Thinking point

Can you think of any other reasons why a person may remain silent when being questioned by the police?

Summary

Balance
- Need to detect *and* protect – give police enough powers to detect crime and also ensure that laws exist to protect individual privacy and other rights.

Key provisions
- PACE (the Police and Criminal Evidence Act 1984) give police powers to detect crime, and also contain safeguards in its Code of Practice.
- The Human Rights Act 1998 makes provisions of the European Convention on Human Rights part of English law and enforceable in English courts.

Stop and search
- Section 1 PACE and Code A – must be reasonable grounds. Problems regarding race in some areas.

Arrest
- Arrestable offences, Section 24; non-arrestable offences, Section 25. Code C – reasonable grounds. Section 30 – taken to police station.

Detention
- Period of detention, Sections 41–43; for custody officer's duties and detainee's rights see summaries in Chapter 9.
- Rights may be withheld under Sections 56 and 58. Covered by Code C.
- Correct obtaining of evidence under interview, Sections 76 and 78.

Caution
- Warned of limitations on right to silence (see Chapter 9).

Tasks

1   Write a brief explanation of the following words and phrases. Use the glossary to help you check your answers.

right   custody officer
PACE   arrestable offence
arrest   detainee
reasonable grounds

2   Some of the rules governing exercise of police powers are found in statutes and some in Codes. What difference does it make whether a rule is in an Act or a Code?

3   How successfully does the law balance the rights of individuals against the necessity of giving police the powers they need to investigate crime? Try answering this question with reference to three sets of powers:

(a) the powers of stop and search;
(b) the power of arrest;
(c) powers of detention.

4   Discuss whether the provisions of PACE are designed to protect the police or the defendant.

5   Consider also the effect of the Human Rights Act 1998 on

(a) the powers of the police to investigate crime;
(b) the rights of an individual when a crime is being investigated.

Part 3

Dispute solving (2): legal personnel

We have looked at the structure of the courts as part of the solution to the problem of solving disputes. Another very important part of that structure is the people who work within the English legal system.

Some of those people are highly paid and qualified lawyers such as:

- barristers;
- solicitors; and
- judges.

Without the help and advice of these people the courts alone would be of limited use to many of those who have legal problems. Since professional lawyers *are* qualified and paid for the work they do, funding of legal services and access to justice is an issue very closely connected with the legal profession, so this is also included in this section of the book.

Other people found within the broad framework of the English legal system are lay people. These are members of the public who are not legally qualified and who are unpaid for their role in the legal system. These include:

- magistrates; and
- jurors.

Magistrates are unpaid, but act as part-time judges in the magistrates' court. Jurors play a key role in trials, mainly in the Crown Courts. They both play a significant role in lay representation within the dispute solving process.

10   The legal profession

Who are the lawyers? A lawyer is a very general word for a person who has studied law or who practises law. The legal profession consists of two main branches or divisions of lawyers, barristers and solicitors. In the United Kingdom, if a person has a legal problem and is in need of advice, a solicitor is approached. The role of the solicitor generally involves contact with the public – enquiring into facts and deciding whether further action is needed. If further specialist advice is needed, or if, at a later date, representation is required in the higher courts, the client is referred to a barrister.

The two branches of the profession have their own areas of expertise and their own governing bodies. These bodies lay down the rules of training, practice and professional conduct, and require certain minimum standards of education. Most other countries do not have such a clearly divided profession, although most lawyers, wherever they practise, specialise in an area of law.

Lawyers begin their training together, but then divide according to whether they are going on to become a barrister or solicitor. In recent years, particularly since the 1990 Courts and Legal Services Act, basic training and areas of practice have become more similar, and there are more areas of overlap between solicitors and barristers. This could be seen as a move towards fusion – the joining of the two branches, or at least as an opening up of the professions.

Barristers

Barristers are sometimes referred to as the senior branch of the legal profession, as historically they were the only qualified lawyers. Solicitors were originally their clerks who split off in the nineteenth century and formed their own professional body. There are about 10,000 barristers in practice in England and Wales, and they are specialists in advocacy (the presentation and arguing of cases in court). They also prepare written advice, called an opinion, if asked to by a solicitor in a particular case.

To train as a barrister it is now a requirement to have a degree of at least at upper second class honours. If the degree is in law, the graduate may proceed to the next stage of training, but if the degree is in another subject then the student must 'convert' it by taking the Common Professional Examination or a Postgraduate Diploma in Law. This is the academic stage of training. Once

Figure 10.1

this has been successfully completed, a prospective barrister must join one of the four Inns of Court:

- Gray's Inn
- Lincoln's Inn
- Middle Temple
- Inner Temple.

Traditionally there is a requirement to 'keep terms'. This had to completed, until recently, by dining at the Inns of Court on 18 occasions. The requirement has now been reduced to 12, and an alternative is now to attend additional educational forums, such as weekend residential courses.

Although this sounds a strange way in which to qualify for a profession, it has its basis in history, and encourages young barristers to meet with more senior members of the profession, as well as make contacts with their contemporaries.

The vocational part of a barrister's training is the Bar Vocational Course. Until recently this could only be done at the Inns of Court School of Law in London, but now several other institutions have been authorised to run the course. This will help those students who may be deterred by the financial difficulties of an extra compulsory year in London at the end of a degree. The course emphasises the development of legal skills such as legal research, fact management and advocacy, as well as the main areas of core knowledge of civil and criminal litigation, evidence and sentencing. Having completed this stage of training, applicants are then 'called to the Bar' – they receive their vocational qualification at their chosen Inn of Court ceremony.

Those who are intending to practise must then spend 12 months doing 'pupillage' with a senior barrister. This stage forms the practical training. Training places, or pupillages, are difficult to find, and there is little financial support for trainee barristers other than from their family or a limited number of discretionary grants. Some chambers (groups of barristers) do pay up to £6,000 for pupillage, but trainees have to find the money for their specialised clothing (including a wig and gown), books, travelling and living expenses.

Figure 10.2

Once qualified, barristers are self-employed, although they normally join a set of chambers where they share the services of a clerk and working expenses. Payment for their services is often up to 18 months late, and the traditional position is that barristers cannot sue for their fees. This may now be changing – and is probably long overdue (see the section on control over barristers, below). About a third to a half of all young barristers leave the profession within the first two to three years due to financial problems. This has led to the criticisms that:

- most barristers come from wealthy middle-class backgrounds, as only they have the resources to withstand the early financial hardships;
- the bar has developed an aloofness from the general population.

A more supportive structure for the early years in a junior barrister's working life would help to avoid such criticism and maintain genuinely high standards.

Once a barrister has been in practice for 10 years, application may be made to become a Queen's Counsel, or QC. Only those at the top of their profession are likely to be selected by the Lord Chancellor for this honour, and it is rare to be appointed on the first application. QCs can command higher fees, and are often accompanied by a 'junior' barrister in court, although this is no longer a formal requirement.

Most judges are appointed by the Lord Chancellor from the ranks of barristers, although solicitors are now eligible to become district judges, circuit judges or recorders, and from there to be elevated to the senior judiciary.

The possibility of appointing solicitors as High Court judges was introduced by the Courts and Legal Services Act 1990, although the numbers of solicitors who are appointed as judges will take some time to come into effect, and it will be some years before the inclusion of this branch of the profession makes any real difference to the public perception of the judiciary as 'white, upper-class men'.

Control over barristers

Barristers are subject to control by the Bar Council, which is made up of senior members of the profession, known as 'benchers'. They may set provisions for training and education of their members, and investigate complaints against their members. The Legal Services Ombudsman may investigate complaints about the way that the Bar Council has investigated a complaint.

Barristers are traditionally not paid a fee, but receive an 'honorarium', which is regarded as a gift in return for their services. The historical aspect of this can be seen by the pouch sewn on the back of their gowns, into which, originally, clients would place their unknown and voluntary contribution. Again, by tradition, there was no contract between the client and barrister, nor between the solicitor and barrister, so barristers could not sue for 'fees', and the client could not sue for negligent performance in court, whether by a barrister or solicitor. This is partly due to policy, in that every dissatisfied client would claim that their failure was due to the advocate's performance rather than their own weak case.

In *Rondel v Worsley* (1969), the precedent was set that bad advocacy could not give rise to negligence actions. This was extended to solicitors as well as barristers. In *Saif Ali v Sydney Mitchell and Co* (1977), however, although confirming the position in *Rondel v Worsley*, the court held that barristers could be held liable for negligent advice before a court action had begun. This meant that barristers and solicitors would be treated alike, in that neither *could* be sued for negligent advocacy, but both would be liable for negligent advice.

Since then, a group of cases of actions against solicitors have recently been heard in the House of Lords, *Hall v Simons* (2000), and these now appear to overrule the traditional position. For both barristers and solicitors, the immunity from legal action while conducting advocacy is removed. Presumably the case will also change the rule preventing recovery of fees, giving barristers normal rights to receive payment for work as in other professions.

Thinking point

- Should there be a right to sue a barrister or solicitor for performance as an advocate?
- How would this performance be measured?

Clearly in most professions a consumer would expect a right to sue if work was not of a satisfactory standard, and in that way the decision in *Hall v Simons* (2000) would merely bring lawyers into line with the expectations of a modern society. There is, however, also a fear of a 'floodgates' effect of unhappy parties, losing their cases, then taking action against a lawyer who has carried out the duty of advocate as well as is possible in the circumstances.

Recent changes to the profession

Until the Courts and Legal Services Act 1990, barristers had a monopoly over advocacy in the higher courts, since only they had rights of audience. Now that solicitors have the right to become certified advocates, the amount of work available for junior barristers has lessened, although the number of graduates wishing to enter the profession is continuing to increase. In March 2001 a report by the Office of Fair Trading called for the abolition of the status of Queen's Counsel. The report said that while recognising that the most experienced barristers may command high fees, it was 'extraordinary' that this should be supported by the government officially, and that it causes distortion in the open market.

The bar has been granted the right to have direct contact in a limited way with corporate clients, such as accountants and surveyors, but there seems no reason at all why the public should not have direct access to barristers, particularly in light of the proposals to widen rights of audience further under the Access to Justice Act 1999.

Solicitors

Solicitors are often referred to as the 'general practitioners' of the legal profession. Approximately 80,000 solicitors are the first point of contact with clients in need of legal advice. Until the Courts and Legal Services Act 1990, they were the only method of obtaining access to barristers, but now other professionals, such as accountants, may approach an advocate directly. Solicitors may specialise in one or more areas of law, such as conveyancing (the transfer of title to land), matrimonial disputes, taxation, probate (the disposition of a deceased's estate) or commercial contracts. Many provincial solicitors, however, deal with the whole range of problems brought to them by clients, relying on the expertise of barristers for any complex legal issues that may arise.

Solicitors are required to have a similar educational background to barristers (a law degree or Common Professional Examination), but their academic training is then geared towards their future practice. They have then to take the Legal Practice Course, which may be taken at a College of Law run by the Law Society or at an authorised university. Having

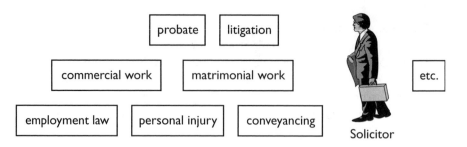

Figure 10.3

successfully completed this stage, a training contract is undertaken with a practising solicitor. During this period, the students are known as 'trainee solicitors' and receive a minimum rate of pay. The Law Society maintains a close watch on this period of training to ensure that all trainees receive a broad-based education and are fully versed in all aspects of solicitors' work. A 20-day Professional Skills Course must also be undertaken. Having completed all parts of the training, solicitors then have their name 'put on the roll' of solicitors, which is kept by the Master of the Rolls.

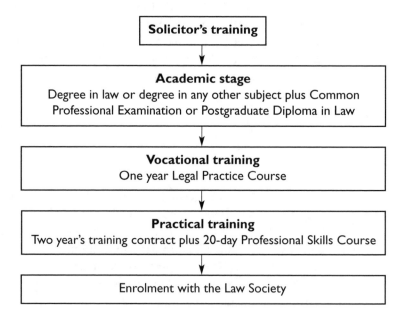

Figure 10.4

Control over solicitors

Solicitors who transgress are subject to the rules of the Law Society, which is responsible for governing education, training and professional conduct. Solicitors tend to work in partnerships, although some may be employed by a firm, while others go into public service with local authorities or other commercial undertakings. Should a complaint be made against a solicitor, it will be investigated by the Office for the Supervision of Solicitors, which may require the offender to appear before the Law Society's disciplinary committee. The Legal Services Ombudsman has the power to investigate the way that a complaint has been handled, but not the complaint itself.

Like barristers, solicitors could be sued for negligent advice or activities (other than advocacy), and are required to carry substantial professional conduct insurance so that a client who has been adversely affected by their careless or wrongful activities can be adequately compensated. Until recently they were not liable for any loss resulting from negligent advocacy, but now will, like barristers, be subject to the judgment in *Hall v Simons* (2000) – see above.

Recent changes to the profession

Solicitors have lost their exclusive right to conveyancing, but have been compensated for the loss of this monopoly by the granting of wider rights of audience and the right to advertise (this was previously viewed as not suitable for the legal profession).

Solicitors have been allowed to represent their clients in the magistrates' and county courts for some time, but since the Courts and Legal Services Act 1990, solicitors who obtain a certificate of competency may also appear in the higher courts. It took four years, following the 1990 Act for the first solicitor-advocate to obtain a certificate, and few took up this opportunity at first. The position then began to change much more quickly, however, and there are now about 1,000 certified advocates. The commitment in terms of time and money needed to obtain the certificate is high, and this could deter otherwise suitable people. There are proposals in the Access to Justice Act 1999 to give all solicitors wider rights of audience.

Figure 10.5

Thinking point

Identify which of the legal professions would be used in each of the following situations (hint – in some cases it will help if you think about which court or courts might be involved):

- a conveyance (transfer of land);
- dealing with a person accused of a summary offence;
- dealing with a breach of contract;
- dealing with a divorce;
- taking an appeal to the House of Lords.

Other professionals

Legal executives

Legal executives are a branch of the legal profession that has developed over recent years to fulfil the need for limited but specialised knowledge and ability. Legal executives are professionals as they belong to a governing body which regulates their education, training and operation, but they have limited responsibility and may only practice under the supervision of solicitors. To qualify as a legal executive, an individual has to have five GCSEs, practical experience and to have passed the appropriate examinations. A trainee legal executive will take the associate examinations, then progress to the fellowship, all of which takes at least five years, during which time they are required to be working under the supervision of a solicitor. Those who have passed all of the examinations may only work under the supervision of a solicitor, and frequently specialise in probate, matrimonial or conveyancing. Their education, training and operation is governed by the Institute of Legal Executives (ILEX) and, as with solicitors and barristers, a disciplinary committee is responsible for their professional conduct. Fellows of the Institute may convert their qualification through a Law Society legal practice course and become a solicitor, even though they do not necessarily have a degree.

Licensed conveyancers

This qualification was first introduced in 1985 in an attempt to break the solicitors' monopoly on conveyancing. Those who wish to qualify must have some practical experience and take professional examinations, but need not work under the supervision of a solicitor. Many licensed conveyancers are now allowed to work for banks and building societies, assisting in their mortgage and conveyancing business under the provisions of the Courts and Legal Services Act 1990.

Para-legals

Para-legal associates have long been a feature of the US legal system, often being employed by lawyers as partly qualified legal secretaries. In England and Wales, however, the Para-Legal Association was only set up in the late 1980s, and is aimed at those who wish to follow a career in the law but who have insufficient educational qualifications to take the ILEX course. Para-lawyers may only work with fully qualified legal personnel, and often carry out the basic work of an office, whether in private practice, local government or commerce.

Summary

The profession	• Two branches of one profession – barristers and solicitors.
Barristers	• About 10,000 in practice. Members of Inns of Court.
	• Training – graduate entry, Bar Vocational Course, pupillage, dining terms and call to the Bar. Wig and gown worn when in court.
	• Practice – sole practitioners, sharing chambers and clerk. Advocacy work with rights of audience in all courts. Viewed as specialists in giving advice (counsel). Some employed. May eventually become Queen's Counsel (but see OFT call for reform).
Solicitors	• About 80,000 in practice as first point of contact for people with legal problems. Members of the Law Society.
	• Training – graduate entry, Legal Practice Course, training contract, enrolment by the Law Society. Now may become solicitor-advocates and then gowns worn in higher courts.
Recent changes	• Abolition of monopolies under the Courts and Legal Services Act 1990; licenced conveyancing; certified advocacy; advertising for solicitors; listing of members of barristers' chambers; possibility of multi-disciplinary partnerships.
Control	• Barristers subject to control of Bar Council and Legal Services Ombudsman. Formerly could not be sued (*Rondel v Worsley* (1969)) but now see *Hall v Simons* (2000).
	• Solicitors subject to the Office for the Supervision of Solicitors and the Legal Services Ombudsman. Could be sued in negligence, but not for advocacy. Now see *Hall v Simons* (2000).

Other professionals

- Licensed conveyancers (e.g. in estate agencies, etc.); legal executives (training and operation governed by ILEX); para-legals.

Tasks

1   Write a brief explanation of the following words:

advocacy   conveyancing
inns of court   Queen's Counsel
benchers   probate

Use the glossary to check your answers.

2   Draw a flow chart illustrating the way in which barristers and solicitors qualify.

3   Describe the work carried out by a barrister and a solicitor. How much overlap is there between the two branches of the profession?

4   Read through the chapter again and note down all the references to the Courts and Legal Services Act 1990. Now try to put them together as a plan for an essay on the effect of that Act on the legal profession.

5   Explain how a client who was dissatisfied with the service provided by a lawyer might seek help. What criticisms could be made of the systems in place?

11 Access to justice – funding advice and representation

When a person believes that they have a legal problem, they need to know first whether they are right, and second what they can do about the problem in terms of obtaining a remedy. Whether the matter is criminal or civil the victim will need access to justice, either against the state or against an individual. We cling to the principle that all people are of equal worth, and that all are equal before the law. People do not all have equal access to the law, however.

The background

Some people do not use the legal system when they may need to do so. For instance, many people suffer personal injury in an accident but do not pursue a claim for compensation. This may be for a good reason, such as the injury not being serious, but in many cases other factors are important. In fact it is estimated that only 20 per cent of potential claimants seek advice on this, but that out of those who do claim, most are successful in obtaining compensation. There are various reasons why obtaining legal advice may be difficult. A person may:

- not be aware of the law, or may not understand that there is a legal problem;
- not have the money that is thought necessary to seek advice or to take an issue to court;
- not know how much a case will cost. The media does not help – the case of Ken Roache suing the *Sun* for libel was reported to have cost £120,000. A person may fear that their own case will be far more expensive than it really is;
- not easily be able to attend a solicitor's office or a court hearing during the working week;
- be unfamiliar with the legal system or afraid of it.

For all of these reasons a person may then be denied access to justice. Steps are being taken to encourage society to be more aware of legal help. Advertising is certainly increasing, even to the extent that lawyers are seen to be vying for trade, nevertheless their opening hours have altered little.

For a number of years the route to help has largely depended on wealth. A very poor person would have obtained Legal Aid. A wealthy person would have paid privately. There was a great gap in the middle, often referred to as 'the unmet need'. This meant that the majority of society could not access the legal system for want of financial help, even though they may have eventually won their cases and obtained compensation and costs.

In order to address this unmet need, the Access to Justice Act 1999 was passed to replace the old Legal Aid scheme. Two new schemes have been established:

- the Community Legal Service for civil cases;
- the Criminal Defence Service for criminal cases.

Funding of civil cases

In April 2000 the Legal Services Commission, under Section 1 of the Access to Justice Act, took over from the Legal Aid Board and took charge of the Community Legal Service Fund. The aim is to use funding available to match legal services to the need for help. The Commission is able to make contracts with solicitors and other agencies to provide services. However:

- the number of contracts available is limited;
- it is alleged by those in practice that remuneration levels are so low that few practices will wish to be involved.

The *Community Legal Service* was set up under the Access to Justice Act and is able to provide:

- legal advice;
- help in settling disputes over legal rights and obligations;
- general legal information and advice over legal services.

The fund excludes personal injury cases apart from medical negligence, conveyancing, defamation, wills and company law. There is, therefore, a need to find some other funding for these. Personal injury is obviously a problem, as that was previously included in Legal Aid – there has already been a huge increase in advertising legal help in this field. This exclusion could cause grave injustice to someone who just cannot obtain help in another way.

The financial conditions for obtaining help from the Community Legal Service Fund will depend on disposable income and disposable capital, where those over the limit may have to pay a contribution on a sliding scale, up to a point where no help at all is available. Certain criteria will be examined, including:

- money remaining in the Fund (there is a fixed budget);
- availability of other funding or services;
- prospects of success;
- the public interest;
- the importance of the matter disputed to the individual;
- the benefit which may be obtained from the claim.

These criteria operate in a similar way to the merits test previously used in assessing Legal Aid, but with the added dimension of priority of government funding. This probably indicates that less funding will be available than under the previous scheme. In that case, it will become more necessary than before to turn to other sources for help.

Alternative provision of legal services

Community-based alternatives

One way of providing help for those who need initial advice is through the Citizens' Advice Bureau and Law Centres. These are often staffed, at least in part, by volunteers, who may not necessarily be able to give very much specific legal advice, but will assist in helping to obtain it. Other advice agencies include motoring organisations, such as the AA, trade unions and specialist groups, such as the Consumers' Association. In addition the Community Legal Service is to establish a website. The aim is to ensure that every public library has Internet facilities by 2002 so that anyone can have access to this service. This is an attempt to provide wide support making general legal help available to the greatest possible number of people. The 'Accident Help Line' has been set up by the Law Society to deal with personal injury cases under this conditional fee scheme, and it covers both legal advice and representation on a no win, no fee basis.

Pro Bono

This is an American idea which has become part of the English process. Many young barristers who are offered places in chambers today will only accept on the basis that they can offer their services to deserving cases free of charge or 'pro bono'.

Conditional fees

Conditional fees, once not allowed on the basis that there was something immoral in paying a lawyer to 'win' a case, are fast becoming the normal way of operating for many lawyers. This has been the case in the United States for some time, lawyers working on the understanding that if they lose the case there will be no payment, but if they win they will be paid a proportion of the money recovered. This basis of charging has been allowed in the English legal system since 1995, a measure introduced in the Courts and Legal Services Act 1990. The amount chargeable on winning (the success fee) must not be more than the usual fee or more than 25 per cent of the damages awarded. Under the Access to Justice Act this uplift on the normal fees is recoverable as costs from the other side on winning the case.

Legal insurance

Yet another way of covering the cost of legal claims is by insurance. Again, this is quite usual in other countries, and is paid as a matter of routine along with health insurance. Premium costs are recoverable from the other party on winning a case.

Funding of criminal cases

The Access to Justice Act also established the Criminal Defence Service which began operation in 2001. This is an attempt to provide a unified defence service which is publicly run, making sure that individuals involved in criminal investigations or proceedings have access to the advice and representation they need. There will be salaried defenders (employees of the government), whose budget will not be capped. In addition the duty solicitor scheme remains, and the budget for the salaried state defenders will not be capped. The provision for criminal help is therefore demand led, with no fixed budget.

This looks good in practice, but it does seem to be somewhat strange to have a state prosecution system on one side of a case and a state defence system on the other side. It is really the same body of expertise prosecuting and defending.

The system will cover advice for those who are arrested and detained in custody, and also representation subject to the following criteria:

- the interests of justice;
- whether there is a likelihood of custody;
- whether it is in the interests of another person that this person is represented.

Summary

Problems   • Reluctance to seek advice; reluctance to litigate; reputation of high costs; effect of media; lack of funds; inaccessible source of advice; unfamiliarity with the law.

Background	• Legal Aid aimed to meet need of funding legal advice and action; unmet need – funded the very poor but not those above social security level.
Current position	• Access to Justice Act 1999 provides access to legal services; Legal Services Commission took over Community Legal Service Fund in April 2000.
Civil cases	• Community Legal Service – to provide legal advice, help in settling disputes, legal information. Dependant on disposable income and capital, and criteria concerning the merits of the case. Funding restricted to set amount per year. Need to use alternatives, such as conditional fees (no win – no fee basis of paying solicitor) and legal expenses insurance.
Criminal cases	• Criminal Defence Service – to provide national service with no set limit. Covers advice for those in custody and representation subject to criteria (interests of justice, likelihood of custodial sentence, in interests of a third party).

Tasks

1 Write a brief explanation of the following expressions. Use this chapter and the glossary to help check your answers.

damages	conditional fees
legal aid	Criminal Defence Service
Community Legal Service	*pro bono*

2 Discuss whether the current funding procedures provide for those on low incomes who need access to justice, both regarding:

   (a) criminal law, and

   (b) civil law.

3 What alternatives exist to obtaining state funding of legal action?

12   The judges

Who are the judges? How does an enthusiastic young lawyer become a judge? The answer is that judges are appointed from barristers and solicitors. Unlike some other countries, where a person can train for a career in the judiciary, in English law experience is gained first by being a practising lawyer. It is, therefore, worth re-reading Chapter 10 on the legal profession.

Those who are selected to serve in the judiciary have qualified as either solicitors or barristers. There is also now provision under the Courts and Legal Services Act 1990 to appoint academic lawyers to the judiciary.

The different types of judges are appointed in different ways, but the Lord Chancellor's department is responsible in some way for all appointments. The Lord Chancellor appoints the lower (or inferior) judges and advises on the appointment of the higher (or superior) judges. The Lord Chancellor's department keeps records on all practising advocates (barristers and solicitors who present cases in court), compiled from comments of judges and other senior members of the legal profession. These records are used when appointments are being considered. A very important feature of the judiciary is that, unlike most other jurisdictions, judges are chosen from among practitioners, rather than forming a separate profession with its own training and career path.

Thinking point

Think of some advantages and disadvantages of the English system of becoming a judge.

Inferior judges

Inferior judges appear in courts lower than the High Court; they are the less senior judges. At this level judges may now apply for posts, whereas previously they were only appointed by invitation.

Inferior judges

District Judge

Recorder

Circuit Judge

Figure 12.1

District judges

District judges and deputy district judges can be barristers or solicitors. They must have been in practice for at least seven years. There are now two kinds of posts for district judges. One of these, the traditional role of a district judge, is in civil law, to administer a county court and to sit as a judge in a county court. The Woolf reforms to civil procedure have added considerably to the workload of district judges in civil law, and additional district judges were appointed when the reforms were implemented. District judges are appointed by the Queen on the recommendation of the Lord Chancellor. This means that in practice it is the Lord Chancellor's department which actually decides who shall be appointed. It is now usual to apply to be a district judge and vacancies are advertised.

> ### Thinking point
>
> Look again at the recent changes to the civil process (Chapter 7). Why do district judges in civil courts now have more work to do?

District judges (magistrates' courts)

This is a new position, where former stipendiary magistrates are responsible for running certain magistrates' courts. The stipendiary magistrate really did the job of the bench of three lay magistrates. To become a district judge in a magistrates' court there is the same requirement as for judges with civil courts – i.e. experience as a solicitor or barrister for seven years. District judges mainly practise within London, although there are district judges in other large city courts, and more have recently been appointed.

Recorders

Recorders and assistant recorders sit in the Crown Court. They are part-time judges, who sit for a certain number of days each year and spend the rest of their time practising as barristers or solicitors. They must have been in practice for at least ten years before appointment as a judge, but it would be most unusual for anyone below the age of about 35 to be appointed.

Recorders are appointed by the Queen on the recommendation of the Lord Chancellor, but their appointments are subject to renewal every three years. This makes a job as a recorder an attractive proposition for a practising lawyer who may wish to become a judge. It is an opportunity to give it a try. If they find that they do not enjoy the job – or that they are not much good at it – they can simply not renew their contract after the first three years. Similarly, the Lord Chancellor's department has the chance to see how a potential judge copes before making a permanent appointment. A general application is made – without knowing if a particular position is available – and then the Lord Chancellor appoints when he has a vacancy.

Circuit judges

Circuit judges are appointed from solicitors or barristers who have practised as advocates for at least ten years or who have been district judges or a recorder. This alternative background provides a route through the judiciary for solicitors, and widens the likely pool from which judges may be drawn (about one in ten circuit judges were solicitors). They sit in county courts, hearing the more difficult or valuable cases, and in the Crown Court. They are appointed by the Queen on the recommendation of the Lord Chancellor.

Practical task

Find advertisements from the appointments section in the quality newspapers for various positions as judge. Photocopy or cut out advertisements for a range of posts. These will give you an idea of the kind of people who are encouraged to apply.

Superior judges

Judges at this level are only appointed by invitation. The Lord Chancellor's department keeps files on people thought to be likely candidates for a senior position. These files contain confidential information which is collected over a period of time. When a position becomes vacant the Lord Chancellor selects a person from these files. This system has been heavily criticised – see the later section on appointments of judges.

High Court judges

High Court judges are appointed from advocates (barristers and solicitor-advocates) with at least ten years' experience or those who have been

Superior judges

Lord of Appeal in Ordinary (Law Lord)	Lord Justice of Appeal	High Court (*puisne*) Judge
House of Lords	Court of Appeal	High Court

Figure 12.2

Circuit judges and academic lawyers. This wider 'pool' of potential applicants was developed from the Courts and Legal Services Act 1990 in a move to provide a wider spread of suitable people with a path through the ranks of the judiciary. Sir Michael Sachs was the first High Court judge who had previously been a solicitor and it is hoped that this move may contribute to the judiciary being drawn from a wider circle.

High Court judges, also known as *puisne* judges, are knighted on appointment and sit in the High Court, the Crown Court for very serious cases and the divisional courts to hear appeals. Since the three divisions of the High Court hear different types of cases, judges usually sit in one in which they have expertise, although in theory they can sit in any division. The current number of judges at this level means that the work load is high and delay is significant. Like the inferior judges, High Court judges are appointed by the Queen on the recommendation of the Lord Chancellor.

Lords Justices of Appeal

Usually, the Lords Justices of Appeal are appointed from among High Court Judges, but it is technically possible for appointments to be made from among practitioners with at least 15 years' experience of advocacy. They are appointed by the Queen on the recommendation of the Prime Minister – although it is openly stated and widely known that the Prime Minister 'receives advice from' the Lord Chancellor's department. Lords Justices of Appeal sit in the Court of Appeal and in the divisional courts of the High Court. As solicitors move through the system, they will eventually be able to become judges at this level, but at present only barristers have become Court of Appeal judges.

There are very few women judges at this level, the first being Elizabeth Butler-Sloss who was appointed in 1988. At first there was not even a title for her, and she was referred to as Lord Justice Butler-Sloss. There is now, since a declaration by the Master of the Rolls in 1994, an unofficial title of Lady Justice Butler-Sloss. She is now Head of the Family Division, and a judge in the Court of Appeal.

The Court of Appeal hears cases on appeal from both civil and criminal courts and this is therefore a busy court, certainly by comparison with the House of Lords.

The Law Lords

These are the most senior judges, and their full title is Lords of Appeal in Ordinary. They are appointed from judges of high office, and in practice this means that they normally are appointed from the Lord Justices of Appeal. Again, then, it is technically possible for an advocate with 15 years' experience to be appointed straight to this position. They are appointed by the Queen on the recommendation of the Prime Minister and sit in the Judicial Committee of the House of Lords and the Judicial Committee of the Privy Council. The House of Lords hears final appeals from Scotland and Northern Ireland, so judges can also be appointed from these areas to the House of Lords.

The House of Lords, as a court, is formally called the Judicial Committee of the House of Lords, and is composed of 12 Law Lords, plus the Lord Chancellor. They are made life peers on appointment, which means that they are entitled to take part in debates in the full House of Lords when it considers new Acts of Parliament. They do not usually do so, however, since:

- they do not have time;
- the country pays these judges high salaries to do a full-time job and they should be seen to be doing it;
- it would not look good to have the most senior judges of the country both forming laws and judging the issues which arise from those laws.

The appeals heard by the House of Lords are those that concern a point of law of general importance. They generally hear less than 70 cases each year, sitting in two courts, so they spend some time forming their judgments. Most of these are civil matters, with just a few criminal cases reaching this level.

Practical task

Find the current holders of the senior posts on the website of the Lord Chancellor's department at:

http://www.lcd.gov.uk/judicial/senjudfr.htm.

Further information of general interest on the judiciary, such as salaries, can be found at:

http://www.lcd.gov.uk.

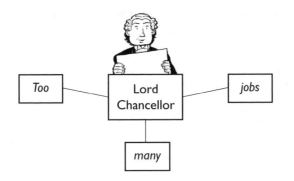

Figure 12.3

The Lord Chancellor

The Lord Chancellor is head of the judiciary, but the position is rather special, being the only person who has powers and responsibilities across all three elements of the legal process.

It has long been recognised that the process of making policy and enforcing the law should be kept separate from law-making and from the judicial process. Read the section in Chapter 3 on *Conflict with the principle of the separation of powers* (pages 34–5).

Montesquieu, an eighteenth-century philosopher, identified the need to keep a separation between those who create the law, those who administer it and those who judge issues arising out of it. In the United Kingdom those three different functions are carried out by:

- Parliament;
- the Cabinet, the Civil Service and other public employees such as the police;
- the judges.

The idea of the separation of powers is that each of the three elements is separate and different, so that the executive devises policy, which then has to be agreed and enacted by the legislature. This law is administered on a day-to-day basis by the executive, and finally, interpreted and applied by the judges. Each of the elements acts as a check on the others, so that no group has absolute power.

The Lord Chancellor is a member of each element. He is:

- a cabinet minister with responsibility for the Lord Chancellor's department, which has responsibility for law reform;
- a member of the House of Lords and chairs its sittings;
- a senior judge, sitting as a member of the Judicial Committee of the House of Lords, and responsible for judicial appointments.

James Pickles, a judge (now retired), in his book *Straight From the Bench*, said that 'the office of the Lord Chancellor is odd. It refutes in one man the idea that we have separation of powers'.

It seems increasingly likely that the Lord Chancellor's position will be changed at some time over the next few years. Just looking at the list of tasks which fall within his role, it is clear that nobody could possibly carry out all of the tasks personally. Indeed, there is enough work for three people taking on the three different aspects of the Lord Chancellor's role. Certainly, it seems likely that an action could be successful, using the provisions of the Human Rights Act, to prevent the Lord Chancellor, a member of the government, sitting as a judge. There have been proposals to replace the Lord Chancellor's role in judicial appointments with a committee of some kind (see the section on appointments later in this chapter).

Practical task

Arrange all the information on judges from the paragraphs above into a table. You might use headings such as Qualification, Court, Appointment, Dismissal – but you can choose your own headings and decide how much information is useful. On the left, list the different kinds of judge and then rule a grid into which the information can be placed. Check your table carefully against the text and, if possible, with a friend. You then have a very useful tool for revision.

The Lord Chief Justice

The Lord Chief Justice heads the criminal court system, sitting in the Court of Appeal (Criminal Division) and in the Divisional Court of Queen's Bench. He is second to the Lord Chancellor in seniority within the judiciary.

The Vice-Chancellor

The nominal head of the Chancery Division is the Lord Chancellor, but the job is done by the Vice-Chancellor, who is also responsible for the civil justice system.

The Master of the Rolls

The Master of the Rolls heads the Court of Appeal (Civil Division). The Master of the Rolls is also the nominal head of the solicitors' profession –'the Rolls' being the list of solicitors who are entitled to practise. Probably the most well-known holder of the post was Lord Denning.

The Law Officers

The following important positions are political appointments:

- The *Attorney-General* is chief legal adviser to the government, and is appointed by the Prime Minister. The person appointed is a Member of Parliament and a barrister, and can therefore represent the government in court hearings.

- The *Solicitor-General* is deputy to the Attorney-General, is a barrister and is also appointed by the Prime Minister.

- The *Director of Public Prosecutions* is head of the Crown Prosecution Service and is responsible for the conduct of criminal prosecutions. The DPP is appointed by the Attorney-General from barristers and solicitors of at least ten years' experience.

The role of the judge and judicial independence

A judge who presides over a trial has a primary duty to ensure a fair trial. This is done by making sure that the rules of evidence and procedure are followed, as these rules seek to ensure that each party's case is heard and that nobody is allowed to act unfairly.

- *In criminal cases* the system is adversarial, which means that the parties run their cases, with the judge acting as referee. The prosecution has to prove its case beyond reasonable doubt and the defence has to challenge the prosecution and put any defence that may be relevant. If there is a jury, the judge has to ensure, as far as possible, that the jury understands the evidence and the issues. The judge will deal with any points of law that have to be decided, and will advise the jury on how to apply the law to whatever facts they find. He will advise the jury on procedure, will explain their duties, and will pass sentence if the defendant is found guilty.

- *In civil cases* the procedure used to be entirely adversarial but, following Lord Woolf's reforms, judges now have to be active in the management of cases. Once a claim has been issued, a judge will decide on the timetable which the parties must follow in bringing the case to court. The judge has an obligation to encourage the parties to use alternative forms of dispute resolution wherever possible (see Chapter 8). By the time the case gets to court the issues should be clearly defined and the judge should be satisfied that litigation is the only appropriate course of action.

  In this move toward acting as case manager, the system is taking a more inquisitorial approach, the judge enquiring into the truth, rather than simply letting two 'sides' argue out their differences. The judge must decide whose evidence is most compelling and apply the law to the facts before deciding on an appropriate remedy.

- *In the higher appeal courts* (the Court of Appeal and the House of Lords) judges do not usually have to concern themselves with issues of fact. They take the facts of the case to be as decided by the trial court. It is their job to interpret the law and to decide whether the trial judge got the law right and applied it correctly to the facts. They may also have to decide whether the sentence or award was appropriate.

As discussed in Chapter 6, judges at the very highest level sometimes make law through the mechanism of precedent and, as discussed in Chapter 5, they have considerable power when deciding what legislation means.

Appointment, training, retirement and removal from office

Appointment

The key person in the appointment system is the Lord Chancellor. He is responsible, either directly or indirectly, for appointments across the whole of the judiciary. Given that he is head of the judiciary, this is not surprising, but on examining his own appointment and role, certain issues arise.

The role of the Lord Chancellor is an openly political one, and in conflict with the separation of powers. There is not a suggestion that he is politically motivated in appointing judges, but the opportunity to be so certainly exists. See the section on the Lord Chancellor above (page 179).

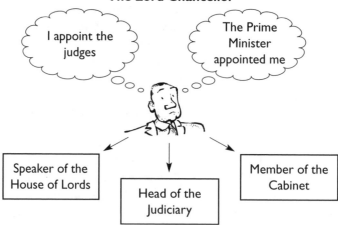

Figure 12.4

Two main criticisms of the judiciary are:

- the age of the judges;
- the background of the judges.

Research shows that these are well-founded criticisms, although there has been some change in recent years.

The average age of the judiciary is higher than other professions both on appointment and on retirement. As the retirement age lowers, this may affect the age at appointment, since there will still be a need for a certain number of judges.

Judges who hold high positions and have *not* been to public school and Oxford or Cambridge are rare. John Griffith found, in research for his book *The Politics of the Judiciary*, that 75 per cent of senior appointments fell into this category. They also visit the same clubs and other social events, and as they come largely from the ranks of barristers, have worked and mixed with each other for the whole of their career. This gives them an image of being out of touch with the rest of society. Lord Taylor, the late Lord Chief Justice, was an exception, being from a state school background and, at 60, was one of the youngest appointments to the position. He was of the view that things were changing slowly, and certainly as the pool from which judges may be appointed widens, this situation may improve.

Superior judges are appointed wholly by invitation. This means that a person may be invited to become a judge in one of the higher courts, but may not apply for the post. It is difficult to think of any other position in modern society where this is the case. Most vacancies in large organisations are advertised, at least within the profession, and those interested may then apply. To have a system where this is not so in the judiciary, where the aim is above all to be seen to be scrupulously fair and independent, leaves the profession wide open to criticism.

In fact the Lord Chancellor selects judges for the higher positions by keeping files on anyone suitable who has been brought to his attention. This raises the issue of exactly what has been brought to his attention and for what reasons. The files are confidential. This is fine in that they are not available to the public, but neither are they available to those whom they concern, and this could mean that inaccuracies are recorded and never corrected.

There is at present a very obvious white male dominance amongst the superior judges. This is not surprising, given the age of the judges in these ranks. They were appointed at a time when there were very few women and members of ethnic minority backgrounds who were eligible for appointment. Even bearing that in mind, however, the figures are changing only very slowly. In March 2003 there were no female Law Lords. Lady Justice Butler-Sloss was Head of the Family Division, there were three Lady Justices of Appeal out of 36 and six female High Court Judges out of 107.

A further problem in appointment is that salaries, although high, are not as high as those of the top barristers. It used to be the case that a barrister would welcome the opportunity to have a pensioned position for the later years of working life, but to obtain a full pension a judge now has to serve for 20 years. There is then little incentive to become a judge for these people.

Lord Irvine, Lord Chancellor, said in a speech to the Third Worldwide Common Law Judiciary Conference, 5 July 1999:

I believe strongly in equal opportunities and encourage applications from any individual who meets the criteria for appointment. However, I am resolutely opposed to any proposition that our courts should be sculpted to conform to any notion of social, political, gender or any other balance.

He then went on to say:

... a modern democracy also demands accountability to Parliament and public for the overall efficiency and effectiveness of the system of justice. This includes the good conduct of the judges and the proper use of public resources. We also need to have procedures for selecting the judges which ensure appointment strictly on merit.

Practical task

In the speech above the Lord Chancellor states clearly the need to encourage applications from anyone 'who meets the criteria for appointment'.

Explain *in your own words* the other main points made by the Lord Chancellor.

Inferior judges are appointed directly by the Lord Chancellor and candidates may submit applications for posts. The positions of circuit judges and district judges are now advertised in the press, but for recorders applications are submitted not knowing whether a post actually exists. A person interested in becoming a recorder submits a general application and the Lord Chancellor keeps it on file until a vacancy arises. This system is not satisfactory in that there is no immediate feedback, so it may be years before a reply is made to the application. The Lord Chancellor has suggested that there may be a move to 'time limited' applications, so that feedback would be given within a certain time.

For circuit judges there is an appointments panel to interview those shortlisted, which was seen as a great step forward from the whole appointment system being in the sole hands of the Lord Chancellor. The following points of criticism may still be made, however.

- The panel consists of a serving or retired judge, an official from the Lord Chancellor's department and a lay person. This is still weighted towards control by the Lord Chancellor.
- The panel does not actually appoint. It merely interviews and passes comments on to the Lord Chancellor who makes the appointment.

The composition of the judiciary at this lower level is also heavily weighted towards males. In April 2001 there were 39 females out of 552 circuit judges, 159 out of more than 1,300 recorders and assistant recorders, and 229 out of nearly 1,400 district judges.

Practical task

Check the latest figures which are available on the website of the Lord Chancellor's department at:

http://www.open.gov.uk/lcd/judicial/womju dfr.htm.

It has been suggested, and was recommended in the Haldane Committee report of 1918, that there should be a ministry of justice, who amongst other things would be responsible for appointments. This could be seen, however, as a move to become even more political, and less open to public scrutiny.

A recent move in an attempt to ensure that the judges are *seen* to be more representative of the society in which they work is the creation of a new Judicial Appointments Commission. The Lord Chancellor has already begun to select members, and the group will oversee in general the appointments procedure and investigate aspects of the appointment judges. The Commission will not actually make the appointments themselves, but it will also investigate any complaints made concerning the appointments procedure in individual cases. This could be seen as a move in the right direction to ensure that the system of appointment of judges carries the respect of society.

Practical task

Imagine that you are a senior civil servant in the Lord Chancellor's department. You have to consider applications for positions as High Court judges and are about to make a shortlist from the applications in front of you. Make three lists:

- personal qualities important in a High Court judge;
- experience necessary for a High Court judge;
- other relevant information.

Compare your lists with those made by other students, and consider the following points.

(a) Is there a point at which information about the applicant is not your business?

(b) Is there a point at which you feel you should know things, but that those things should not be made public?

Training

Until quite recently, judges were not thought to need training. Being experienced practitioners, they were deemed to know enough to enable them to do the job. Fortunately, it is now recognised that the qualities that make a good judge are not necessarily the same as the qualities of a good barrister or solicitor. The Judicial Studies Board provides training for all new judges, especially in sentencing, and updating courses. Recent training has been concentrated on teaching judges how to use information technology, which was seen by Lord Woolf as a very important element in running the civil courts more efficiently, and preparing judges for implementation of the Human Rights Act 1998, which will bring the European Convention on Human Rights into English law. Judges also receive training in issues of race and gender equality. The Board states in its report for 1999–2000 that the aim is for all judges to have training as an integral part of their sitting days (allocated working days).

Practical task

Read more of the work of the Judicial Studies Board on its website at http://www.jsboard.co.uk.

Make a list of some aspects of training of judges with which the Board is concerned.

Quality of judicial performance is monitored by the Lord Chancellor's department by keeping a record of complaints and of appeals against a judge. The Court of Appeal may, very occasionally, criticise something that a judge has done or said and this would be carefully noted. This is a form of accountability and therefore a record of quality of performance, but there is no formal system of quality control within the judiciary.

Retirement and removal from office

All judges retire at the age of 70. This is a fairly new requirement. Judges used to be able to stay in office long after the usual retirement age – previously they were only required to retire at 75. The Judicial Pensions and Retirements Act 1993, which came into force in 1995, provides that no one except the Lord Chancellor may sit judicially in the House of Lords beyond the age of 75.

It could be argued that the age of 70 is still too old. Most people retire before or at 65 in comparable professions, and earlier retirement would give opportunities for appointment at a younger age. The argument against this is that many important and influential judgments have been made by judges when over 65 years old. That is not to say, however, that a slightly younger judge could not make similar judgments.

District judges, recorders and circuit judges can be dismissed by the Lord Chancellor for incapacity or misbehaviour. Incapacity relates to matters of health and one hopes that a judge whose powers were failing could be persuaded by friends to resign before the Lord Chancellor's department had to intervene. Misbehaviour amounts to conduct which is seen as inappropriate in a judge. A conviction for a criminal offence would be an example of misbehaviour. Judges who are caught speeding usually do not have to resign, but will expect a rebuke from the Lord Chancellor's department and a second offence would be unlikely to be tolerated.

High Court judges, Lords Justices of Appeal and Lords of Appeal in Ordinary can be removed from office only at the request of both Houses of Parliament. Only one judge has ever been removed through this process.

Judicial independence

Judges must be independent from the legislature and free from political bias. Those who are members of the House of Lords never take part in controversial debates, unless the issue is one of law, when they tend to take on the role of advisers, rather than adopting a political stance. Lord Taylor, for instance, took a very active part in the debate over minimum sentences. Full-time judges cannot sit in the House of Commons and no judge may be a member of a political party.

Judges are perceived as being pro-establishment, however. Some cases do support this view, notably the GCHQ case of 1984, which supported the withdrawal of the right to join a trade union for those civil servants employed at the national intelligence headquarters in Cheltenham. This was countered by Lord Taylor, however, in the Dimbleby lecture in 1992 when as newly appointed Lord Chief Justice he said that cases such as that involving the Greenham Common protest showed that judges were not as pro-establishment as may be thought. He said that the judiciary was 'more deserving of public support than ever before'.

Judges should also be independent from the executive. They are in that they cannot be dismissed by the government. The role of the Lord Chancellor in appointment of judges raises issues regarding this aspect of independence, however. See the section on appointments (pages 182–5).

The parties to a case are entitled to have it heard by a judge who does not have a personal interest in the outcome of the case. If a judge has some connection with the subject matter of a case then this should be stated to the advocates, before the case begins. Either side may then express the wish to have the case heard by a different judge and that wish will be respected. Judges are expected, as a result of their training, experience and habits of mind, to be able to apply an open mind. This means not an absence of

Defendant   Standing down

Figure 12.5

opinion but an ability to put a personal opinion to one side while hearing argument, and to make a judgment based on evidence and argument.

When Senator Pinochet of Chile was held in custody while extradition proceedings were heard, his case was due to come before the House of Lords. One of the parties to the case was the human rights organisation Amnesty International, who were granted permission to put an argument as to why Pinochet should be extradited to Spain. Lord Hoffman, one of the Lords of Appeal in Ordinary who heard the appeal to the House of Lords, had been an active supporter of Amnesty International. He should have made this known to the barristers for each side. They would then have discussed the matter with their clients and have been free to ask Lord Hoffman to step down. Lord Hoffman did not raise the issue and it was subsequently the subject of an appeal. The House of Lords had no option but to quash their decision and have the issue heard again by a differently constituted House of Lords.

There was no real dispute as to Lord Hoffman having made an error in not declaring his interest. It gave rise to a lot of press coverage, however, and a wide-ranging debate on how much the public, and, in particular, parties to litigation, should be entitled to know about the judge hearing their case. In the United States there is a whole industry devoted to studying individual judges and trying to manipulate the system so that the judge allocated to a case is likely to take a favourable view of the arguments for the party doing the manipulating. This clearly goes too far, as effectively, it amounts to looking for a judge with prejudices and then making use of those prejudices.

Judges also have to be free from financial pressures that might tempt them into corruption, and from physical and other threats that might influence decisions. Financial independence is ensured by paying judges a high salary out of the consolidated fund which does not need authorisation from Parliament. Because of the level of salary judges do not need to become involved in the world of business and industry. Their salaries are not now as high as many lawyers, however, and this could be open to criticism.

Judges have absolute privilege in respect of everything they say in court. This means that they can never be sued in respect of those things. They also have power to protect themselves from abuse or physical threat through the law of contempt of court. If a person abuses a judge they can be sent to prison until they apologise. In practice, this means cooling off in the cells for an hour or two and then being brought before the court to apologise.

Summary

Inferior judges	• District Judges, District Judges (magistrates' courts) – formerly stipendiary magistrates – recorders, Circuit Judges.
Superior judges	• High Court Judges (Puisne Judges), Lords Justices of Appeal (Court of Appeal judges), Law Lords (Lords of Appeal in Ordinary).
Lord Chancellor	• Three-fold role – head of judiciary, speaker (chairman) of House of Lords and seat in the Cabinet. Conflicts with theory of separation of powers. • A political appointment – appointed by Prime Minister. • Responsible for appointment of judiciary.
Other senior posts	• Judicial appointments – Lord Chief Justice, Master of the Rolls, Vice Chancellor. • Political appointments – Law officers: Attorney General, Solicitor General, Director of Public Prosecutions.
Role	• Judge manages cases and ensures that rules of evidence are followed; sometimes decides verdict; decides sentence in criminal cases and awards remedy in civil cases. Decides appeals in higher courts. • Independent politically, financially, commercially, academically.
Structure	• Appointments – responsibility of Lord Chancellor. Criticised regarding age and background. System criticised for lack of openness; many posts not advertised and appointments to highest posts by recommendation not application; interview panel exists but does not appoint; Appointments Commission to oversee system, but not to appoint. • Training – very little initially (a few days). Judicial Studies Board aims to train all judges specifically in application of Human Rights Act 1998.

- Retirement/removal from office – at 70 (previously no set age). Inferior judges can be dismissed by Lord Chancellor for incapacity or misbehaviour. Superior judges can be dismissed at request of both Houses of Parliament.
- Composition – white male-dominated and from similar backgrounds, but solicitors now entitled to be considered for appointment.

Tasks

1   Write an explanation of the following words and phrases. Use this chapter and the glossary to help check your answers.

academic lawyers	jurisdictions
incapacity	inferior judges
executive	superior judges
legislature	advocates

2   (a)   Explain the rules governing the appointment of judges.

   (b)   What recent changes have taken place?

   (c)   Is any further reform necessary?

3   (a)   What is meant by the term judicial independence?

   (b)   Does the judiciary have such independence?

4   Consider whether:

   (a)   a recorder, and

   (b)   the Lord Chancellor

   may be described as 'independent'.

13 Lay people in the legal system

Lay people have no legal training. Why, then, should we be discussing such people in a book on the English legal system? In fact, lay people play an important part in the legal system as representatives of the public in the form of jurors, magistrates and lay members of tribunals. Their major importance lies in:

- demonstrating that the law is not a mystery understood only by lawyers;
- ensuring public accountability, in that the public see openly what goes on in court;
- maintaining public confidence in the system.

Lay people show, therefore, that law is not only for clever people who have passed lots of examinations, but is an important element in ensuring a just society. In any situation in which lay people are involved in making decisions, lawyers cannot communicate solely with other lawyers, using specialised concepts and language. They have to make the effort to communicate in ordinary language and to explain legal concepts in a manner that any intelligent person can understand. This helps to make sure that important issues are accessible to ordinary people.

The involvement of lay people also means that decisions are made by ordinary people from a wide variety of backgrounds. One of the issues you will see with regard to jurors and magistrates is whether the system provides lay people from sufficiently different backgrounds or whether much the same sort of people get to serve on juries, or to be magistrates, because of the way the selection processes operate.

Care has to be taken when discussing the involvement of lay people because it can be a very emotive issue. There seems to be a deeply held cultural belief that any attempt to reduce the role of lay people is an attempt to reduce the freedom of the individual and their protection from the power of the state. This can, at times, override practical arguments about the efficiency and effectiveness of using lay people.

Jurors

The role and function of jurors

Juries sit in less than 4 per cent of all criminal trials, since most cases start and finish in the magistrates' court. The jury is only needed in those cases which go on to the Crown Court (where trial is on indictment – see Chapter 7), and then only where the defendant pleads not guilty. The law on juries is found in the Juries Act 1974, little bits of various other statutes, and in cases decided by the courts.

Historically the jury was a group of people who knew the defendant or the victim, or who had seen the incident, or who lived near to where it was alleged to have taken place. The jurors were really witnesses. Today it is the reverse situation in so far as the jury is said to be anonymous and amorphous – that is unknown to those taking part in the trial, and not a permanent body of people.

> *Bushell's Case* (1670)
> The independence of the jury was established, as it was held that the jurors were the only judges of the facts, even if this went against the opinion of the judge.

The function of jurors is to decide on matters of fact. They are mainly found in criminal trials in the Crown Court and their job is to listen to the evidence presented to the court and to decide who did what, so that they can announce a verdict.

A group of people will be called to serve as jurors at a certain court. They will have received some information about their duties with the jury summons, which is the document that tells them where and when to attend for jury service. They are also now normally shown a video about serving as a juror.

Figure 13.1

There will be several jury trials going on and, when a court is ready to swear in a jury, a group of potential jurors will be taken into the court, from which 12 people will be called. Names are read out by the court clerk one at a time and each potential juror comes into the jury box to be sworn. The oath is as follows:

I swear by Almighty God that I will faithfully try the defendant and give a true verdict according to the evidence.

Figure 13.2

A juror may choose to take the oath on a holy book other than the Bible, or may alternatively choose to affirm, that is to solemnly promise to try the defendant and give a true verdict according to the evidence, but with no reference to religion.

The prosecution may ask a juror to leave the jury box before he or she is sworn in. This right is very rarely used and will be exercised only by agreement with the defence advocate where both advocates believe that an individual is not fit to serve on the jury.

The defence has no right to challenge any one juror, but can complain that the group as a whole (the 'array') does not accurately reflect the local population.

After the evidence has been presented by both sides, the judge sums up at the end of the trial and explains to the jurors what they have to decide.

Thinking point

In a case involving an alleged assault, the judge might have to explain to the jury that they have to decide whether the defendant intended to hit the victim or whether the defendant was reckless as to whether the victim would be struck and that, in either case, their verdict should be guilty. If, however, they believed that the defendant was simply negligent in what he or she did, the defendant would be not guilty. This involves the jury in a difficult decision about what was in the defendant's mind at the time of the incident. They will have heard and seen the witnesses and have to decide what they believe. What kind of things might influence the jurors' decision as to whether the defendant is guilty?

The jury retires to the jury room to consider the verdict. Usually, the jury's verdict must be unanimous, but a judge may, if the jury have been deliberating for over two hours, tell them that a verdict may be accepted which is that of 10 or 11 of them. This is known as a majority verdict, and the aim is to speed up a decision, or make it possible to reach one, where most jurors are in agreement.

Jurors may make notes during the trial, and if a juror has a question which arises during deliberations in the jury room, it has to be written on a piece of paper and handed to the judge. The judge will then call the jury back to court to answer the question. Jurors are excluded from court while points of law are argued between the advocates for each side.

The jury's decision is made in private and no one else is allowed in the room while they are deliberating. They select a foreman, who will tell the court their decision.

The selection of jurors

Jurors are selected from the electoral roll, that is, the list of people entitled to vote. They must be at least aged 18 and not older than 70. Between the ages of 65 and 70 there is a right to refuse to do jury service. Otherwise, it is a duty to serve as a juror if selected. Jurors must have been resident in this country for at least five years since the age of 13. Twelve people are needed for each jury, although a larger number are called, forming a 'pool' to ensure that there is a full jury in each court.

Various people are exempt from jury service for different reasons.

- *Ineligible*. This group includes:
  - those concerned with the administration of justice, i.e. police officers, barristers and solicitors;
  - those with a religious vocation, i.e. priests, etc.;
  - those who are mentally ill.
- *Disqualified*. This group includes those with certain criminal records, including anyone who has:
  - served any period of imprisonment; or
  - received a suspended sentence; or
  - received a community service order during the previous ten years.
- *Excused*. This group includes two categories:
  - Those who are excused as a right. These people are excused automatically, but can serve if they choose, but do not have to do so. The group includes doctors, MPs, members of the armed forces and those who have served on a jury during the previous two years.
  - Those who are excused by the discretion of the judge. These people may be asked to serve at another time. This includes, for example, mothers with small children, students with examinations, those with booked holidays.

The different categories are excluded for different reasons. People who are excused are people who would be regarded as suitable but who are doing something else which at the particular time is either more important or, at least, important enough to allow them to defer their service. People who are disqualified are regarded as unsuitable for a reason to which no blame attaches, such as being closely connected with the legal system, but which might sway their judgement.

Service on a jury is a civic duty and compulsory unless a person falls into one of the above categories. Jurors have a right to time off work to serve and, if their employer does not pay them for the time they are away (which is usually two weeks), they can claim loss of earnings up to a certain amount and travel expenses. If a trial is going to be a long one, the judge makes sure that potential jurors will be available for the whole of the trial before the jury is chosen.

The theory is that the jury is drawn at random from society as a whole and that any form of tampering with this process is wrong. Very occasionally, if national security is involved and some or all of the hearing is to be in private, the Attorney-General may give permission for potential jurors to be vetted. This means that an investigation is carried out into their backgrounds and anyone who may hold strong views likely to affect their judgment in the case would not be summoned. This does not arise very often, and the general principle is that the jury consists of 12 citizens who are a randomly selected cross-section of society, representative of the people involved in the trial. This is known as trial by one's peers.

It is argued, however, that the concepts of ineligibility, disqualification and excusals effectively exclude large sections of the community. In particular, it is argued that the middle and upper-middle classes are largely exempt. Looking at the list of exemptions, those who are lawfully exempt include a number of professional categories, and those who are eligible to serve can often argue successfully to be excused.

The Auld Review has recommended that in future those who are at present ineligible or excused as a right should serve. This has been included in the proposed Criminal Justice Act 2003.

Practical task

Watch the progress of this legislation through Parliament

In her research as a juror, Penny Darbyshire's article 'Notes of a Lawyer Juror' finds that out of a block of 200 summoned for jury service, only 100–120 will actually serve, the rest having lawful reasons not to serve. She also found that there was 'wide-spread reluctance to serve'. In general it seems that the public support the idea of the jury as a principle, and would not want to lose it, but do not personally want to carry out jury service. The extent of reluctance to serve is shown in an article by Sean Enright,

'Britain's Reluctant Jurors', where he discusses the extent of personation – people who send others to do their jury service for them.

Practical task

Visit your local Crown Court and watch parts of some jury trials. Attempting to watch the whole of a jury trial would probably take several days. If you can, watch a jury being sworn in. Try to see a jury hearing prose-cution evidence and then one hearing defence evidence. You will find that court ushers are very helpful in directing you to the appropriate court rooms if you tell them what you would like to see.

Think about the composition of the juries you saw.

- How would you describe the jurors in terms of gender, age and race?
- Were jurors making notes?
- Did they seem interested in what was going on?

Like all researchers into juries, you will be frustrated by the provisions of the Contempt of Court Act, which make it an offence to discuss any aspect of a case with any member of the jury. Try nevertheless to form some broad views about how the jurors approach their job by watching them at work.

Civil juries

We have already seen that juries are only used in a small proportion of trials. Juries in civil actions are much rarer still. There is a right to a jury trial only in cases of:

- defamation;
- malicious prosecution;
- false imprisonment;
- fraud.

Even here the judge may refuse a jury if the trial will involve a lot of documen-tary evidence or scientific or accounting material. For example, the 'McLibel trial', which involved a defamation action brought by McDonalds against two environmental campaigners, was heard by a judge alone. It was probably a good decision to refuse a jury, as the trial turned into the longest ever civil trial.

In practice, trial by jury in civil cases is not of major importance since it happens in so few cases. This has become so largely because of its unsuit-ability in personal injury cases for reasons which were restated by Lord Denning in *Ward v James* (1966).

- Experience is needed to assess compensation fairly (jurors do not have such experience).

- Only by legal training and practice are people be able to apply the law with uniformity and treat like cases alike (jurors do not have legal training or practice).
- Out of court settlements depend on predictability – most problems arising do not result in legal action, and society therefore needs consistent application of law.

In the Queen's Bench Division jury trial is granted at the discretion of the court, rather than as a right, and is now extremely rare.

Coroners' juries

Coroners occasionally summon a jury for inquiry into the circumstances of death. This is a less formal hearing and the jury will consist of between seven and eleven people.

The arguments for and against juries

Many long-standing arguments exist both for and against the retention of the jury as the flagship of criminal trials in the English legal system. These have recently been revived by the government's attempts to restrict the number of jury trials in criminal cases by removing the right of the defendant charged with an offence triable either way to opt for jury trial (see Chapter 7 on the court structure). The government's argument is that the decision as to which mode of trial is appropriate should be made by magistrates, rather than the defendant. The proposal to restrict the right to choose jury trial was made by the Runciman Commission. It recommended that if the prosecution and defence could not agree whether a defendant should be tried before magistrates or at the Crown Court, the magistrates should decide, taking into account the gravity and complexity of the case, the likely effect on the defendant of a conviction.

Arguments for trial by jury

- Trial by peers is a popular concept.
- Maintains public confidence in the legal system.
- Lay representation counteracts the remote image of the law.
- Twelve opinions are seen to be fairer than one.
- Limited ability of jurors to mitigate the harshness of the law.
- Juries generally get the verdict 'right'.
- Local people understand local problems and are good judges of fact.

Figure 13.3

Arguments in favour of trial by jury

The arguments in favour of juries were eloquently put by Lord Denning in the following civil case.

> *Ward v James (1966)*
> Lord Denning said:
>
> > Let it not be supposed that this court is in any way opposed to trial by jury. It has been the bulwark of our liberties too long for any of us to seek to alter it. Whenever a man is on trial for serious crime, or when in a civil case a man's honour or integrity is at stake, or when one or other party must be deliberately lying, then trial by jury has no equal.

Another well known statement in support of jury trial was made by Lord Devlin in his book *Trial by Jury* (1956) where he referred to this kind of trial as 'the lamp that shows that freedom lives'.

The following are further arguments in favour of retention of the jury for criminal trial.

- Trial by peers meets with favour generally and is a popular concept, raising public confidence in the legal system. As seen above, however, although jury trial is favoured, there is reluctance to serve.

- The notion of trial by peers assures the public of their rights regarding civil liberties. This may, however, be seen as less important since the passing of the Human Rights Act 1998.

- Lay representation in the criminal justice system helps to counteract the rather remote image sometimes portrayed by the legal profession. This is especially important in an adversarial system of trial.

- Up to 12 people may be perceived by the public and the defendant as making a fairer decision than a single judge.

- The jury represents a limited ability of the public to change the law, or at least to criticise its harshness.

For example in the nineteenth century many crimes were punishable by death, including theft of goods stolen which were less more than five shillings. This led juries to find goods of less value, showing disapproval in such a harsh sanction. Again, in more recent times, there was a reluctance to convict for motor-manslaughter which carried a life sentence, and this led to the creation of the offence of causing death by reckless driving, which carries a lower custodial sentence of up to five years.

McCabe and Purves said, in *The Jury Trial at Work* (1972), that 'the jury … can bend the law without breaking it'. It could be said that in expressing a view of the law in this way the jury operates as a barometer of public opinion on the state of the legal system.

- Recent research is limited because of the Contempt of Court Act 1981, but shadow jury research has been carried out (using a 'mock' jury alongside a real one, and recording their debate). This has generally shown that juries on the whole do get the verdict right, although the work done by Baldwin and McConville in Birmingham in 1979 suggests that up to 5 per cent of jury trials could result in the wrong verdict.

- It is said that juries are well placed to judge which witnesses are telling the truth, and in addition, as local people, understand the needs of the area which they represent. The argument at its core is that jurors are 'ordinary people', but, as we have seen, it may be nearer to truth that there is over-representation on juries of the young unemployed, middle-aged housewives and retired people because of the rules on eligibility and excuse.

Arguments against trial by jury

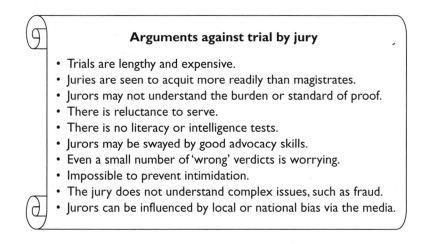

Arguments against trial by jury

- Trials are lengthy and expensive.
- Juries are seen to acquit more readily than magistrates.
- Jurors may not understand the burden or standard of proof.
- There is reluctance to serve.
- There is no literacy or intelligence tests.
- Jurors may be swayed by good advocacy skills.
- Even a small number of 'wrong' verdicts is worrying.
- Impossible to prevent intimidation.
- The jury does not understand complex issues, such as fraud.
- Jurors can be influenced by local or national bias via the media.

Figure 13.4

There are prominent people who do not view criminal trial by jury with favour. Professor Hogan once said: 'Trial by jury has long outlived its usefulness. We preserve it because it's a sacred cow'. He meant by this that the jury (in his opinion) did not, any longer, perform a useful task and that the legal system would work just as well without it. There is a reluctance to get rid of it, however, as people would disapprove.

Sir Robert Mark, former Commissioner of the Metropolitan Police, also said that confidence in the jury system is 'based on practically no evidence whatsoever'. As mentioned above, research is limited by the Contempt of Court Act 1981, so that it is an offence to disclose statements made or votes cast by a jury. This is a valid attempt to stop jury 'nobbling'– putting pressure on jury members to vote in a particular way – but it does also prevent legitimate research which may help to improve the system.

The following are further arguments against the retention of the jury in criminal trials.

- Jury trial is expensive. Certainly jury trials are more expensive than trial in the magistrates' courts or trial by single judge. There is a heavy administrative burden, the jurors are paid expenses, the advocates are highly paid, the preparation necessary is more complex and therefore more expensive. In addition the trial itself is much longer because of the need to explain everything to the jury.

- Juries tend to acquit more readily than magistrates. The argument about acquittal rates is interesting. It could be that juries are more prone to give the benefit of the doubt (to which the defendant is entitled in any event) or it could be that a higher proportion of those opting for jury trial are innocent of the offence charged.

- It is said that defendants 'play the system' by opting for jury trial, so prolonging time spent out on bail or in prison on remand under a slightly easier regime than that for convicted prisoners, and then changing their plea to guilty when the time comes for their trial at Crown Court.

  It does happen that the Crown Prosecution Service will agree to drop a more serious charge and replace it with a less serious charge, making this decision between the committal proceedings and the jury trial. A defendant who would not have pleaded guilty to the more serious charge might decide to plead guilty to the lesser charge. This would account for at least some apparent changes of mind before jury trial.

- Jurors tend not to understand the burden or the standard of proof (beyond reasonable doubt) in criminal cases, applying instead the civil standard (on the balance of probabilities). They tend to ask the question: Does it seem more likely than not that the defendant did this?

- There is no literacy or intelligence test, and the jury could be swayed by good advocacy rather than facts.

- Local or national bias may sway the opinion of the jury.

- It is impossible to guarantee no corruption or intimidation, although this has been improved by screening the jury from public view in some courts.

- Jurors may not be capable of understanding complex fraud issues. The Fraud Trials Committee 1986 recommended replacing the jury with a small panel of experts, and there have been repeated calls since then for reform in this area.

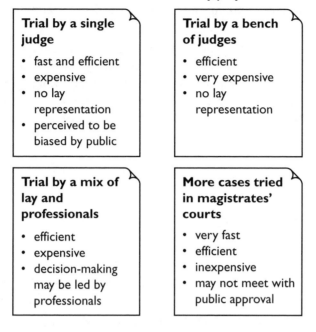

Figure 13.5

Possible alternatives to trial by jury

There are various alternatives to trial by jury in the criminal courts. The factors to consider are:

1   whether the new method of trial would be effective;
2   whether the public would find the new method of trial acceptable;
3   whether the cost would be greater.

Possible alternatives include:

- Trying more cases in the magistrates' court, with the most serious being tried by district judges (formerly stipendiary magistrates). This would be effective and inexpensive, and although it may not meet with full public approval, the government has proposed it as a way forward following the Auld Review.

- Removing the jury and trying cases with a single judge. Judges are likely to handle cases more quickly (courts like this, known as Diplock courts, have been running for some time in Northern Ireland), and therefore at less expense. The decision would be by a trained and practised lawyer, but the system would be unlikely to meet with public approval and would lack lay representation.

- Trial by a bench of three judges. This would be efficient, with high quality decision-making, but would be expensive and would lack lay representation.

- Trial by a composite panel – a 'mini-jury' – made up of professional and lay people. This has been favoured by some leading lawyers, including Professor Zander. The decision-making would probably be of good quality, lay representation would be retained, but it could be argued that professionals would dominate the discussion and decision-making process.

Practical task

Think about where you stand on the issue of jury trial in criminal courts. Do you think juries are an expensive waste of time, or an essential element of a just society?

- List the arguments on each side and decide which you find most convincing. Some arguments can be countered by a suggestion for reform.

- The examiner will not mind what your view is – remember that there are high profile people with differing views on jury trial. You must, however, back up your opinion by good arguments.

- You cannot form a reasonable opinion unless you consider not only the advantages and disadvantages, but also the available alternatives.

- Holding more trials in the magistrates' courts is one alternative. See if your decision is different when you have considered the alternative to jury trial in criminal cases.

Magistrates

Magistrates' courts are very busy courts which are found in most towns and deal mostly with criminal cases (see Chapter 7 for revision of the criminal courts).

The role and function of magistrates

Magistrates' courts may be run in one of two ways. They are mostly staffed by lay magistrates with the help of a court clerk. Alternatively there are some courts where a stipendiary, or paid and qualified magistrate, sits alone. These are now known as District Judges (magistrates' courts) and will be discussed below. Most of the material in this book on magistrates refers to lay magistrates.

Lay magistrates

Most magistrates are lay magistrates, also known as Justices of the Peace. They number about 30,000 and sit as benches of three, mostly in criminal cases, in magistrates' courts across the country. They are appointed by the Lord Chancellor on the advice of advisory committees for each area. Sometimes vacancies for magistrates are advertised, sometimes people are recommended to the area committee by individuals or by local organisations. The extraordinary thing about these magistrates is that they work free of charge for the country, by giving up at least 26 days of service in court, plus training and preparation time, each year. Some give much more than that. They are not legally qualified and undertake the work out of a sense of citizenship, recognising the need for lay representation in the legal system.

Candidates must be aged between 21 and 60, although the advice given to advisory committees is that nobody under 27 would normally be appointed. Most are at least 40. The committees aim to achieve a balance of age, race and gender on the bench in their area. They should be of good character – which means they must not have criminal convictions – and must show qualities such as the ability to assimilate information, understand argument and reach a reasoned decision. They are from the area that they serve, living within 15 miles of the court area.

Magistrates are legally entitled to time off work but employers are not obliged to pay for this time. If magistrates lose pay as a result of sitting, they can claim loss of wages and they can also claim travel expenses.

Magistrates attend a training course and watch other magistrates working before they are allowed to sit in court. They then have to attend training sessions from time to time. Many magistrates develop some kind of specialisation, like family work, traffic or the youth court.

Magistrates' civil jurisdiction consists of licensing and family matters and some debt work. The youth court is also, strictly, civil jurisdiction. In criminal cases they conduct summary trials, sentence defendants who plead or are found guilty, and hold committal proceedings in indictable offences and hybrid offences when the defendant has opted for trial in the Crown Court. Magistrates grant bail, issue warrants and hear appeals from their clerk's refusal to grant legal aid. In short, they have a varied jurisdiction.

As magistrates are lay people they have advice available from the court clerk. Many court clerks are not themselves qualified, although the Clerk to the Justices (who is in charge of the administration of the court) must be a qualified barrister or solicitor. The clerk's job is to give technical advice on matters of law and procedure but the clerk must not be involved in the magistrates' decision as to a person's guilt, nor in deciding what sentence is appropriate.

District Judges (magistrates' courts)

In large cities with busy courts there may be a stipendiary magistrate recently renamed District Judge (magistrates' court). This will be a paid professional lawyer (i.e. one who receives a stipend). This person sits full-time as a judge in the magistrates' court, and carries out work as a career, just like any other judge. This system has been so successful that the number has been increased recently to 98 District judges and 166 Deputy District judges.

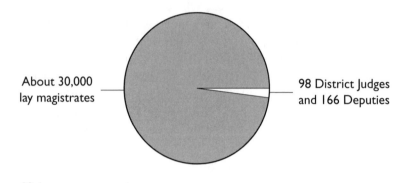

About 30,000 lay magistrates   98 District Judges and 166 Deputies

Figure 13.6

Practical task

Visit your local magistrates' court. There may well be more than one court sitting if the court is in a city or large town. Watch the cases being dealt with.

Who seems to be running the court? It should be the chair of magistrates (the magistrate sitting in the middle), but in some courts it often looks more as if the clerk is running things.

Does the chair seem to be making most of the decisions, or can you see the three magistrates discussing things as they go along?

Prepare and deliver a brief talk to your group about what you saw and heard during your visit. Note:

- the offences charged – whether the defendant was male or female, and the approximate age;
- the process followed – was there a full trial, an adjournment, or was the hearing just for sentencing?
- the sentence – if one was given.

Advantages and disadvantages of lay magistrates

Criticisms – or disadvantages

Magistrates have been criticised for being:

1 unrepresentative of the community as a whole – it is often said that they are middle-aged, middle-class and middle-minded;

2 inconsistent with other benches of magistrates elsewhere in the country in the sentences they pass, so that for similar offences people may receive different treatment;

3 more likely than juries to convict.

These criticisms may be answered as follows:

1 Magistrates can be chosen only from those who come forward. Middle-aged and middle-class people are more likely to have sympathetic employers who will not make it difficult for their employees to become magistrates.

2 One of the benefits of having magistrates is that justice is given a local flavour and magistrates can decide to take a stronger line with particular offences in their area. Also, it would be impossible, given the number of cases arising on a daily basis, to report and digest all cases immediately, which is what would be needed to ensure complete consistency.

3 It is possible that defendants who are not guilty are more likely to choose jury trial where that option is open to them, so leaving a higher proportion of guilty defendants who make a not guilty plea in the magistrates' court.

Advantages

• Magistrates are a much cheaper way to administer justice than using juries or professional judges. They save the country enormous sums of money and it would therefore be very difficult indeed to replace them.

• It is also argued that they prevent the administration of justice falling totally into the hands of lawyers, and so preserve lay representation and public confidence in the system.

• Their local knowledge and understanding of the needs of people within an area helps to administer justice in a fair way.

• Although they tend to be middle-class, magistrates are probably nearer in social context to defendants than judges.

• Improved training programmes operated by the Magistrates' Committee of the Judicial Studies Board are compulsory. This means that although they do not have extensive legal knowledge, magistrates are trained in the areas of law which commonly arise before them.

Practical tasks

I   Contact your local magistrates' court and ask if a magistrate could come to give a talk to your class or year group. The Magistrates' Association organises this on a national basis, so most courts will have magistrates who will give such talks. Prepare by understanding how magistrates are chosen and what they do. Do ask lots of questions and see what the magistrate has to say about the common criticisms of magistrates.

2   Imagine that you have been charged with shop lifting (an offence of theft, which is a hybrid offence). On the evidence of what you have observed in visiting magistrates' courts and the Crown Court, where would you prefer to be tried?

Summary

Jurors	• Role – sit in Crown Courts; 12 members of public hear cases on indictment; decide verdict, not sentence.
Selection	• Taken from electoral roll; aged between 18 and 70, right of refusal 65–70; some disqualified, ineligible, excused, either as a right or at the discretion of the court. Reluctance to serve.
Advantages and disadvantages	• Popularity of trial by peers, maintains public confidence, understanding of the plight of the defendant, a collective decision, *but* reluctance to serve, difficulty of understanding burden and standard of proof, or complex issues, costly.
Alternatives	• Single judge, bench of three, composite jury (lay and professionals), increased trial by magistrates.
Magistrates	• Role – sit in magistrates' courts, hear all criminal cases, try summary offences and those triable either way remaining with magistrates.
Selection	• Mostly lay people (some stipendiaries – see Chapter 12).
	• Over 30,000, unpaid, unqualified legally, of 'good standing' in the community, from local area.
	• Appointment by Lord Chancellor by recommendation and application.

Advantages and disadvantages	•	Inexpensive, lay representation, understand needs of the local area, *but* of similar backgrounds, lack of legal training, inconsistent sentencing.
Alternatives	•	Trial by stipendiary magistrates – now known as District Judges (magistrates' courts).

Tasks

1   Write a brief explanation of the following words and phrases. Use the glossary and this chapter to help check your answers.

lay	remand
indictment	acquittal
anonymous	stipendiary
jurisdiction	civil
stipendiary	summary offences
amorphous	committal proceedings
unanimous	bail
defamation	

2   Recent reforms and proposed reforms of the criminal justice system have been designed to provide a more economic system.

     Is it an essential ingredient of a justice system that it should be affordable, or does an emphasis on saving money threaten to destroy the justice system?

3   Having prepared the above topic as an essay, now use it for a debate. A good starting point is to list arguments for each proposition and find some evidence in support of those arguments.

4   Consider this statement by Lord Denning: 'Whenever a man is on trial for serious crime ... then trial by jury has no equal'.

    (a)   Briefly explain the trial process which will apply to a person accused of a serious crime, and suggest why that person may face jury trial.

    (b)   How will the jury for the trial be selected?

    (c)   Why does Lord Denning place such importance on trial by jury?

5   (a)   Consider the advantages and disadvantages of trial by jury.

    (b)   What alternatives could be suggested for this kind of trial?

6   (a)   Briefly explain who lay magistrates are.

    (b)   What criticisms could be made of the system of lay magistrates?

    (c)   Are these criticisms justified?

    (d)   Consider any advantages of using a system of lay magistrates.

Part 4

Introduction to substantive law

So far this book has investigated the way that the English legal system operates, including the way in which the law is formed, the courts and the people who work in them, the role played by the police, etc. The next part of the book provides an introduction to aspects of two areas of substantive law:

- criminal law; and
- tort.

It then considers the sanctions and remedies which may flow from these.

The material studied in this part of the book will be useful for examination purposes as it will provide you with illustrations and examples to support your previous studies, as well as introducing you to particular rules of law.

Central to this part of the book is the concept of liability. The term 'liability' means responsibility for a person's actions towards others in society, whether in civil or criminal law. The distinction between civil and criminal law is discussed in the next two chapters, although some differences have already arisen in Chapter 7 (the court system). In general the criminal law is concerned with upholding a standard of behaviour by punishing those who offend, while the civil law is concerned with compensating the victim.

This part of the book only deals with liability for non-fatal offences against the person in criminal law, and negligence causing personal injury and damage to property in tort, plus related sanctions and remedies. For A-level candidates the topics are developed further in modules of the A2 specification. AQA candidates should be able to explain the rules of law covered here, and apply them to a factual problem situation. The topics will then be developed further in modules 4 and 5. OCR candidates will study *one* topic out of criminal law, contract law, or the law of tort in depth for A2.

The skills of applying law to factual situations, which are needed for all of these areas of study, are further explained and developed in the final part of the book.

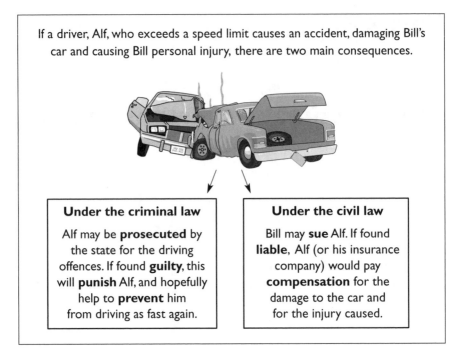

If a driver, Alf, who exceeds a speed limit causes an accident, damaging Bill's car and causing Bill personal injury, there are two main consequences.

Under the criminal law

Alf may be **prosecuted** by the state for the driving offences. If found **guilty**, this will **punish** Alf, and hopefully help to **prevent** him from driving as fast again.

Under the civil law

Bill may **sue** Alf. If found **liable**, Alf (or his insurance company) would pay **compensation** for the damage to the car and for the injury caused.

Figure P3.1

14 Criminal law

Criminal law is the branch of law that you will study which deals with offences against the state, or society in general. They are regarded as being so serious that the state is obliged to take action against the accused and, if convicted, the offender is subjected to punishment rather than just paying some form of compensation.

The terminology used reflects the seriousness of the situation. As the criminal law is regarded as being more serious, and having more repercussions on the accused's reputation, and, possibly, ending in a loss of liberty, the standard of proof is higher than that imposed in a civil case. In a criminal case the prosecution must prove its case *beyond reasonable doubt*, which means that the jury must be very clear that they believe that the accused is responsible for the crime. If the jury believe beyond reasonable doubt that the defendant, or accused, is responsible for the criminal action, they will return a verdict of *guilty*, and the offender will be sentenced by the judge.

The majority of crimes consist of two elements:

- The *mens rea* is the mental element of a crime, and is the state of mind of the person committing the crime. This could be, for example, intention to carry out an act, or recklessness over it.
- The *actus reus* is the prohibited conduct which forms the crime, and could be an act or an omission to act.

These phrases come from a Latin maxim '*Actus non facit reum nisi mens sit rea*', which means that an act does not create guilt unless the mind is also guilty. Crimes, whether statutory or common law, are usually defined in terms of the appropriate elements, and the definition of most crimes includes both *actus reus* and *mens rea*. So, for example, in murder, causing the death of another person is the *actus reus*, and the intention to kill or seriously harm is the *mens rea*.

Figure 14.1

Actus reus

This is the physical element of a crime – the wrongful act or prohibited action or failure to act (omission). The act or omission must be voluntary, that is it is carried out by the accused who has some control over his or her physical actions.

Many crimes are statutory in nature, in other words they have been created by an Act of Parliament, such as the non-fatal offences against the person. Other crimes, however, are common law in nature, having been developed over the years by the courts, such as murder and involuntary manslaughter. In both cases, the definition will include a specific reference to the *actus reus* required for the particular offence, which may not only refer to the act, but also to the consequence, such as an assault or a battery resulting in actual bodily harm. Part of the issue is therefore the result, which should be considered as well as the act. The act must *cause* the result, which is another aspect of the *actus reus*. So, you should consider:

- the voluntary act or omission
- which causes
- the result and
- (in some cases) the circumstances surrounding the event.

Conduct – act or omission

Either a positive act or an omission could amount to the *actus reus*, so:

- the accused may commit a positive action which results in the prohibited consequence; or
- the accused may fail to carry out an action which they are obliged to do, resulting in the prohibited consequence.

The law does not place a general duty on people to help others, so there are not many circumstances where failure to act results in criminal liability. There are some occasions, however, where an omission can form the *actus reus* of an offence. An example is where there is a relationship between two people where one cares for the other. Failure to care for a child can be seen in *R v Gibbins and Proctor* (1918) where a couple were found guilty of murder having starved a child to death. In *R v Pittwood* (1902) a gatekeeper opened the gate of a railway crossing to let a car through, and forgot to close it – an omission, since his contracted duty was to open and close the gate at the right times. He was convicted for manslaughter of the driver of a hay cart who later went over the crossing and was killed by a train.

Where the accused has created a dangerous situation, causing danger or harm to the victim, and fails to do anything to remove the harm or help the victim, then this may amount to an *actus reus*. This is illustrated in the following case.

R v Miller (1983)
Miller was a squatter in a house. He was convicted of an offence of criminal damage because, having accidentally started a fire in a room, he failed to do anything to put it out or summon help, but left the room to sleep in another one.

The following recent case shows again a failure to act when there could be said to be a duty, even if not strictly part of the contract of employment or law of the land, amounting to the *actus reus* of an offence.

R v Naughton (2001)
An off-duty police officer who did not intervene when one of his friends attacked a restaurant owner was convicted of misconduct in a public office.

Voluntary act

It is said that an act must be voluntary, meaning that the accused's behaviour, whether by way of an act or omission, is as the result of a physical action over which there is some control, as opposed to a reflex reaction where the accused has no control. The general defence of automatism covers this situation and will be addressed at A2 level for those who study criminal law.

Examples include various forms of automatic physical action over which a person does not have control. This could be due to a reflex reaction, such as being stung by bees, or an uncontrolled activity such as being concussed and wandering about, slipping on ice or sleepwalking. The important point is that to form the *actus reus* of an offence the action is subject to some degree of physical control.

Causation

Causation needs to be established for many offences. This is clearly seen in murder, were the accused must have done, or omitted to do, something which caused death. If the victim does not die, despite the action of the accused, there is not a conviction of murder. When considering whether or not the act or omission of the accused has caused the consequence, the courts must look at two issues:

- causation in fact; and
- causation in law.

Causation in fact

Causation in fact relates to whether or not the actions of the accused were the factual cause of the consequence. The test adopted by the courts is the 'but for' test. Here the court asks whether the victim would have suffered the injury 'but for' the actions of the accused. Compare the following cases.

> *R v Pagett* (1993)
> Pagett fired at the police, who responded by firing back at Pagett. He held his girlfriend in front of him as a shield when the police fired at him. Although it was actually the police bullets that caused her death, the action of the accused was held to be the factual cause of her death as, 'but for' his actions, she would not have died.
>
> *R v White* (1910)
> A lady was given a drink which contained potassium cyanide by her son, White. She was later found dead on her sofa. The son was not convicted of murder because medical evidence showed that the lady had not taken the drink, but had died of a heart attack. The consequence of death would have happened anyway, without the dose of poison. The son certainly had intent to kill her, but had not factually caused the death (he was, however, convicted of attempted murder).

Causation in law

Causation in law relates to whether or not the consequence was caused by the actions of the accused or whether the accused made a significant contribution to it. The defendant's actions do not need to be the sole or even main cause of the consequence. There must not be another act between that of the accused and the consequence which breaks the chain of causation.

If A hits B on the head thereby fracturing B's skull, and B dies, A has caused B's death. If, on the other hand, C hits D on the head in a spate of anger, but then D recovers from the blow and later steps into the road where he is killed by a passing vehicle, C cannot be said to have killed D. The case of *R v Smith* provides a case example of the difficulties of the chain of causation.

> *R v Smith* (1959)
> Smith, a soldier, stabbed another soldier while posted in Germany. The victim was dropped twice by other people on the way to hospital, and when there he received poor medical treatment and subsequently died.

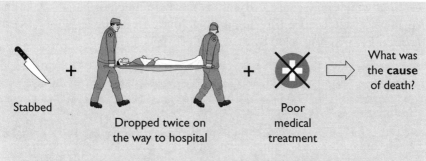

Stabbed + Dropped twice on the way to hospital + Poor medical treatment ⟹ What was the **cause** of death?

Figure 14.2

The court held that the fact of having been dropped *and* the poor treatment were not enough to break the chain of causation and prevent Smith's conviction, as the original wound was still the 'operating and substantial' cause of death.

We are looking, then, at a situation where the actions of the accused have begun a chain of events, but there has been some other, intervening act by a third party which may have broken the chain of causation. This may have superseded the initial act or omission as the substantial cause of the final consequence. If this has happened, the defendant would not be guilty, but courts are unwilling to allow a defendant to 'escape' responsibility. Consider the two cases of *Blaue* and *Cheshire*. In neither case did the intervening events break the chain of causation.

R v Blaue (1975)
The victim, a Jehovah's Witness, refused a blood transfusion after being attacked by the accused, and bled to death as a result of her injuries. The defendant was held to be liable for causing her death. The victim would not have been in hospital at all 'but for' the action of the defendant. Lawton LJ said that 'those who use violence ... must take their victim as they find them'. The victim's religious beliefs did not therefore break the chain of causation.

R v Cheshire (1991)
The victim was recovering in hospital after being attacked by the defendant, but medical complications resulted from the insertion of a tube in his throat (a tracheotomy), and he died as a result. The Court of Appeal held that the defendant had caused the death, as 'but for' the defendant's actions the victim would not have died, and the defendant's actions made a 'significant contribution' to the death. Only in the most extraordinary case would medical treatment break the chain of causation.

One area which may cause difficulties is where a doctor has to make the decision to switch off a life support machine. An example is the case of *Malcherek* which was heard by the Court of Appeal.

R v Malcherek (1981)
Malcherek's wife was admitted to hospital after Malcherek had stabbed her nine times. She appeared to recover, but suffered a set-back and had to have open heart surgery. Brain damage had been sustained, however, and the doctors eventually had to switch off the life support equipment. Malcherek was convicted of murder, even though there was medical intervention, and the final act was that of the doctor switching off the equipment sustaining the wife's life.

In *Airedale v Bland* (1993) the court had to make a decision authorising doctors to switch off the life support equipment for Tony Bland, a Hillsborough football disaster victim. It was said that a doctor was 'simply allowing the patient to die in the sense that he was desisting from taking a step which might prevent his patient from dying as a result of his pre-existing condition'.

Thinking point

Can you think of any occasions, however unlikely, when a doctor may commit a criminal offence by switching off life support equipment?

An interesting recent case concerning causation is that concerning the separation of conjoined twins, where the decision had to be made to either leave both to die in the near future or to save the life of one at the expense of the other. Does this give rise to criminal liability?

Re A (Children) (2000)
Doctors had to decide whether to operate to separate 'Siamese twins' Jodie and Mary. They were joined in such a way that Jodie's heart and lungs were providing oxygenated blood for both twins, and they were likely to die within months if nothing was done. The court was asked for authorisation to separate the twins.
   The difficulty was that separation would probably save the life of Jodie but cause the death of Mary. In law, the surgeon operating to save Jodie would have caused Mary's death intentionally, even though that would not have been his primary motive. Mary's death could, however, be seen as a side-effect of treatment that was in her best interests overall.

Circumstances

In some crimes, the surrounding circumstances may also be relevant. For example, assault is an offence, but if the victim happens to be a policeman who is assaulted in the course of his duty, then the defendant would be charged with a more serious offence. The particular offence would have arisen out of circumstances. Similarly, if a person is drunk at home, that is not an offence; being drunk in a public place is, however. The difference is the circumstances in which the action takes place.

Thinking point

Consider these facts.

George throws a ball at Fred, which misses and bounces off a wall hitting Harry. Harry's grandmother, Isobel, sees the incident, faints, and hits her head on a brick, causing a skull fracture.

On the way to hospital, the ambulance in which she is travelling is involved in a traffic accident, causing further injuries and a delay in getting to hospital.

When she gets to the Accident and Emergency unit, she is seen by a young and inexperienced doctor who does not realise how serious her injuries are, so that by the time she is treated her condition is much more severe and the consequences much more serious than they need have been.

Taking account only of the issues of *actus reus* discussed above, consider:

- whether George *may* be held liable, following case law;
- whether George *should* be held liable.

Mens rea

Apart from the action of committing an offence, such as shooting a gun and causing death, most offences require some mental element to be present, such as the intention to kill or cause really serious injury. This mental element of a crime is known as the *mens rea*, literally the 'guilty mind', and again is specified by the definition of the offence. A person would only be convicted of the full offence if both of these elements are present. There are two basic categories of *mens rea* recognised by law:

- intention;
- recklessness.

Each criminal offence has its own particular *actus reus* and *mens rea*, both of which have to be satisfied in order for the accused to be guilty of the offence. In statutory offences, the *mens rea* is often defined by terms such as 'knowingly', 'maliciously', intentionally', 'wilfully', 'permitting', 'suffering', 'recklessly' and so on. Some offences require a much higher level of *mens rea* than others.

Thinking point

Consider the problems of interpreting the words above according to the rules of statutory interpretation studied in Chapter 5.

Specific intention

For some offences, such as murder, or causing grievous bodily harm with intent, it is necessary to have a specific intention, and in *R v Mohan* (1976) it was said that this is 'a decision to bring about, as far as it lies within the accused's power, [a specific consequence] no matter whether the accused desired that consequence of his act or not'.

The two offences in Sections 18 and 20 of the Offences Against the Person Act 1861 require a similar *actus reus*, but it is the *mens rea* which makes the offences different.

Practical task

Read carefully Sections 18 and 20 of the Offences against the Person Act, given below. What is the *actus reus* of these offences? From the wording decide which parts of the offences amount to the *mens rea*, making one offence more serious than the other.

Offences Against the Person Act 1861

18. Whosoever shall unlawfully and maliciously by any means whatsoever wound or cause any grievous bodily harm to any person with intent to do some grievous bodily harm to any person or with intent to resist or prevent the lawful apprehension or detainer of any person, shall be guilty of [an offence], and being convicted thereof shall be liable to imprisonment for life.
20. Whosoever shall unlawfully and maliciously wound or inflict any grievous bodily harm upon any other person, either with or without any weapon or instrument, shall be guilty of [an offence triable either way], and being convicted thereof shall be liable to imprisonment for five years.

Oblique intent

When a person actually desires the result of their action they are said to have direct intent. So, if A intends to throw a brick at B and cause serious harm and does so, that is direct intent. Difficulties arise when a person did not really intend the consequence of an action.

Suppose A throws a brick at B realising that (a) serious harm may be caused to B, and (b) that B's glasses may be broken, but does not really want to break B's glasses. If A nevertheless goes on to throw the brick at B and causes both serious harm and breaks B's glasses, there will be said to be oblique intent regarding the glasses. A, although not really desiring an outcome, has realised that it will occur, and has gone on to carry out the *actus reus* anyway.

A recent House of Lords case has laid down the current guidelines for oblique intent.

> *R v Woollin* (1998)
> Here it was said that the jury should be directed that they are not entitled to find the necessary intention unless they feel sure that the consequence was a virtual certainty as a result of the defendant's actions and that the defendant appreciated that such was the case.

Recklessness

Recklessness is a lower level of *mens rea* than intention. There are two kinds: subjective and objective recklessness.

Subjective recklessness

This is where a person does not necessarily set out to bring about a desired result, but realises that it could occur from a course of action, and continues with that action anyway. This kind of recklessness applies to the offences of assault – assault causing actual bodily harm and malicious wounding – and it was explained in the following case.

> *R v Cunningham* (1957)
> Cunningham ripped a gas meter from a wall to steal money from it. Gas leaked from where the meter had been and made a woman living there ill. The word 'maliciously' was held to mean either
>
> *continued*

- intending to do the particular harm that was done; or
- being reckless in realising that the defendant realised that there was risk of such harm occurring.

The second of these is now known as subjective recklessness, as the individual knows of the risk and goes on to carry out the deed. Here Cunningham could only be guilty if he knew that the gas escaping could be harmful.

Objective recklessness

Where a defendant does not realise that there is a risk, but an ordinary person – described in *MPC v Caldwell* (1981) as 'an ordinary prudent individual' – would have done so, recklessness is said to be objective. This could make a defendant liable for an offence even if that particular person did not realise that there was a risk. This applies to criminal damage.

Transferred malice

If a person intends to harm a person and carries out the *actus reus* to do that, but by some chance the act causes harm to another person, the intention is said to be transferred to the offence against the person harmed. For example, if A intends to shoot B, but aims badly and shoots C, A cannot claim that there was no offence because there was not an intention to harm C. This is said to be transferred malice.

Strict liability offences

Some offences can be committed by the *actus reus* alone, without the need to show any *mens rea*. These are known as strict liability offences. When a statutory offence is unclear as to the *mens rea* required, the courts have the task of deciding if the offence is intended to be one of strict liability. The case of *Sweet v Parsley* (1969) provides a good illustration of this.

Sweet v Parsley (1969)
A landlady was convicted of being involved in the management of premises used for the consumption of illegal drugs, even though she did not know of the activities of her tenants. The House of Lords held that the conviction was wrong, because they felt that Parliament could not have intended this to be a strict liability offence, and implied that they had meant to include the word 'knowingly' within the definition. Lord Pearce said:

Before the court will dispense with the necessity for *mens rea* it has to be satisfied that Parliament so intended. The mere absence of the word 'knowingly' is not enough. But the nature of the crime, the punishment, the absence of social obloquy, the particular mischief and the field of activity in which it occurs, and the working of the particular section and its context, may show that Parliament intended that the Act should be prevented by punishment regardless of intent or knowledge. The innocent hotel-keeper, the lady who keeps lodgings or takes paying guests, the manager of a cinema, the warden of a hostel, the matron of a hospital, the housemaster and matron of a boarding school, all these, it is conceded, are on the respondent's argument liable to conviction the moment that irresponsible occupants smoke cannabis cigarettes.

Who decides on strict liability?

Few offences will be found to have strict liability, so how is it decided which these should be? It is true to say that most offences which are now recognised as ones of strict liability are statutory offences, but it is also true that in the statutes creating these offences it does not say 'This offence does not need *mens rea*. It is strict liability.' In fact, referring back to Chapter 5 on statutory interpretation, one of the *presumptions* of interpretation is that criminal offences *require mens rea*. If a statute is interpreted in such a way as to put into practice the intention of Parliament, then it should be clear from the wording of the statute that Parliament intended there to be strict liability in some circumstances, without the words actually being in that form. Otherwise the courts should go back to the presumption of some degree of *mens rea* being necessary. The House of Lords stressed this in the following case.

B v DPP (2000)
The Divisional Court of Queen's Bench had upheld the conviction of a 15-year-old boy for an offence of inciting a child under 14 to commit an act of gross indecency, finding that it was an offence of strict liability. The House of Lords overruled this decision, emphasising that where the statute makes no mention of *mens rea* there is a presumption that it is required and that the presumption is particularly strong if the offence is serious.

Why is liability sometimes strict?

Some offences which are classified as being strict liability are those where it would be extremely difficult to prove the *mens rea*, such as parking and speeding offences, and without strict liability guilty people would probably escape conviction. In other cases the consequences are so severe that it is felt that criminal sanctions are required as a matter of social policy, such as selling food unfit for human consumption, or a breach of some of the Health and Safety at Work legislation. In some cases the imposition of strict liability operates as a deterrent. The following examples show the practicality of strict liability in some situations.

- A butcher who buys meat pies from a manufacturer or wholesaler, and sells them to the general public, may be guilty of a strict liability offence if those pies are unfit to be eaten, even if the butcher had no knowledge that the pies were contaminated. This may seem to be unfair, but it encourages people to be especially careful in situations where the consequences might have severe results.

- It is a requirement that moving parts of machines should be guarded to protect workers from harm. The employers will be strictly liable under the Health and Safety at Work Act 1974 if they fail to comply with these requirements.

- Under the Trade Descriptions Acts 1968 and 1972 there is a strict liability offence of displaying goods with the incorrect price or description.

These are not absolute liability offences, as defences may exist. In the Health and Safety at Work Act, for instance, the duties imposed are only 'in so far as is reasonably practicable', which means that an employer could use the defence that to protect the workforce fully would be so expensive as to be prohibitive. The availability of defences means that liability is not absolute, but is strict.

The following are examples of absolute liability, where the defendant could offer nothing at all as a defence.

Larsonneur (1932)
The defendant, an illegal alien, was deported from Eire, and brought to England under police custody. She had no permission to land in England, but was held in a police cell in Holyhead. She was convicted of being an illegal alien 'found' within the United Kingdom without permission.

The court relied on *Larsonneur* in deciding the following case.

Winzar v Chief Constable of Kent (1982)
The defendant was taken to hospital, was discovered to be drunk and told to leave. He was then seen slumped in a seat in a corridor and taken by the police to their car, where he was arrested for being drunk on a highway. The circumstances of 'being found' constituted the offence.

Coincidence of *actus reus* and *mens rea*

The *actus reus* and *mens rea* together form a complete offence, and having formed one without the other will not lead to conviction. The two elements must occur at the same time or very near to each other in time. In some circumstances the *actus* could be a continuous act, and if the *mens rea* is formed at some time during the occurrence of the *actus reus*, that will still amount to an offence. So if A takes a book, intending to return it, but then decides to keep it, this still may amount to the total offence of theft. An example is seen in the following case.

Fagan v Metropolitan Police Commissioner (1969)
When asked to pull in by a policeman, Fagan parked his car, not realising that he had done so, on the policeman's foot. When the policeman asked him to move the car, he refused, saying 'F*** you, you can wait', and switched off the engine. He later started the car again and slowly moved the car off the policeman's foot. Fagan was charged with assaulting a police officer in the execution of his duty. Although it was not clear whether Fagan drove on to the policeman's foot accidentally (and if he did, he would have carried out the *actus reus* without the required *mens rea*), the magistrates were convinced that when he 'knowingly, provocatively and unnecessarily allowed the wheel to remain on the foot' he had the required *mens rea* for the offence. They then saw the act of leaving the car there to be a continuing one, which coupled itself with the *mens rea* at a point during this act, to form an offence. An offence is only committed when the two elements were both present – not when Fagan parked the car, as at that point he had no *mens rea*, but only when he refused to move it.

Fagan
unintentionally
parked on the **+** leave the car
policeman's foot
(*actus reus*)

He then
decided to
there
(*mens rea*)

Figure 14.3

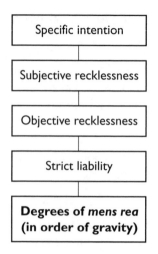

Figure 14.4

Non-fatal offences against the person

We are going to examine the area of criminal law which involves offences against the person which do not result in death. These offences can be placed in rank order of seriousness from assault upwards.

Assault

Assault was once based wholly on common law, but there is now reference to it in statute. The statute does not define the offence, however.

Section 39 of the Criminal Justice Act 1988 states that assault is a summary offence for which the maximum sentence is six months' imprisonment or a fine. That tells us about the sentence, but the common law is needed to define the offence itself.

The *actus reus* of assault is an act which puts a person in fear that unlawful force is about to be used on them.

Figure 14.5

From this it can be seen that it is not even necessary to touch the other person to commit an act of assault. Just causing fear, for example raising an arm above someone suddenly as if to hit that person, would amount to assault. Clearly the fear has to be real, and there is doubt over whether the use of words alone would always be enough to amount to assault, although in *R v Ireland* (1997) it was held that unwanted and threatening telephone calls to women could amount to assault. The context will be important, however. Compare the following cases.

Read v Coker (1853)
Coker and his servants surrounded Read, who was there to collect rent, they rolled up their sleeves and threatened that they would break his neck unless he left the premises. Read clearly feared that the threat would be carried out and this amounted to an assault.

Turberville v Savage (1669)
The defendant placed his hand on the hilt of his sword, and said 'If it were not Assize time I would not take such language from you'.

In the first case the court held that even though the threat was conditional, it did amount to an assault because of the real fear. In the second case, however, the court held that there was no assault as what the defendant was actually saying was that he was not going to attack the claimant as it was Assize time and there were judges about.

It is also a requirement that the fear must be immediate.

Smith v Chief Superintendent, Woking Police Station (1983)
The victim looked through the closed bedroom window of a ground floor flat, late at night, to find the defendant looking in. Under the Vagrancy Act 1824 the defendant was convicted of trespassing with an unlawful purpose. Regarding the 'unlawful purpose' the court agreed that his actions amounted to assault. The victim had been sufficiently and immediately afraid to constitute assault even through a closed window.

The *mens rea* of assault is either:

- intention to cause someone to fear that they would receive unwanted force; or
- recklessness – knowing that there was a risk that the victim might fear unwanted force (known as *Cunningham* recklessness – see pages 219–20 above).

Battery

Battery is often linked with assault, just because the offences are often committed together. They are two different offences, however. Like assault, battery is stated in Section 39 of the Criminal Justice Act 1988 to be a summary offence carrying a maximum of six months' imprisonment or a fine.

The *actus reus* of battery is applying unlawful force to another person. Clearly, reasonable social contact is allowed and will not amount to a battery, although if the force is unwanted then just touching could, in some circumstances, amount to battery. This was explained in the following case.

Collins v Wilcock (1984)
Goff LJ said:

> Nobody can complain of the jostling which is inevitable from his presence in, for example, a supermarket, an underground station, or a busy street; nor can a person who attends a party complain if his hand is seized in friendship, or even if his back is slapped … Another form of conduct long held to be acceptable is touching a person for the purpose of engaging his attention, though of course using no greater degree of physical contact than is reasonably necessary in the circumstances for that purpose.

There is no need to prove that the person was injured or that harm or pain was caused. Battery is usually imagined to be one person striking the other in some way, but it could be caused indirectly. See *Fagan* (page 223) and the following cases for examples of force applied indirectly.

DPP v K (a minor) (1990)
A 15-year-old left a Chemistry lesson to go to the toilet, and put acid into the hot air drier in the school toilets. The next person to use the drier was sprayed with acid. This amounted to battery, even though the force was indirect.

R v Haystead (2000)
A punch to a person holding a child caused the child to fall to the floor. This was held to be a battery, even though the force was indirect.

The *mens rea* is again intention to cause unlawful force or recklessness as to whether it is caused (*Cunningham* recklessness, as for assault).

Assault causing actual bodily harm

An assault is generally seen as more serious if in the course of the action a person is injured. Section 47 of the Offences Against the Person Act 1861 makes it an offence to commit 'any assault occasioning actual bodily harm'. This is a crime requiring a particular outcome, or a 'result crime', but the accused does not have to intend the result or be reckless as to actual bodily harm. The offence is triable either way and carries a maximum penalty of five years in prison.

The *actus reus* is causing an assault *or* battery (see above for both of these) and in doing this causing (or occasioning) actual harm or injury. The development of this offence has depended greatly on the interpretation of the statute, firstly in allowing the word 'assault' to mean assault or battery, and secondly in giving some meaning to 'actual bodily harm'. In fact this has in the past been interpreted widely, with very little harm occurring, but the current interpretation is found in the case below.

> *R v Chan-Fook* (1994)
> The Court of Appeal said that 'the word 'actual' indicates that the injury (although there is no need for it to be permanent) should not be so trivial as to be wholly insignificant'.

Since the phrase 'actual bodily harm' could be open to differing interpretation, the issue was bound to arise as to whether psychological harm was included. The answer is that 'bodily harm' is not limited to physical harm and can be psychological injury, such as shock, but must be recognised by medical practice. In *Chan-Fook* it was said that the offence 'does not include mere emotions such as fear or distress or panic, nor does it include, as such, states of mind that are not themselves evidence of some identifiable clinical condition'.

The *mens rea* of a Section 47 offence is the same as that of assault and battery. If a person has the *mens rea* required for battery, but the victim is injured, then this may amount to a Section 47 offence.

> *R v Roberts* (1971)
> The defendant had attempted to remove the coat of a girl in a moving car. She believed that he meant to assault her, so she jumped from the car and was injured. The Court of Appeal held that the issue was one of causation – were the victim's actions the natural result of the defendant's conduct? It did not matter whether he foresaw that she would jump and be injured. The only *mens rea* required was his intention to commit a battery.
>
> *R v Savage* (1991)
> The defendant threw a glass of beer over the victim. The glass shattered and the victim was injured. It could not be shown whether the
> *continued*

defendant had let go of the glass deliberately or accidentally, so the Court of Appeal held that this could not amount to malicious wounding under Section 20 of the Act, but could be an offence under Section 47, as throwing the beer over the victim indicated a level of *mens rea* sufficient for battery.

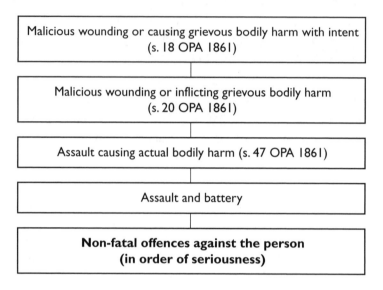

Figure 14.6

Wounding and inflicting grievous bodily harm

The two more serious offences under the Offences Against the Person Act 1861 were examined in connection with *mens rea*, but the exact wording of the Act is important and it is therefore considered again here.

Offences Against the Person Act 1861
18. Whosoever shall unlawfully and maliciously by any means whatsoever wound or cause any grievous bodily harm to any person with intent to do some grievous bodily harm to any person or with intent to resist or prevent the lawful apprehension or detainer of any person, shall be guilty of [an offence], and being convicted thereof shall be liable to imprisonment for life.
20. Whosoever shall unlawfully and maliciously wound or inflict any grievous bodily harm upon any other person, either with or without any weapon or instrument, shall be guilty of [an offence triable either way], and being convicted thereof shall be liable to imprisonment for five years.

These are both statutory offences, and the *actus reus* is almost identical. The difference lies, then, in the *mens rea* required. The offence under Section 18 is clearly more serious, as seen in the maximum sentence of life imprisonment, compared with five years for Section 20.

The *actus reus* for both offences consists of 'wounding' or 'grievous bodily harm'. In the case of *DPP v Smith* (1961) it was said that grievous bodily harm meant really serious harm, and *R v Saunders* (1985) confirmed this, but said that there was no difference between the meaning of 'serious' and 'really serious'.

Wounding means an external injury including the breaking the skin. Both the inner and outer layers of the skin must be broken, so that a bruise alone is not sufficient, and neither is a broken bone or internal injuries unless the skin has also been broken. A cut or graze, however, may, according to the strict wording, be enough to amount to the *actus reus*.

Thinking point

Is it satisfactory that a minor external wound could, in theory, lead to conviction while a more serious internal wound would not do so?

In fact, although the legal boundaries of wounds leading to grievous bodily harm are unclear, there are guidelines for the police in the 1994 charging standards. The level of wounding expected to lead to a charge of grievous bodily harm includes:

- injury resulting in permanent disability;
- permanent loss of any sensory function;
- significant permanent visible disfigurement;
- broken or displaced limbs or bones (including fractured skull, compound fractures, broken cheek bone, jaw, ribs, etc.);
- injuries causing substantial loss of blood, usually requiring a transfusion; and
- injuries (physical or psychiatric) resulting in lengthy treatment or incapacity.

It would be good, however, to see some clearer legal definition.

C (a minor) v Eisenhower (1984)
A child was shot by an air gun, the pellet ruptured a blood vessel in the eye, causing internal bleeding. Since the victim suffered internal injuries but no breaking of the skin, this did not amount to an offence under this statutory provision.

Section 18 uses the word 'cause' and Section 20 uses the word 'inflict'. Until recently the word 'cause' was thought to be wider (and therefore easier to prove) than 'inflict'. In 1997, however, the House of Lords decided unanimously that there was no difference between the two words.

R v Burstow (1997)
The defendant was charged with inflicting grievous bodily harm when he caused his victim psychiatric harm by stalking her. He sent her hate mail, made malicious telephone calls, stole garments from her washing line and passed around intimate personal details about her family. The question arose as to whether Burstow had 'inflicted' the harm. It was held that there was no need to prove a direct use of force. Lord Hope said, 'For all practical purposes ... the words "cause" and "inflict" may be taken to be interchangeable.'

Section 20

The *mens rea* for the offence generally known as malicious wounding under Section 20 is based on the word 'maliciously'. Malice in this context does not necessarily mean the same as the old idea of evil or wicked, but it was said in *Cunningham* that in this context 'maliciously' meant intentionally or recklessly (remember the *Cunningham* sense of the word reckless – pages 219–20).

Thinking point

Do you think that offenders or juries would generally understand the issue of recklessness? There has been some confusion in cases over the kind of recklessness required, but it is generally thought to be the *Cunningham* kind. This is certainly an area where clarification is needed as part of a general reform of assault offences.

R v Mowatt (1967)
The defendant sat on the victim, hit him in the face and banged the victim's head on the floor. The Court of Appeal held that that there was no need to intend wounding or grievous bodily harm or even to be reckless in this respect, but that it was enough to have 'foreseen that some physical harm to some person, albeit of a minor character, might result'. The level of *mens rea* required for this offence, then, is quite low compared with that in Section 18.

A new offence has been created, or really added on to those already existing. If a person commits an offence under Sections 20 or 47 of the Offences Against the Person Act 1861 and the offence is aggravated by racial issues, then an offence is also committed under Section 29 of the Crime and Disorder Act 1998. This allows the court to apply a higher maximum sentence. An offence is racially aggravated if the offender demonstrates hostility towards the victim based on the victim's actual or presumed membership of, or association with, a particular racial group, or if the offender is motivated wholly or partly by hostility towards members of a racial group in general (Section 29).

Section 18

The *mens rea* for the offence generally known as wounding with intent under Section 18 is one of specific intent, and makes the offence the most serious of the assaults. The *mens rea* required is that the defendant acts with intent to:

- do some grievous bodily harm;
- resist or prevent lawful arrest or detention.

So intention must be to cause grievous bodily harm (whereas in a charge under Section 20 the intention to cause some harm would be enough). The word defendant must also have acted maliciously, as with Section 20.

Practical tasks

1 Look in your local newspapers for cases relating to these offences over a period of one month.

- Note the facts, the offence with which the defendant has been charged, which court deals with the issue and the penalty imposed.
- Compare the number of each type of offence over a period of a month.
- Can you draw any conclusions from these figures?

2 Visit your local magistrates' court and Crown Court and observe the proceedings.

- Are any of these offences are being tried? Note if the solicitors, barristers or judge use terms such as *mens rea* or *actus reus*. Listen for terms such as 'causation', 'intention', 'maliciously' or 'recklessly'.
- Do you understand what these terms mean? Think back to your work on juries in the Crown Court (Chapter 13). Do you think that a jury in a Crown Court would understand the meaning of these terms?

Proposals for reform

The area of non-fatal assaults is badly in need of reform. The requirements for proof in terms of *actus reus* and *mens rea* are complex, and anomalies are bound to arise. The requirement of intention, for instance, is open to interpretation by different people and from decisions in cases. The Law Commission suggests that the defendant must have realised that the consequences are 'near inevitable', giving as an example a situation where an explosion is designed to destroy the cargo in a plane in mid-air but it inevitably will kill the crew and passengers.

Even at the House of Lords level there has been confusion over the exact level of *mens rea* required for some offences. In addition, although a Section 20 offence of malicious wounding is viewed as more serious than the Section 47 offence of assault causing actual bodily harm, the maximum penalty is the same. Words and concepts have changed since the Offences Against the Person Act 1861 was produced 140 years ago, and clarification is needed to make interpretation relevant to society today.

The Law Commission has reported on this area, and proposed a new structure to the offences. The Labour government issued a document containing a draft Bill, 'Violence: Reforming the Offences Against the Person Act 1861, Draft Offences Against the Person Bill 1998', but no further action has been taken. We await developments.

Summary

Terminology	• The defendant, if *prosecuted* and found *guilty* beyond reasonable doubt, will be *sentenced*.
Elements	• *Actus reus* – the prohibited conduct; • *Mens rea* – the mental element of the crime.
Actus reus	• A voluntary act or omission which causes a result or circumstance.
Causation	• In fact – 'but for' the prohibited act would this result have arisen (*R v Pagett* (1993))? • In law – a new event must not have intervened to break the chain of causation (*R v Blaue* (1975)).
Mens rea	• Two main categories – intention and recklessness. Often indicated by words such as 'maliciously, intentionally'. • Levels of *mens rea* – specific intention (*Mohan*); subjective recklessness (*R v Cunningham* (1975)), objective recklessness (*MPC v Caldwell* (1981)), strict liability (offences under the Health and Safety at Work Act 1974).

Non-fatal offences against the person	• Assault – putting a person in fear of being subject to unlawful force, with intention to do so or with subjective recklessness (*Read v Coker* (1853)).
	• Battery – applying unlawful force to a person, with intention to do so or with subjective recklessness (*DPP v K* (a minor) (1990)).
	• Assault occasioning actual bodily harm – Section 47 of the Offences Against the Person Act 1861. Causing an assault or battery and causing actual bodily harm, with the same *mens rea* as for assault or battery (*R v Savage* (1991)).
	• Malicious wounding – Section 20 of the Offences Against the Person Act 1861.
	• Maliciously wounding or inflicting grievous bodily harm upon a person, intentionally or with *Cunningham* recklessness (*R v Mowatt* (1967)).
	• Wounding with intent – Section 18 of the Offences Against the Person Act 1861.
	• Maliciously wounding or causing any grievous bodily harm to a person, with intent to do some grievous bodily harm, or with intent to resist or prevent arrest.
Reform	• Law Commission proposes a set of new offences to avoid current confusion in a Draft Offences Against the Person Bill 1998. No action taken so far.

Tasks

1 Write a brief explanation of the following words and phrases. Use the glossary and this chapter to check your answers.

omission	battery
causation	transferred malice
actus reus	assault
intention	wounding
recklessness	grievous
mens rea	strict liability

2 Explain more fully the concepts of (a) *actus reus* and (b) *mens rea*, citing authorities for each.

3 Explain the differences between causation in fact, and causation in law.

4 Jo has been attacked by someone and is hurt. Without knowing any further facts, and on the basis of the law covered in this chapter, explain to Jo what offences might have been committed towards him.

[As you do not know all the facts, you will need to advise Jo ... if ... then.]

15　The law of tort

What is the law of tort? It is part of the *civil* law, and rather than punish the person doing wrong, the law of tort is concerned with *compensating the victim* who has suffered by the actions of another person doing wrong.

The terminology is worth learning correctly. Unlike criminal law, there is *not* a finding of guilt – mainly because a person may be responsible for a wrong act without meaning to do wrong. If I let my car roll into another vehicle because I did not put the brake on properly, I may not have intended to do that as a deliberate act. However, the car is mine, and the damage to the other vehicle is still my responsibility and I am at fault. I would therefore not be found guilty, but *liable* for compensation to the owner of the other vehicle.

The standard of proof is also different from criminal law. It is necessary to find someone liable *on the balance of probabilities*. This means that if all the evidence is considered for both sides, it is more likely than not that I have caused the damage. Clearly this is a lower level of proof than in criminal law, where someone's freedom may be at stake.

It is difficult to state exactly what a tort is, but one fairly simple definition is that given by Martin and Gibbins who suggest that a tort is:

> 'a wrong which entitles the injured party to claim compensation from the wrongdoer'.

An action in tort, then, is usually brought by someone who has suffered loss at the hands of another person who has done something wrong. The loss might be financial, physical or loss of reputation (in the case of the tort of defamation – see below).

Figure 15.1

There are many different torts, but they all have one thing in common. They set a standard of behaviour by which we must all abide – so:

- the tort of negligence imposes a duty to be careful;
- nuisance requires us to use our land so as not to interfere with our neighbours;
- trespass to the person imposes a duty to respect the autonomy of others;
- defamation imposes a duty to tell only the truth about others;
- occupiers' liability imposes a duty to compensate others for harm caused by dangerous premises.

For AS law you will be studying the tort of negligence which is arguably one of the most important of the modern torts. If you choose to go on to study for the full A level (A2), you will have the opportunity to develop your knowledge of negligence and to study other torts.

The tort of negligence

The tort of negligence is quite a recent development of the civil law, and reflects society's view that wrongdoers should pay compensation for the damage they have caused. The principle of tort was explained in the following case which we first met in Chapter 6.

Donoghue v Stevenson (1932)
Lord Atkin said that the tort was 'based upon a general public sentiment of moral wrongdoing for which the offender must pay'.

However, life would be impossible if every time something went wrong we were presented with a bill for the money to cover the loss. Where would we find the money either to pay the bill or to pay insurance premiums to cover us for the risk? Over the years, judges have developed principles which help to decide when an obligation to pay arises and how much should be paid.

Definition

An ordinary person may well define the word 'negligence' as 'carelessness', while the dictionary suggests 'lack of proper care in doing something' (*Shorter Oxford Dictionary*). The law defines the word as meaning that when a person has a duty to act, a person injured by failure to perform that duty in a reasonable way is entitled to compensation.

In order to make the concept of negligence easier to deal with, it is traditionally considered in three parts:

- duty of care;
- breach of that duty;
- resulting damage.

This book follows the traditional pattern of looking for a claim in negligence in these parts, but you must remember that each part of negligence is part of the whole, and that *all three parts* need to be looked at when answering examination questions.

Reminder

Duty of care + breach of duty + resulting damage = negligence

---

Duty of care

Although the judges have tried to devise a general principle which tells us when a legal duty of care is owed, they have found it difficult to be precise. They now ask three questions:

- Is the loss foreseeable?
- Is there proximity between the parties?
- Is it fair to impose a duty of care?

Is the loss foreseeable?

Lord Atkin's test is probably the best known and is based on what he called the 'neighbour' test. He said that we owe a duty of care to people if it is reasonable to foresee that they might suffer harm as a result of our act or omission.

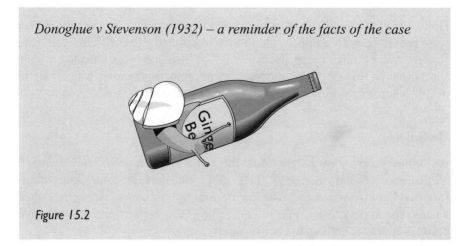

Donoghue v Stevenson (1932) – a reminder of the facts of the case

Figure 15.2

Mrs Donoghue went to a cafe with a friend who bought her a bottle of ginger beer. The bottle was opaque so that the contents could not be seen and it was sealed as it had been when it left the manufacturers. Mrs Donoghue drank half the ginger beer but when the rest was poured into her glass, out floated the remains of a decomposing snail. Mrs Donoghue was made ill by the experience and wanted compensation. She could not use the law of consumer protection as it stood at that time as she had not bought the ginger beer herself. She brought a case against the manufacturers alleging that it was their fault and that they should pay damages. The court agreed and held that, based on the neighbour test, the manufacturer owed Mrs Donoghue a duty of care.

In deciding whether the possibility of injury was foreseeable, common sense will often give the answer. It is obvious, for example, that we may injure someone else if we drive too fast or ride a bicycle at night without lights. There are, however, occasions when the risk is not obvious and it is in these cases that the courts have tried to provide guidance.

Is there proximity between the parties?

Common sense also suggests that there has to be some limit on the people to whom the duty is owed. The law therefore says that there should be a *sufficient relationship of proximity* between the wrongdoer and the victim – in other words, should the wrongdoer have foreseen that the victim might be affected? By proximity, the law really means 'closeness' between the person causing the wrong and the victim. The Case of the Pregnant Fishwife (properly known as *Bourhill v Young* (1943)) is one example.

Bourhill v Young (1943)
Mrs Bourhill was a fishwife who was travelling on a tram. As she got off the tram and picked up her basket, a motorcyclist passed the tram on the side away from Mrs Bourhill and some 45 metres away crashed into a car and was killed.

The rider was clearly negligent but the question was – did he owe a duty of care to Mrs Bourhill? She had not seen the accident but went over to have a look at the site, seeing the blood on the road. She said that as a result she suffered shock and gave birth to a stillborn child about a month later.

The court held that the rider owed no duty to Mrs Bourhill – she was standing behind a solid barrier, not within the rider's field of vision, and was in no way at risk from his speed.

In *Bourhill* the harm that was suffered was a kind of psychiatric harm, and here the courts look for a very close degree of proximity. This is also true where loss of money is involved. The most recent attempt to provide a general test is found in the following case.

Caparo Industries v Dickman (1990)

We see from this case that three questions will be asked by the court:

1. Was the damage reasonably foreseeable?
2. Was there sufficient proximity between claimant and defendant?
3. Is it just and reasonable to impose a duty of care?

The claimants were shareholders in a company. After reading annual accounts which are sent to all shareholders, the claimants bought more shares and eventually took over the company. Only then did they discover that the accounts were wrong. The company had in fact made a loss rather than the profit shown by the accounts.

In the circumstances, as the accounts had not been prepared with a possible takeover in mind but merely as required by law for the information of shareholders, the court held that damage of the kind suffered by the claimants was not reasonably foreseeable, there was no sufficient proximity between the claimants and the accountants and therefore it was not just and reasonable to impose a duty of care on the accountants.

It could be said that the company had not foreseen that the particular claimants in *Caparo v Dickman* would be making use of the accounts, only people in general. A contrasting case follows.

Law Society v KPMG Peat Marwick and Others (1999)

The Court of Appeal held that the defendant accountants owed a duty of care to the Law Society when preparing a report for a firm of solicitors because they knew the report would be used by the Law Society in deciding whether the firm was complying with solicitors' accounts rules. This case can be distinguished from Caparo v Dickman because the accountants knew that the accounts would be seen and relied on by the Law Society, even though they had been prepared under a contract with the firm of solicitors.

Is it fair and reasonable to impose a duty of care?

This is a matter of policy – a general principle to be followed. *Should* the defendant owe a duty of care? The court held in *Anns v Merton London Borough Council* (1978) that the council were negligent in not checking that building plans were satisfactory. They said that there was a two-stage test:

- Is there a relationship of proximity?
- If so, is there anything to negate or limit a duty of care?

Later, however, the courts have realised that asking these two questions together may result in a lot of people claiming that they should 'escape' from a duty of care. In *Caparo v Dickman* (above) it was said that the question to be asked is whether 'the situation should be one in which the court considers it fair, just and reasonable that the law should impose a duty of a given scope on the one party for the benefit of the other.'

Thinking point

Describe three everyday situations where it is foreseeable that a person may be injured or property damaged.

There are some recognised situations where it has been decided, for various reasons, that there is *not* a duty of care.

Professional immunity

People in most professions owe a duty of care towards their clients in respect of advice given and work done. Generally, if work is not up to a reasonable standard the client can sue for breach of contract. The law of negligence, however, acts as a safety net in circumstances where there is some reason why the law of contract does not protect adequately the client suffering loss.

In *Rondel v Worsley* (1969) the House of Lords decided that barristers owed no duty of care in negligence to their clients (see Chapter 10 on the legal profession). This was later extended to solicitor advocates. However, the position has changed with the decision in *Arthur Hall v Simons and others* (2000) where it was held that solicitor advocates could sue for fees, and that this would probably extend to barristers.

The decision in *Rondel v Worsley* was important because it prevented cases being reopened for discussion, and prevented every disgruntled losing party from taking revenge on the barrister presenting the case. However, we can see that in today's society it is not necessarily appropriate to totally exclude a whole profession from an important area of law which lays down professional standards. In this way we can see the courts shaping the policy on principles of fairness.

Police and rescue services

The courts have been reluctant to impose a duty of care on public bodies such as the social services, police, army, fire brigade and rescue services. Consider the following three cases.

> *Mulcahy v Ministry of Defence* (1996)
> It was held that no duty of care was owed to a soldier injured in 'battle conditions'. The claimant had suffered damage to his hearing when a gun captain ordered that a gun be fired while the claimant was not in a safe position.
>
> *OLL v Secretary of State for the Home Department* (1997)
> It was held that the Coastguard did not owe a duty of care in negligence in respect of rescue operations unless their activity led to greater injury than would have occurred had they not been involved.
>
> *Hill v Chief Constable for West Yorkshire* (1988)
> The House of Lords decided that the police did not owe a duty of care to individual members of the public to identify and apprehend an unknown criminal.

It is true that it must be possible for public services to operate freely, to the best of their ability, without the constant pressure of being sued at every turn. The message of these cases is that the public can only expect a reasonably high level of skill, not 100 per cent perfection.

The Human Rights Act 1998 has brought some changes. In *Z and Others v UK* (2001) the European Court of Human Rights made it clear that it must be possible for someone who has been injured by a *negligent* action of a public servant to bring an action for compensation.

> *Z and Others v UK* (2001)
> In a case about children who suffered 'the worst neglect' that a doctor had ever seen, social workers failed to take the children away from their parents and as a result all the children had serious problems when then grew up. The English courts held that they could not make a claim for damages but the European Court of Human Rights held that this was a breach of the children's rights under the European Convention on Human Rights and they were given compensation.

This means that members of the public do have a right to bring an action where they have suffered as a result of the negligence of a public servant. There is still no right to expect perfection, just a reasonable standard in performing the duties which are part of the job.

> **Thinking point**
>
> Do you think that the way in which the courts decide if there is a legal duty of care reflects Lord Atkin's view that it is based on what the public would believe to be moral wrongdoing?

Breach of duty

In order to decide whether a person is in breach of the duty of care, it is essential that there should be some standard by which they can be judged. If the law is to be fair, it must be applied according to specific rules. Judges cannot simply decide each case on the basis of their personal views (see Chapter 6 to revise certainty in relation to the doctrine of precedent). The next step, therefore, in proving negligence, having shown that there is a duty of care, is to show that there is a breach of that duty. Baron Alderson explained how that duty may be breached in the following case.

> *Blyth v Birmingham Waterworks Co* (1856)
> He said, 'Negligence is the omission to do something which a reasonable man guided upon those considerations which ordinarily regulate the conduct of human affairs would do, or doing something which a prudent and reasonable man would not do'.

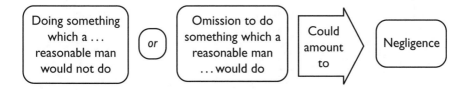

Figure 15.3

In relation to breach of the duty of care, we are judged by the standard of the 'reasonable man'. This person is also known as 'the man on the Clapham omnibus', or the ordinary man in the street. While these descriptions may not be politically correct in the early twenty-first century, they have stuck although the phrase *reasonable person* is becoming more generally used. Whatever the person may be called, the important thing is that the rules provide an acceptable standard of behaviour for a particular act against which others can be measured.

Reasonable person

Figure 15.4

It must always be remembered that the standard is objective – the personal characteristics of the defendant are rarely relevant. The matter is looked at from the point of view of the claimant who is entitled to expect the courts to give protection from actions which do not comply with an acceptable standard. A doctor, for example, is expected to reach the standard of the reasonable doctor.

> *Bolam v Friern Hospital Management Committee* (1957)
> It was held that a doctor will not be regarded as having been negligent if he or she has followed practice accepted by a responsible body of medical opinion.
>
> *Nettleship v Weston* (1971)
> A car driver is expected to reach the standard of a reasonable car driver even when the driver is a learner driver.
> However, children are expected to be less prudent than adults, so a lower standard is expected of children than of adults in a similar situation.
>
> *Mullin v Richards* (1998)
> Two 15-year-old girls were play-fighting with plastic rulers. One of the rulers broke and one of the girls was blinded in one eye by a fragment of plastic. The other girl was held not have been negligent because the risk of injury in these circumstances was held not to have been one which the reasonable 15-year-old would appreciate. Similarly, if the claimant is a minor suing an adult, the adult will be expected to have taken the age of the claimant into account when deciding whether a particular situation was dangerous.

The reasonable person reaches a decision which carefully balances all the known facts and those other facts which can be anticipated, to enable any risk to be identified and action taken to eliminate the risk or to reduce it. Over the years cases have provided some useful examples of things which ought to be taken into account, but remember that each case will be decided on its own particular facts.

The degree of risk

In the following case the likelihood of injury being caused was the important issue. As there was very little risk of a cricket ball being hit outside the ground, the likelihood of injury was small.

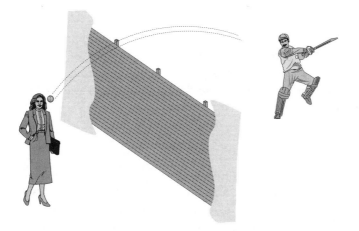

Figure 15.5

Bolton v Stone (1951)
The claimant was standing in the street when she was hit and injured by a cricket ball which had been hit out of a cricket ground nearby. She was about 90 metres away from the wicket and the ball had gone over a 5 metre high fence. The evidence showed that a similar incident had happened only six times in the previous 25 years and that on each of the previous occasions no one had been injured and nothing had been damaged. The claimant received no compensation as in the circumstances the cricket club had done all that it was reasonably required to do to minimise the risk.

The potential seriousness of injury

If there is a risk of very serious injury, the defendant would be expected to be very careful. In the following case it was held that although the likelihood of injury was very small, the reasonable person would also take into account the seriousness of any injury which might be caused.

Paris v Stepney Borough Council (1951)
The claimant was employed to do a job which involved a very slight risk that his eyes could be injured. The accident happened and he was blinded in one eye. The risk for Mr P was no greater than that for other employees but it was decided that he was entitled to compensation. His employers knew that he had already lost the sight in one eye so that the accident left him totally blind, a much more serious consequence than damage to one eye alone. A reasonable employer would have provided him with protective eye-wear.

The cost of precaution

The cost of providing precautions may be taken into account. The cost of preventing a cricket ball escaping in *Bolton v Stone* would have been that of building a very high fence or wall around the whole of the pitch. As the cricket ball rarely went outside the pitch, the cost was not justified. This principle is illustrated by the following case.

Latimer v AEC Ltd (1952)
An employee was injured by slipping on an oily floor. The management had tried to minimise the risk by putting down sawdust and it was held that this was sufficient to fulfil the duty of care. Even though all risk could have been eliminated by closing the factory, to require this would have been unreasonable.

Thinking point

Can you think of any situations in which it may be reasonable to expect a factory to close to protect its employees from risk?

The importance of the activity

Some risk may be acceptable if the task being undertaken is socially important. This point is illustrated in the following case. An action against the police was unsuccessful, showing the importance of their activity of detecting and preventing crime.

Marshall v Osmand (1982)
The plaintiff had been a passenger in a stolen vehicle. He was injured when the police stopped the vehicle and he tried to run away. Milmo J said:

> 'A police officer driving a motor car in hot pursuit of a person or persons, whom he rightly suspects of having committed an arrestable offence, does not owe that person the same duty of care which he owes to a lawful and innocent user of the highway going about his lawful occasions. He must not deliberately injure such a person unless it is reasonably necessary to do so in order to arrest him, and his actions must not be judged by standards which would be applicable if the situation were such that the officer had time to consider all possible alternative courses of action that he could have taken to discharge his duty successfully.'

Thinking point

How far should this case protect police action? In what kinds of situations might the police be considered to have acted inappropriately?

Learners and professionals

The reasonable man test applies to all, but common sense says that there are some, notably beginners and experts, who ought to be judged differently. The courts do, however, bear in mind the needs of the 'innocent' victim.

In the case of someone who is inexperienced, the courts will disregard that lack of experience. In *Nettleship v Weston* (1971) a learner driver was judged against the standard of a qualified driver, and in *Wilsher v Essex Area Health Committee* (1987) a junior doctor was judged against the standard of a doctor who was experienced in carrying out the particular treatment.

In the case of professionals or others who are expert in a particular skill, the position is more difficult as the judges are not, and do not claim to be, experts themselves. They have to rely on evidence given to them, often by members of the same profession as the defendant, as to what the claimant was reasonably entitled to expect. Most of the cases which have come before the courts relate to medical negligence but the rules are the same for all professionals.

In deciding whether or not a reasonable and competent degree of skill was used, the judges apply the Bolam Test (from *Bolam v Friern* – see page 242) which says that a doctor is not guilty of negligence if he has acted in accordance with a practice accepted as proper by a responsible body of medical men skilled in that particular art. This can leave a profession open to the accusation that it acts as judge and jury in its own cause – in other words the profession is able to close ranks.

> *Bolitho v City & Hackney Health Authority* (1997)
> The court made it clear that the practice approved by a responsible body of similar professionals must be capable of withstanding rigorous analysis before the judges will accept that it is a proper practice.

Children

Where a child is the wrongdoer, there is no specific reason why the child should not be held accountable for its actions but this is an area where there is little English law. An Australian case, *McHale v Watson* (1966), held that a child should be judged by the standard of an ordinary child of the same age as the defendant. In a recent English case, *Mullin v Richards* (1998), the Court of Appeal held that a trial judge had been wrong in ignoring the fact that both the claimant and the defendant were only 15 years old.

> *Mullin v Richards* (1998)
> Two girls, Teresa and Heidi, had a sword fight with plastic rulers one of which broke. A piece of plastic flew into Teresa's eye. The trial judge held that Heidi owed Teresa a duty of care, that the injury was foreseeable and that Teresa was entitled to compensation. The Court of Appeal, taking into account the girls' age, held that what had happened was simply a children's game and that Heidi was not liable in negligence.

In reality it would rarely be the case that damages were sought from a child as the child is unlikely to have any money to meet the bill. It is a source of continuing argument as to whether or not parents should be liable for torts committed by their children. Under English law, a parent will only be liable for damage caused by their child if the parent can be shown to have been at fault, for example by giving a child a dangerous implement but not making sure that the child is taught how to use it properly and responsibly.

In cases where the child is the claimant, the child is not expected to have the same level of understanding of danger as an adult and will be judged by what can reasonably be expected of a child of that age.

Thinking point

At what age do you think that a child should have to take full responsibility for its own actions?

  Should parents be responsible for the child's negligent acts?

Damage caused

Having established

- a duty of care, and
- a breach of that duty

there is then a need to show that damage has been caused as a result of the breach.

A person will only be liable for damage which they have actually caused the victim. The same rules apply whether the damage has been caused to a person or to property.

Causation – the 'but for' test

The cause of the damage is important, and a test has been developed known as the 'but for' test. This test simply asks the question – 'Would the damage have happened had it not been for the breach of duty?' The answer to the question will in many cases be obvious. One of the best known examples is given by *Barnett v Chelsea & Kensington Hospital Management Committee* (1969) in which the claimant was able to prove the existence of a duty of care and breach of that duty but was unable to prove damage.

Barnett v Chelsea & Kensington HMC (1969)
A man went to an Accident & Emergency department complaining of vomiting and feeling very ill but was sent home without being seen by a doctor. He was told he should go to his own GP. The man died later the same day. There was no doubt that the hospital and its staff owed him a duty of care and were in breach of that duty. However, the evidence proved that he died as a result of the arsenic poisoning which he had got from drinking some tea before he felt ill. Even if the hospital had treated him properly, the man would still have died as he had too much arsenic for his life to be saved. The widow could not prove that the hospital's action (or, rather, inaction) had in any way contributed to her husband's death.

If the act can be shown to be *one* of the causes of the damage, then the claimant may well succeed. An example of this can be seen in the following case.

Bonnington Castings Ltd v Wardlaw (1956)
Mr Wardlaw worked in an atmosphere in which he inhaled silica dust. He contracted pneumoconiosis. This was caused in part by the dust in the atmosphere, not all of which resulted from his employer's failure to maintain a dust extraction machine properly. Enough silica dust was left in the atmosphere to be a significant contributory factor to his illness and so he was awarded damages.

Where there is more than one possible cause, it used to be thought that it must be proved that the act complained of was the actual cause, as the courts would not allow a claim where it was merely a possibility.

> *Wilsher v Essex Area Health Authority* (1987)
> A child was born very prematurely. One of the problems of such babies is that oxygen deficiency may cause brain damage. The child was monitored but the equipment measured the oxygen in the veins rather than in the arteries. The result was that the child received too much oxygen. It was later discovered that the child had suffered brain damage as a result of which his sight was badly damaged. The problem with his sight could have been caused by the excessive amount of oxygen or by the fact that he was born too soon for his eyes to be properly developed. As it was not possible to prove which had caused the damage, the child was not able to obtain compensation.

In a recent case, the House of Lords has held that, where the actual cause of the injury is known although it is not possible to pinpoint exactly when it happened, it is possible to claim against a person who may have contributed to the injury even though actual contribution cannot be proved. The facts of the case make this rather complicated situation clearer.

> *Fairchild v Glenhaven Funeral Services and Others* (2002)
> Mr Fairchild died of a rare form of lung cancer (mesothelioma) caused by inhaling asbestos fibres. He had worked for several employers and had could have inhaled the fibres at any time in each of his employments. His last employment was with the defendant and he was exposed to the same risk in that employment. Doctors have no idea how the illness is actually caused and it was impossible to say when the illness was actually triggered. As it could have been caused by the defendant's negligence in exposing Mr Fairchild to the risk, his widow was entitled to claim compensation on his behalf.

The difference between *Wilsher* and *Fairchild* is that the actual cause of the baby's problem was unknown, whereas in the case of Mr Fairchild, the cause was known, all that was unclear was when it happened. As there was a possibility that the culprit was his last employment, those employers could be found to be liable.

Foreseeable damage

Another hurdle for the victim is that the damage must be of the type or kind that was reasonably foreseeable. The events leading to the damage may not have been precisely what anyone could have imagined but it is sometimes the end result that counts. This rule of foreseeability of the type or kind of damage comes from a case usually known as *The Wagon Mound*.

> *Overseas Tankship (UK) Ltd v Morts Dock & Engineering Co Ltd (1961) (The Wagon Mound)*
> Oil had been spilled into Sydney Harbour. The defendants were liable for the spillage but not for a fire which occurred when the floating oil was set alight. It was not foreseeable that a fire would be caused.

Another example of how the rules work is seen below.

> *Hughes v Lord Advocate* (1963)
> Some workmen left a manhole open, covering it with a tent and drawing up the ladder. Paraffin lamps were left so that people could see the danger. Hughes was ten years old, and when playing in the area knocked one of the lamps into the hole where it caused an explosion and as a result Hughes was burned. The court held that it was foreseeable that a child might be burned by the lamps even if the precise sequence of events was unforeseeable. Hughes was therefore awarded damages.

Practical task

Read the facts of the case of *Jolley v Sutton LBC* (1998):

> Two boys found an abandoned boat and decided to repair it. They jacked the boat up to work underneath it and one of the boys was seriously injured when the jack collapsed and the boat fell on him.

Now consider the following issues:

- Should the defendant be found liable for negligence for abandoning the boat if anyone – even an adult – was injured by being on or in it?

- Should the defendant be found liable if children were injured while playing in the boat?

- Should the defendant have foreseen the actions of these particular children and be found liable to them?

When you have answered each of the above points, giving your reasoning, look at the finding of the court at the end of the Tasks section, page 253.

A kind of exception to this principle of foreseeability exists. Once it is shown that the damage was caused by the incident and was of the type foreseeable, then defendants have to 'take the victim as they find him'. This is known as the 'thin skull rule'. It means that if the damage is worse for the particular victim because of some peculiarity of the victim (e.g. having a thin skull), the defendant is liable to compensate for the actual damage suffered even if someone else would have been, for example, stronger and therefore less seriously injured.

Smith v Leech Brain & Co (1962)
A workman was scalded on the lip when molten metal splashed him due to his employer's negligence. The burn was only minor but it started a cancer which had been dormant. His death from cancer was not foreseeable but the injury caused by the burn was, and the cancer was caused by the burn. The employer was liable on the basis that the victim had to be taken as he actually was, not as another victim might have been.

Thinking point

Do you think that the rules relating to causation and remoteness of damage are fair? Think of how they apply

- to the victim;
- to the defendant.

The law of torts and criminal law

The law of torts and the criminal law work side by side in many cases. The tort of negligence is based on the fault of the defendant who did not take sufficient care. This differs from the usual criminal requirement that, to be guilty of a crime, the defendant must have intended to commit the wrongful act (i.e. the requirement of the so-called guilty mind or *mens rea*). Although at times, for example in the case of a road traffic accident, a driver may be guilty of a road traffic offence and also liable in negligence for causing injury to someone, the two cases will be heard in different courts and subject to different rules. It must be remembered that a person may be found liable for the tort but be found to have committed no criminal offence.

The law of torts, especially the tort of negligence, has developed to protect people from actions by others which do not meet an acceptable standard. The rules are sometimes said to try to make sure that people behave in an acceptable way as they know that they may have to pay compensation to anyone injured by their failure to do so. It can be argued that the existence of insurance to cover such payments, for example the compulsory insurance that all drivers must have, dilutes the effect but even so, the rules probably do still help because if the insured person makes too many claims, insurance premiums will go up and they may be refused insurance cover.

Practical task

Look in the newspapers each day for a few weeks and find some examples of actions in negligence. Keep a scrapbook of cuttings, photocopies or brief notes of each case you find.

Remember the elements needed to prove negligence:

- a duty of care;
- breach of that duty;
- damage caused as a result.

Summarise the facts of each case you have found.

Identify the claimant and the defendant. Note whether a duty was owed and, if so, the way in which the defendant fell short of the standard required. Note the outcome (if it is reported). This part will be useful to you in thinking about remedies.

Summary

Terminology	• If the defendant is *sued* and found *liable* on the balance of probabilities, the plaintiff will be given a *remedy*.
Negligence	• A breach of a duty of care resulting in damage to another. • The person suffering the damage is entitled to a remedy.
Duty of care	• Is the loss foreseeable? Neighbour test – *Donoghue v Stevenson* (1932).
	• Is there proximity between the parties? *Bourhill v Young* (1943), *Law Society v KPMG* (2000). • Is it fair to impose a duty of care? *Hill v Chief Constable for West Yorkshire* (1988).
Breach of duty	• Doing something which a reasonable man would not, or omission to do something which a reasonable man

would do – *Blyth v Birmingham Waterworks* (1856). The standard is objective – *Nettleship v Weston* (1971).

Factors
- Degree of risk – *Bolton v Stone* (1951).
- Potential seriousness of injury – *Paris v Stepney Borough Council* (1951).
- Cost of precaution – *Latimer v AEC Ltd* (1952).
- Importance of the activity – *Marshall v Osmand* (1982).
- Learners and professionals – *Wilsher v Essex Area Health Authority* (1987); *Bolam v Friern* (1957).
- Children – *Mullin v Richards* (1998).

Damage caused
- Damage may be to a person or property.
- Causation – would the damage have happened had it not been for the breach of duty? *Barnett v Chelsea & Kensington HMC* (1969).
- Must be of the type that was reasonably foreseeable – *The Wagon Mound* (1961), *Hughes v Lord Advocate* (1963).
- The 'thin skull rule' – the defendant must take the victim as they find him – *Smith v Leech Brain & Co.* (1962).

Relationship with crime
- Unlike crime, no need to prove deliberate intention to do wrong – just fault, and this may arise out of being responsible for something, e.g. owning it (such as a car which rolls into a wall). Liability may exist for a tort without being guilty of a crime.

Tasks

1   Write a brief explanation of the following words. Use this chapter and the glossary to check your answers.

prosecuted	sued
claimant	duty of care
defendant	breach
liable	objective
proximity	thin skull rule

2   (a) Explain the stages of proving negligence in a case.

(b) Referring to the cases in this chapter, consider whether these stages of proof result in a standard of liability which the public would find acceptable.

3   'It is not enough that a duty was owed and the defendant fell short of the standard of the reasonable man'.

Explain, using cases to illustrate your answer, what else must be proved to make the defendant responsible for the claimant's loss.

4   Refer back to Chapter 6 and look at the headnote to the report of *Reeves v Commissioner of Police of the Metropolis* (see pages 86–8). In your own words, explain why the police owed a duty of care and how they were in breach of it.

Findings of the Court of Appeal in the case of Jolley v Sutton LBC (1998) – see the Practical Task 245.

- The defendants had been negligent in leaving the boat where it was and would have bee liable for injuries to children playing on the boat.
- The court held that it was not forseable that children would decide to try to repair the boat and be injured in doing so, and the defendants were therefore not liable in these particular circumstances.

---

16 Sanctions and remedies

The end result of either a criminal case or a civil case needs to be effective in some way, or the whole point of the court process would be lost. The two kinds of law have very different aims (see the beginning of this part of the book, page 209), so the outcome is also different.

- The aim of criminal law is to punish the offender and prevent a repeat of the crime.
- The aim of the civil law is to compensate the victim for harm suffered.

The outcome of a criminal case in which the defendant is convicted is therefore the imposition of a sentence of some kind by the court, while in a civil matter, a successful claimant will be awarded a remedy.

Sanctions

When considering what may happen to a person convicted at the end of a criminal trial, there are two considerations.

- What, as a matter of sentencing policy, should we be aiming to achieve by the sanction?
- What particular measures are available to a judge, and which one(s) would be most effective?

Sentencing policy or aims

Sentencing policy is generally a matter for Parliament, so it is for Parliament to decide what sentences are available and, in broad terms, what type of sentence should be used for each crime. The policy chosen will depend on what Parliament believes the purpose of sentencing to be. This policy will then, hopefully, be made clear through statute. There are two main themes of sentencing policy, punishing or helping. We say that these policies are:

- *retributive* – looking at the crime and punishing for it; or
- *utilitarian* – aiming to make the sentence achieve a useful purpose.

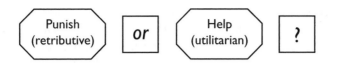

Figure 16.1

Retributive aims were popular in the Victorian period, basing justice on 'an eye for an eye' principle of an offender deserving to be harshly treated. They are also popular with governments, who want to be seen to be tough on crime in order to achieve an effective law and order policy. These aims include retribution and denunciation – the idea that a criminal should get just deserts – in other words be punished in a manner deserved, and suited to the offence committed.

The utilitarian aims try to make sentencing serve a purpose useful to society, either in a general way (for example by protecting society from offenders), or by improving the individual offenders so that they are once more useful to society. These aims include reform and rehabilitation, protection of society and deterrence.

Retribution

Retribution means punishment. As an objective of sentencing it is very simple: a person who has broken the rules shall be punished. It is very attractive option if one has been the victim of crime. There is a basic need to feel that the person who has made you suffer will suffer in turn. This superficial attraction makes it equally attractive to politicians, as a good vote-winner.

Retribution is provided through imprisonment and, to a lesser extent, the imposition of a fine. Logically, the worse the offence, the longer the prison sentence or the greater the fine. This is also attractively simple but does not address any issues to do with the individual offender. Hogan views this as a 'relic of barbarism', and it is seen by many not to be useful as a single aim of sentencing.

Denunciation

The objective of denunciation is to send clear messages about what a society will tolerate and what it will not, and in doing so to lay down the boundaries of what is seen as crime by current society. If particular conduct is seen to carry a harsh sentence, that conduct and those who involve themselves in it are seen to be denounced by society as a whole. The life sentence for murder, for example, gives a clear message of denunciation.

Each of these policy approaches could provide a framework for sentencing. Unfortunately, such a framework does not exist because the policies are so different and, as a society, we do not have a clear preference.

Governments introduce new initiatives which are generally recognisably driven by one approach or another, but when there is a change of government the policy is changed and the initiative is abandoned, sometimes before it has even been implemented. For example, the Crime (Sentences) Act 1997 provided for a new system of releasing prisoners after their sentence, but the system was never introduced and the relevant sections of the Act, Sections 10–27, were repealed by the Crime and Disorder Act 1998.

Reform and rehabilitation

The purpose of reform is to change the offender so that he or she will not want to reoffend. It is therefore a process of education. A policy of reform would result in resources being used to provide good educational facilities in prisons and considerable support for newly released offenders. It would also favour the use of sentences, other than imprisonment, designed to improve the offender's sense of self-worth.

Critics of reform are sceptical about its chances of success. Certainly, it is difficult to measure the success of reform without knowing exactly what happened to individual offenders – did they reoffend and get caught, reoffend more efficiently and so not get caught, or offend in some other way (changing, for example, from offences of violence to offences of dishonesty)? Would the last possibility be regarded as any kind of success?

Deterrence

This aim of sentencing is to deter both individuals, and people generally, in society from committing crime. It can be viewed, then, in two ways:

- *individual deterrence*, which aims to stop the person who has committed an offence from reoffending;
- *general deterrence*, which aims to send out messages to society that those who offend will be punished.

A policy of deterrence would promote unpleasant sentences and, possibly, longer sentences of imprisonment. The difficulty with a policy of deterrence is that it supposes that people think before they commit crime. Much crime is related to drink or drugs, which is likely seriously to impair a person's capacity for measured consideration of the consequences of their actions. The majority of offenders (based on statistics of recorded crimes) are young males – a group not always given to cool reflection before action. Even if a person does coldly weigh the possible consequences of his or her actions, such thought is more likely to be directed to the possibility of being detected, rather than the likely sentence for the offence. The social consequences of being caught – such as the reaction of friends and family – are perhaps also more likely to act as a deterrent than the legal consequences. Certainly reoffence rates indicate that individuals are not deterred by most sanctions.

Protection of society

A very basic aim of sentencing is to protect society. The burglar who is in prison cannot, for the time being, commit burglary. Unless the death penalty is favoured for murder and other serious offences, or for surgical intervention to 'cure' those who commit sexual offences, protection is necessarily a short-term aim. In the short term it is undeniably successful but it does not pretend to address the long-term issues and applies, of necessity, only to more serious offences. It could be argued that since custody is seen as a 'university of crime', where an offender mixes with other offenders, and learns of new ways to offend, that person could emerge from prison a greater danger to society than before.

Sentencing practice

The sentence imposed in each individual case is a matter for the magistrates or the judge, but there are some guidelines and other help available.

- A maximum sentence for each offence is laid down by statute.
- Guidance on the kind of sentence to impose is laid down in the Powers of Criminal Courts (Sentencing) Act 2000 – for example when to impose a custodial sentence (imprisonment or youth custody), the use of combined sentences, etc.
- Guidance is provided by the Criminal Division of the Court of Appeal under Section 80 of the Crime and Disorder Act 1998 – though it had been providing guidance for a long time before this statutory provision was made.
- Section 81 of the same Act provides for a Sentencing Advisory Panel.
- If the defendant is on bail when the offence is committed, under the Powers of Criminal Courts (Sentencing) Act 2000 this will be an aggravating factor.
- The Crime (Sentences) Act 1997 provided, for the first time, minimum sentences in certain circumstances. There is now an automatic life sentence for a second conviction for attempted murder, rape or armed robbery; a minimum of seven years' imprisonment for a third conviction for a Class A drug-trafficking offence and a minimum of three years' imprisonment for a third conviction for domestic burglary.
- There is also a sense of a 'normal' sentence for each offence. This is known as a 'tariff'. If, for example, the maximum sentence for a particular offence is six months' imprisonment, the tariff might be a fine or two months' imprisonment. The magistrates or judge would consider whether there were factors about the offence or the offender that should influence them either to sentence below the tariff level or above it. Information about the offence and the offender comes from a range of sources.

Plea in mitigation

There will be a plea in mitigation by the offender's solicitor or barrister. This is a speech made after the defendant has pleaded guilty, or has been found guilty, and consists of an attempt to explain why the offence was committed and why the court should look favourably upon the defendant. Nothing in the plea in mitigation has to be proved and there is no right of reply for victims.

Antecedents

This is information provided to the court by the Crown Prosecution Service. It includes the offender's criminal record, but also anything to their credit and general background information about domestic circumstances.

Pre-sentence report

The pre-sentence report is prepared by a probation officer. It is always good practice to have one but it is obligatory before a person can be sentenced to imprisonment or a community sentence. It consists of an assessment of the offender's family and social background, employment and the circumstances of the offence.

Victim impact statement

This is provided by the victim, explaining the effect that the offence had on him or her. The judge or magistrates have no obligation to take it into account. There may also, if it is appropriate, be medical reports and character witnesses.

Practical task

Local papers regularly report on sentences passed in local magistrates' courts and Crown Courts. Make a note over a period of four weeks the mains facts of offences and the sentences given.

For each case, try to decide, from the material outlined above, what factors the court might have taken into account when sentencing and what policy the court appeared to be following.

Sentencing options

The sanctions available to a judge are varied. When a person stands before the court having been convicted of an offence, the judge has to bear in mind the aims of sentencing, and then endeavour to impose a sanction which best achieves the desired aims.

Imprisonment

The ultimate sanction in English law is a sentence of imprisonment. There is a tendency for people in general to assume that imprisonment ought to be used and that almost anyone who is convicted and is not sentenced to imprisonment has in some way been 'let off'.

The reality of imprisonment is difficult to imagine but it is a good start to look around the room at college or in school, and imagine that instead of going home at the end of the afternoon you will move to a different part of the building to eat. You will be in the company of the people you see around you now, whether you would choose their company or not. Soon, well before the time you would normally go to bed, you will be locked into a small room, quite possibly with one or two other people even though the room was designed as a single cell. You have no choice as to who those people are, what you will eat, what you will wear. You cannot choose to take a shower, watch television, use the telephone or go to the bathroom.

All these things may be available, but you do not have a right to them and availability will, in practice, depend on staffing levels within the prison. You will have little privacy and little to do. This will not be just for today, but every day for weeks, months and years.

Imprisonment often means the loss of a job, a home and sometimes family or friends. It is very difficult indeed for a person who has been in prison to find a job on release. The whole fabric that keeps a person within society and out of trouble will either have disappeared or have been placed under considerable strain.

Oscar Wilde, who was imprisoned for homosexual acts that are today legal, wrote in *The Ballad of Reading Gaol*:

> ... every prison that men build
> Is built with bricks of shame,
> And bound with bars lest Christ should see
> How men their brothers maim.

Section 1(2) of the Powers of Criminal Courts (Sentencing) Act 2000 provides that imprisonment is to be used only if:

(a) the offence(s) is/are so serious that only such a sentence can be justified; or

(b) for violent or sexual offences, only imprisonment will protect the public from serious harm from this offender.

The court has to give a reason for imposing a custodial sentence. Prisons remain overcrowded and over-used, however. The Chief Inspector of Prisons told a Home Affairs Committee that produced the report *Alternatives to Prison Sentences* in September 1998 that about 70 per cent of women prisoners and 30–40 per cent of young offenders did not need to be in prison.

In March 2003 there are nearly 73,000 people in custody in England and Wales, representing a significant increase on the previous year. Some of them were on remand, that is, they had been convicted and were awaiting sentence or they had not yet been tried but had been denied bail – so they might not be guilty of any offence. Over 11,000 of that total were young offenders, who are almost always held in separate institutions, rather than in adult prisons.

Figure 16.2

To look after, and maintain security of, about 73,000 prisoners there are over 45,000 members of staff (obviously needed for 24 hours a day duty, and therefore employed on a shift basis). This and the cost of buildings, maintenance and administration, means that prison is a costly exercise. It costs approximately as much to keep one person in prison for a night as it does for a person to stay at the Ritz hotel.

Practical task

Keep up-to-date with the current statistics on the prison population on the Internet at this website:

http://www.hmprisons.gov.uk

It was expected that the effect of the Power of Criminal Courts (Sentencing) Act 2000 would have been to reduce the number of people in prison. In fact, in 1987 the total number of people in custody was 48,963 of whom 8,676 were young offenders, so recent years have seen a large increase in prisoners.

A person serving less than 12 months' imprisonment is released unconditionally after half the sentence has been served. In addition, prisoners may be released earlier provided they agree to wear an electronic tag and be bound by a curfew.

Practical task

The statistics for the number of people in custody come from the *Annual Abstract of Statistics*, published each year by the Office for National Statistics. The following figures, from the Office for National Statistics, relate to the length of sentence being served by adults.

Length of sentence	1987	1997
up to 18 months	9,074	9,724
18 months to 4 years	10,283	10,777
over 4 years, including life	8,963	19,950

1 What conclusions can you draw from these figures about trends in sentencing practice?
2 Read more about criminal statistics at the following website:

http://www.homeoffice.gov.uk/rds/prisons1.html

and make further observations about sentencing practice based on the figures you find.

Consecutive and concurrent sentences

If a person is sentenced to prison for several offences, the sentences are normally served at the same time – concurrently. This means that a person who was given four sentences each of five years may only serve five years in total. In certain circumstances the judge will impose consecutive sentences, especially if there is felt to be a need to exceed the maximum sentence allowed.

This happened in March 2001 when a driver killed six people, three in his own vehicle and three in another vehicle, having consumed 13 pints of lager. The driver was sentenced to five years concurrently for each of the

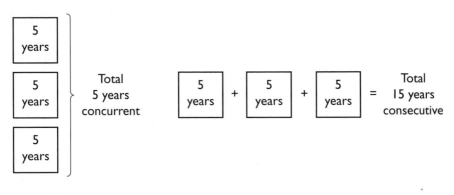

Figure 16.3

three in his vehicle, and ten years concurrently for each of the three in the other vehicle – but the ten years were to be serve consecutively from the five, going beyond the maximum allowed in normal circumstances.

Automatic life sentences (other than for murder)

The Crime (Sentences) Act 1997 provides that where a person has committed two serious offences a life sentence should be automatic. It also provides, however, that a court can impose a sentence less than life where the circumstances are exceptional so that an offender does not present a significant risk to the public. In the case of *R v Offen* (2000) the court said it would do so where there was a long gap between the two offences in which no other offences were committed. It would also consider the effect of two very different offences, or the age of the offender. Apart from being reasonable in itself, this policy would accord with the Human Rights Act 1998 in imposing reasonable sentences.

Community-based sentences

Community sentences are designed to punish by deprivation of liberty without resorting to imprisonment. They may be imposed only if the offence carries the possibility of imprisonment. The court may make one or more of the following orders.

Community rehabilitation order (formerly a probation order)
The court may place the defendant on probation for a period of between six months and three years, and may impose additional requirements, for example, where the defendant must live. The defendant keeps in touch with a probation officer who helps the defendant to cope with housing, job and family problems. If the defendant breaks a condition of the order the court may sentence the defendant again in respect of the original offence.

The present Home Secretary has expressed concern that probation officers are seen as too tolerant and has proposed changes that will reduce the perception that probation is a 'soft option'. There is some tension between two opposing views of the purpose of probation. On the one hand probation is a way to try to change the offender and help him or her to cope with life. On the other it is a form of punishment. The new name for this shows that at present it is seen, at least in part, as rehabilitative.

Community punishment order (formerly a community service order)
A defendant who has committed an offence punishable with imprisonment may be ordered to do between 40 and 240 hours of work over a period of 12 months. The work is on projects of value to the community. If an offender has a job, the community punishment order operates at weekends or other times that do not conflict with the offender's employment.

The community punishment order deprives an offender of liberty, so is retributive (as its new name indicates), but also involves elements of making reparation to society and, perhaps, of rehabilitating the offender.

Community punishment and rehabilitation order (formerly a combination order)

Under the Criminal Justice and Courts Service Act 2000 the court may combine the above two orders, so that a person has to both report to the probation office (hopefully to give advice and support to reform and rehabilitate), and also to do community service, which serves a retributive purpose.

Two new orders have been introduced:

- an *exclusion order*, which prohibits the offender from certain places;
- a *drug abstinence order*, which prohibits the offender from taking specified Class A drugs.

Fines

A fine is a sum of money payable to the Crown. This should not be confused with a compensation order, which is for a sum of money to be paid by the defendant to the victim. Fines are very common for motoring offences and for comparatively minor offences such as failure to buy a television licence. Fines might be regarded as retributive (a form of punishment) and also, perhaps, as in some way a kind of reparation in as much as the offence is against society as a whole and the fine goes into society's coffers.

There are problems in deciding the appropriate level of fines. Clearly, it is not enough to have a tariff that relates only to the offence committed (the more serious the offence, the bigger the fine). This would mean that rich people would be punished comparatively little and poor people would be faced with fines they were quite unable to pay.

An attempt was made to address the problem in 1991 by the introduction of a unit fine system. Judges and magistrates carrying out sentencing had to apply a formula based on:

- the severity of the offence; and
- the means of the offender.

The system was based on a system of multiplication, and received bad press because of anomalies which arose, mainly when people had not filled in forms before the trial and were given sentences of maximum fines for trivial offences. The arrangements were fiercely criticised and were abolished by the Criminal Justice Act 1993, although the principles of considering severity and means are seen as sound.

The statute that creates the offence will lay down the maximum fine. Magistrates' courts can fine up to a maximum of £5,000. The Magistrates' Association issues guidance to magistrates on the level of fine appropriate for particular offences and they then take into account any circumstances relating to the offence, the offender, or both, which would lead them to impose a larger or smaller amount than the tariff.

Other orders

Courts may make a range of other orders, either instead of a sentence or in addition to one. For example, an absolute discharge or a conditional discharge may be granted. The defendant is not sentenced immediately, but if the discharge is conditional, sentence will be given in respect of the original offence if another offence is committed within a specified period.

The Crime and Disorder Act 1998 provides that a court may make an anti-social behaviour order (ASBO) in respect of any person aged over ten who has acted in an anti-social manner, that is to say, a manner that caused or was likely to cause harassment, alarm or distress to one or more persons not of the same household as the offender. The order must be necessary to protect people in the area from further anti-social acts. Anti-social behaviour orders are civil orders, but if a person is in breach of an ASBO there are criminal penalties. This type of hybrid order is very unusual and there has been some disquiet expressed about how these powers may be used.

Reconviction rates

The success, or otherwise, of sentencing may be measured to some extent by looking at reconviction rates. That is, how many offenders have been convicted again within two years of being sentenced for their original offence. Over 75 per cent of young male offenders in recent years have reoffended within two years of release.

Practical task

Statistics are compiled by the Home Office and can be found in Criminal Statistics in England and Wales kept in the reference section of public libraries and on the Home Office website at:

www.homeoffice.gov.uk

- Using the Home Office statistics, consider whether there is any marked difference in reconviction rates between those sentenced to imprisonment and those sentenced to a community sentence.

- Then try to find out the cost of keeping a person in prison, compared with the cost of organising community sentences.

- Armed with this information, and bearing in mind the cost of prison, write a brief report addressed to judges in Crown Courts, advising them on economical and effective sentencing.

Young offenders

'Young offender' can mean any offender under 21 years old, although some provisions apply to those under 18 years old, some to those under 17 and some to under-16s. Offenders under 18 are dealt with by youth courts, staffed by magistrates. An exception to this is that, at present, a young offender charged with murder is tried in an adult court, as is a young offender who has been charged with committing a serious offence with adults.

The European Court of Human Rights found that the trial of Venables and Thompson in an adult court for the murder of James Bulger had not, in some respects, been fair, and it is likely, therefore, that this practice will be changed.

As is the case with adults, the policy behind sentencing young offenders changes over time. There is agreement that there is more chance of changing the behaviour of young people, but disagreement as to whether this is best done by deterrence or by reform and re-education.

Section 37 of the Crime and Disorder Act 1998 says that 'it shall be the principal aim of the youth justice system to prevent offending by children and young persons'. Section 41 of the same Act provides for a Youth Justice Board to monitor the operation of the youth justice system, advise the Home Secretary and identify and promote good practice. Every local authority must establish a youth offending team for each area to coordinate provision of youth justice services and to report annually to the Youth Justice Board.

Young offenders are not sent to adult prisons. They go to young offender institutions. The Crime and Disorder Act 1998 introduced detention and training orders, replacing secure training orders from April 2000.

Young offenders may be made the subject of community sentences, although community rehabilitation orders for young offenders are called 'supervision orders'. The Crime and Disorder Act 1998 also provides for Action Plan orders. The offender is placed under supervision and, for a period of three months, may be required, for example, to report to an attendance centre, stay away from certain places or go to school. Clearly, this is an attempt to push young offenders towards sorting out their lives and addressing the behaviour that get them into trouble.

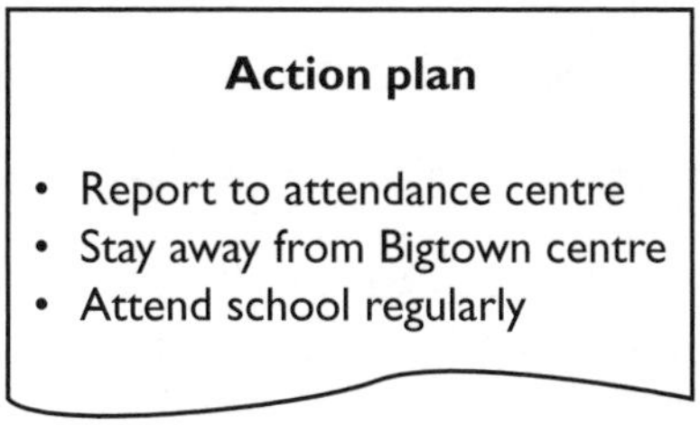

> **Action plan**
>
> - Report to attendance centre
> - Stay away from Bigtown centre
> - Attend school regularly

Figure 16.4

The Crime and Disorder Act 1998 also introduced reparation orders, which require the young offender to compensate the victim or society at large in some way. The order may be for up to 24 hours' work, to be completed within three months.

Young offenders may be fined and parents of under-16s are responsible for payment of fines. The Act also gives courts the power to make parenting orders, which require parents to attend counselling or guidance sessions and to comply with conditions such as escorting a child to school.

A young person who admits an offence may be given a reprimand by the police, provided that they have no criminal convictions. This means they will not be charged with an offence, but the reprimand is recorded. Rather more serious matters may receive a warning. A young offender who is warned is referred to the youth offending team, who may arrange a rehabilitation scheme.

The 1998 Act gave local authorities the power to make local curfew orders in respect of children under ten, covering a specific area for up to 90 days between 9.00 p.m. and 6.00 a.m.

Thinking point

Consider whether each of the measures discussed above for young offenders is retributive or utilitarian in aim, or a mixture of both.

The age of criminal responsibility is ten, so a child under ten cannot be dealt with by the Youth Court, but the Crime and Disorder Act 1998 gives the family court power to make a child safety order in respect of a child under ten who has committed an act that would have been a criminal offence if he or she had been over ten, or broken a curfew order, or committed the sort of behaviour that could have led to an ASBO if he or she was over ten. The child is placed under the supervision of a social worker or a member of the Youth Offending Team and may be required to attend school, avoid certain places and/or people and be at home during certain hours. The order is for a period of three months, but may be extended for up to twelve months.

Thinking point

What evidence can you find among the provisions of the Crime and Disorder Act 1998 that its aim is to prevent offending among young people? What do you think causes young people to offend? Do you think the provisions will help to reduce offending?

Remedies

The civil law offers a range of remedies, including:

- *damages* – payment of money as compensation;
- *injunction* – an order, usually to stop doing something;
- *specific performance* – an order to perform a task agreed in a contract.

Damages

Following a successful claim in the tort of negligence, the remedy the claimant wants is damages, that is, a payment of money. The purpose of damages is to compensate claimants by putting them in the position in which they would have been if the wrong had not been committed. This is known as the reliance basis of assessment.

Damages for a person who has been injured will consist of general damages and special damages.

General damages

General damages are paid for pain and suffering and loss of amenity (things the person can no longer do). Both these sums are difficult to quantify and judges have up to date information, supplied by the Judicial Studies Board, about the amounts awarded to claimants suffering similar losses to ensure that there is consistency in the awards made by different courts.

This information is also available to practitioners, so they can advise clients about the amounts likely to be awarded. This should help claimants and defendants to agree a settlement in cases where there is no dispute as to liability.

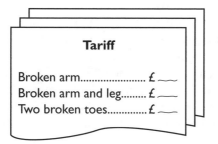

Tariff

Broken arm........................ £ ～～
Broken arm and leg.......... £ ～～
Two broken toes.............. £ ～～

Figure 16.5

Special damages

Loss of earnings up to the time of trial, damage to property and medical expenses are much easier to quantify. Specific sums of money have been lost or spent and evidence, in the form of wage slips and receipts, can be produced to prove this. These are known as special damages. The claimant lists these amounts when making a claim and brings the list up-to-date later in the action.

If an injury will prevent a person working after the trial, an award is made for future loss of earnings. This is calculated by taking a figure for net annual earnings and multiplying it by a number, known as the multiplier, which represents the number of working years a person has left, minus a factor to deal with unknown future happenings – such as redundancy, illness or death from a cause unconnected with the defendant's negligence. It is assumed that the claimant will invest the damages to produce income. This means that the multiplier will generally be no larger than 17 or 18.

Claimants have often claimed social security benefits because they have been off work after an accident. Solicitors have to deduct any benefits received from the damages awarded (except those relating to pain and suffering) and repay that amount to the Department of Social Security. Generally, this would mean that a person who was awarded damages for loss of earnings covering a period for which they had claimed unemployment benefit, for example the amount of unemployment benefit they had received would be deducted from their damages.

Damages are usually paid in a lump sum. This means the claimant may receive a substantial sum of money as a one-off payment. This can cause problems if the claimant decides to spend the money and not make provision for the future. There are alternatives. If both the claimant and the defendant agree, damages may be paid by periodical payments. This addresses the problem of expecting a claimant to manage one large sum.

Sometimes it may be unclear at the time of trial how serious the claimant's injuries are. In this situation the Supreme Court Act 1981, as amended, allows the claimant to claim provisional damages and come back to court later if there is a deterioration. Similarly, if the defendant is an insurance company (as is usually the case) or a public authority, the court may order an interim payment if the defendant is clearly liable and the only argument is about how much should be payable as damages. This avoids subjecting the claimant to a long delay in receiving any money while the details are argued out. It is important because, especially for a seriously injured person, money is often needed immediately after an accident to provide suitable accommodation and other large capital items.

	week 1	week 2	week 3	week 4
or	£	£	£	£

Damages can be a lump sum *or* regular payment

Figure 16.6

Death

As the purpose of damages is to compensate the claimant, one might take the view that a dead victim is beyond earthly compensation and so no damages are payable. Nevertheless, it is possible to claim damages in respect of a death. A dependant may sue under the Fatal Accidents Act 1976. Such a claim is available to spouses, heterosexual co-habitants, children and other relatives of the victim. The claimant has to prove that they were financially dependent on the deceased victim. If a person dies after an accident but not immediately, their estate can make a claim under the Law Reform (Miscellaneous Provisions) Act 1934 for loss of earnings up to the time of death, pain and suffering, loss of amenity and funeral expenses.

The Administration of Justice Act 1982 allows close relations to claim a fixed sum for bereavement. If a person died immediately and had no financial dependants this will be the only claim in respect of their death. The instantaneous death of a child in a road accident, for example, would give rise to a claim under the 1982 Act but no other claim would be possible.

Damages for breach of contract

Damages may be recoverable for a breach of contract. Here, it would not necessarily compensate properly by making payment on the reliance basis, as loss of profits may have been sustained as a result of the breach. The court therefore aims to put the claimant in the position in which they would have been had the contract been properly performed. This is known as the loss of bargain, or expectation, basis of assessment.

Exemplary damages

There are circumstances in which damages over and above an amount required to compensate the victim will be ordered. Exemplary damages may be ordered if the defendant committed a tort willfully, that is, knowing that they were doing so and deciding to carry on, or if a bank wrongly dishonours a cheque. Such an order is very rare because the primary aim is compensation, not punishment.

Nominal damages

Occasionally there are circumstances in which a court will order a very small sum to be paid. In a defamation action it is possible that a claimant may win but that the court may disapprove of their having brought an action. In such a case, the court can order contemptuous damages as low as 1 penny.

Sometimes a claimant will bring an action in order to prevent a defendant's tortious conduct, even though there has been no financial loss to the claimant. This could happen in an action in trespass or in nuisance. Here the court may order nominal damages to acknowledge the claimant's rights.

Other remedies

The civil law provides other remedies that are suited to specific circumstances.

Injunctions

An injunction is a court order to the defendant. It is often a case of the court wanting to control action rather than prevent it altogether. For instance, if a factory began to send unpleasant fumes into the surrounding area, the neighbours would not want compensation in the form of money – they would not want to suffer from the fumes.

The court could issue an injunction ordering the factory to cease production as this would stop the fumes altogether. Recognising the need for goods to be produced, however, the court may accept evidence of modified methods of production and order the factory to put some system into place by a certain date under which the fumes would not be emitted.

- A prohibitory injunction orders the defendant not to do something.
- A mandatory injunction is an order to do something.

A defendant who does not comply with an injunction is in contempt of court and might be sent to prison. A claimant may apply to the court for an interlocutory injunction, to stop the defendant doing something before the case is heard in court. If, for example, a person is planning to build on land over which a neighbour claims to have ownership, the neighbour might apply for an interlocutory injunction to prevent the building work beginning until the court has decided who owns the land.

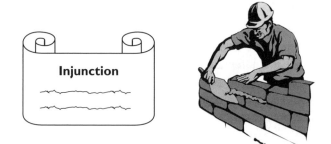

An interlocutory injunction could be used to stop a person building on a neighbour's land, until the problem is heard by the court in a full hearing

Figure 16.7

Specific performance

Occasionally it is possible to obtain an order of specific performance, requiring the other party to a contract to do what they have promised to do under the contract, for example, to move out of a house which someone else has bought.

Summary

Remember	<ul><li>Criminal law – to punish the offender and prevent a repeat of the crime.</li><li>Civil law – to compensate the victim for harm suffered.</li></ul>

Sanctions

Sentencing aims	<ul><li>Retribution (punishment), denunciation (disapproval), reform and rehabilitation (to 'normal' life), deterrence (preventing further offending), protection of society (from danger). Overall aim – to bring about justice.</li></ul>
Sentencing practice	<ul><li>Guidelines include: statutory maximum sentences, Powers of Criminal Courts (Sentencing) Act 2000, Crime and Disorder Act 1998, Crime (Sentences) Act 1997, tariffs.</li><li>Plea in mitigation, antecedents and pre-sentence report and victim impact statements may raise issues.</li></ul>
Sanctions	<ul><li>Custody (prison or youth custody) may be concurrent or consecutive; community rehabilitation order (formerly a probation order); community punishment order (formerly a community service order); community punishment and rehabilitation order (formerly a combination order); fine; electronic tagging (curfew); discharge.</li></ul>
Young offender	<ul><li>Under-21s, but under-18s to be dealt with in a youth court. If murder, tried in an adult court at present. Age of criminal responsibility is 10.</li></ul>

Remedies

Principles	<ul><li>Compensation (often in money) to cover harm suffered.</li><li>Tort based – to restore victim to original position as if the harm had not arisen.</li><li>Damages for breach of contract – puts victim in position as if contract had been performed.</li></ul>

Damages	• General – for pain and suffering and loss of amenity – tariff for injuries.
	• Special – for loss of earnings, damage to property, medical expenses, etc.
	• Exemplary – to show disapproval.
	• Nominal – after winning, when a court does not approve of the action.
Other remedies	• Injunction – a court order over some action. May be to control action rather than to stop it altogether. Can be prohibitory or mandatory.
	• Specific performance – to enforce an action, such as a duty owed under a contract.

Tasks

1 Write a brief explanation of each of the following words and phrases. Use this chapter and the glossary to check your answers.

deterrence	antecedents
retribution	community sentence
denunciation	general damages
sanction	multiplier
custody	interim payment
tariff	injunction
mitigation	specific performance

2 Tom has been convicted of theft.

(a) Explain the aims of sentencing which a judge must bear in mind when sentencing Tom.

(b) Consider the sanctions which would may be imposed on Tom.

3 (a) Consider what alternatives a judge has to sending a person convicted of an offence to prison.

(b) Why should the judge wish to do this?

4 Explain why the traditional lump sum method of paying damages may not always be suitable and consider the advantages and disadvantages of periodical payments.

Part 5

Key skills and practice in examination questions

This part of the book aims to give practical advice and help in preparing for examinations and key skills assessments. It is also important to remember that you will need to develop the skills which you use to study law at AS-level if you plan to continue to the full A-level in law.

Contextual skills

Law is not a subject which can be studied satisfactorily in isolation. It changes constantly, if rather slowly at times, in response to society. This makes the study of law interesting and exciting, and it is important, therefore, that throughout your study of law you begin to think about the wider issues raised. You will obviously obtain marks in examinations for repeating the facts that you have learned, but you can make that material go further, and therefore receive more marks, if you can analyse the law that you know and comment on whether it is satisfactory.

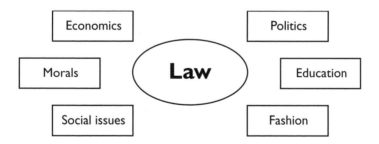

Figure P5.1

Law and morals

Fairness, or justice, is an important principle in forming laws, and is hopefully reflected in statutes (as Parliament lays down rules for an ordered society) and in case law (as judges form precedents for others to follow).

As you learn about different areas of law you will be able to distinguish between using law as a set of rules for convenience and using it to uphold morals. A good distinction is to compare the following issues, both of which may result in a case at the magistrates' court:

- a person not buying a television licence, but nevertheless using a television; and
- a person stealing from an elderly lady.

There is a lot of overlap between legal and moral issues, for example in imposing fines on poor people found guilty of stealing, or in deciding whether a doctor should be allowed to switch off a life support machine.

The law generally develops to reflect changes in society and in current thought. Many examples can be found from your study of the English legal system, for example, in the case of *British Railways Board v Herrington* (1972) the House of Lords used their new Practice Statement powers to overturn previous law and encourage large organisations, like British Rail, to ensure that the environment was a safe place for everyone, including children.

Policy issues

We can often see the principles of a particular government emerging through the law, particularly in the creation of statutes. Principles are unlikely to be extreme at present, since the political tendency of the elected House of Commons is generally subject to the support of the non-elected, and more traditional, House of Lords. Statutes laying down the law over issues such as sentencing and police powers often reflect current political policy, however.

17   Key skills

Be reassured – key skills are nothing new. They are really ongoing skills that you will have largely acquired in your journey through education. Just as it is expected that you can write an essay in order to pass AS-level law, it is also expected that you can read, summarise, form an argument, present your work in a reasonable way, etc.

There is now, however, a greater need to *show* that you have achieved a reasonable level of proficiency in these skills. To a prospective employer, or a university admissions tutor, they are an integral and essential part of your attainment. This is an encouragement to think positively and enthusiastically about key skills, because if you are studying A-level subjects, you should find it a reasonably straightforward task to assemble the evidence needed, provided that you are organised.

The government and examination boards have set out guidelines on what is expected and how this can be achieved. Activities are suggested below, which can be included in your portfolio of key skills, and which can, as a routine part of your study, help you to provide evidence that you are working at an appropriate level in the particular areas of skill.

Figure 17.1

Key skills to be assessed

The main key skills at level 3 are:	*The 'wider' key skills at level 3 are:*

- C3 Communication
- N3 Application of number

- IT3 Information technology

- WO3 Working with others
- LP3 Improving own learning and performance

- PS3 Problem solving

 To achieve a qualification in key skills, both internal and external assessment is involved. You will have to compile a portfolio of tasks undertaken across your studies, showing evidence that you are competent in each area of skill. This need not be a particularly difficult task, or much more than you would do in the normal course of studying at A-level. The ideas here will provide opportunities for you to demonstrate that you have the skills within the various categories, which you can use to compile your portfolio. It is difficult in an essay-based subject to show evidence of the skill of application of number, but there are many opportunities of using the other skills in achieving your goal of success in A-level law. The following are suggestions, pointing you to an area of study covered in most cases by this book where you can find material to help you.

Communication

C3.1a: contribute to a group discussion about a complex subject

- It is said that Parliament can create any law. How are its powers limited by membership of the European Union? (Chapter 1)
- Does our national Parliament reflect the views of the people it serves? (Chapter 2)
- How can Parliament be persuaded to change the law? (Chapter 4)
- Is it really the judges, rather than Parliament, who decide how statutes should apply? (Chapter 5)
- How can a judge avoid an 'awkward' precedent? Should they do so? (Chapter 6)
- Which cases succeed in reaching the House of Lords? Why is this? (Chapter 10 – and you may wish to refer back to Chapter 6)
- Why are alternatives to court increasingly necessary? (Chapters 8 and 11)
- Does the system of training of lawyers provide the legal services needed by a modern society? (Chapter 10)
- 'Wanted – two new judges for the Court of Appeal.' Will this advertisement become a reality?

You will need to consider the following:

– Should judges' positions be advertised?

– Who should be able to apply?

– By whom should judges be appointed? (Chapter 12)

- 'Joe public likes the jury.' Is this true? (Chapter 13)
- 'Lay magistrates are here to stay because they are cost effective.' Do you agree? (Chapter 13)
- Do the police have the powers which are needed to catch criminals? (Chapter 9)

C3.1b: make a presentation about a complex subject, using at least one image to illustrate complex points

- Explain an area of law, ready for use on an overhead projector, using a diagram – some of the diagrams in this book are a good starting point for gathering ideas, such as the formation of a statute (Chapter 2), the structure of the courts (Chapter 7), the criminal process (Chapter 7). All of these lend themselves to a flowchart-type of illustration (see diagrams in the chapters).
- Find a picture of a magistrates' court or Crown Court, or draw a diagrammatic one, labelling the people involved in the court process (judge or magistrates, clerk, solicitors, barristers, jury (if appropriate), defendant, usher, press, public).
- Explain the training route to becoming a solicitor or barrister, using a diagram to help illustrate it (Chapter 10).
- Choose some cases from either criminal law or the law of tort (Chapters 14 and 15) and make either a set of posters for the wall or a set of overhead projector sheets, containing a very brief summary of the case details and a picture to illustrate each one. You may like to refer to the cases in Chapter 6 for some ideas. These will help you to remember the cases.

C3.2: read and synthesise information from two extended documents that deal with a complex subject. One of these documents should include at least one image

- Finding an extended document to read should not be a problem. Look in the quality press and in law journals, and choose an article on law or a case report. Summarise your findings to use in essays.
- There are articles in the *Times Law Supplements* and other leading newspapers. Other possibilities include articles in the *New Law Journal* or on the Internet. Many articles will be illustrated with pictures, and

those on criminal statistics may include graphs or charts. Choose two different articles on a theme, make notes on what you find and write a report on the topic.

• The local press will report on cases arising in the area, and often contain an illustration. These reports may continue over several days for cases heard in the Crown Court. Make a note of the facts, any legal points arising and the sentences given.

C3.3: write two different types of documents about complex subjects. One piece of writing should be an extended document and include at least one image

• Create a mini-project on a subject of interest to you, for example, the training of solicitors or barristers (Chapter 10), the role of lay people in the legal system (Chapter 13). Find out further information about these topics from other sources, for example, from the Law Society or the General Council of the Bar (Education and Training) for the legal profession, or the clerk to the local courts for lay people. Obtain more information from the Internet. Include images from material you have obtained in your work.

• Create a revision file on the non-fatal offences against the person (Chapter 14) or the duty of care in tort (Chapter 15). You could include an account of some leading cases and illustrate some of them using diagrams.

• Draft advice to a client based on a scenario from a part of the syllabus. The following are suggestions.

  1 Ben is playing football in his garden with his son, Craig. The football smashes a pane of glass in Ali's greenhouse (the football often goes over the hedge into Ali's garden, but this is the first time that any damage has occurred). Advise Ali.

  2 Jill punches Ken during an argument and her ring causes a small cut to his cheek. Advise Jill as to any offences with which she may be charged.

Information technology

IT3.1: compare and use different sources to search for, and select, information required for two different purposes

• There is a selection of Internet website addresses in the resources list of this book. Using these and others, you can read the case reports from the House of Lords, find statutes which have been passed recently, read about miscarriages of justice, find out in more detail the results of enquiries into the legal system, such as the Woolf report or the Auld review, learn more about the training of barristers, solicitors and legal executives, and find a list of senior members of the judiciary.

- Use a CD-Rom to research a topic of law, for example, *The Times* reports on CD-Rom or Lawtex (see Legal Resources list on page 171).

IT3.2: explore, develop and exchange information and derive new information to meet two different purposes

- Create a database of cases in criminal law or the law of tort, using one field to contain a key word to identify the main topic of the case. You could work as a team on this, so that a larger number of cases can be entered. This could be used for:
  - fellow students to access a set of cases on a topic by performing a query;
  - the production of a Law magazine (again, working as a team);
  - emailing a list of cases on a particular topic in response to requests by other law students.

IT3.3: present information from different sources for two different purposes and audiences. Your work must include at least one example of text, one example of images and one example of numbers

- Create a report for members of staff, describing how your compiled the database described in *IT3.2* (above). Illustrate how the system works, and how it is possible to incorporate some of the results into a magazine. Show on a spreadsheet a record of cases requested by other students, and construct a chart to show how many times they were requested.
- Create a presentation to explain the criminal court structure to non-lawyers. Explain the difference between summary and indictable offences, and list the courts in which they are tried. Use a pie chart to show the proportion of offences tried summarily and on indictment.

Working with others

The evidence for this area of skill needs to be presented in at least two substantial activities that each include tasks for *WO3.1*, *WO3.2* and *WO3.3*. You need to show that you can work in a group and in one-to-one situations. The aspects of activity for which you need to provide evidence are:

- *WO3.1*: plan a group activity, agreeing objectives, responsibilities and working arrangements.
- *WO3.2*: work towards achieving the agreed objectives seeking to establish and maintain cooperative working relationships in meeting individual responsibilities.

- *WO3.3*: review the activity with others against the agreed objectives and agree ways of enhancing collaborative work.

Suggested activities

The organisation of a debate based on one of the issues suggested in *C3.1a.* The stages could be:

- Meet as a group and organise the breakdown of tasks, for example, there will need to be agreement on pairs or small groups researching different legal aspects of the problem, including obtaining articles and perhaps case details and references, and preparing speeches for presentation. Appoint a leader to coordinate the exchange of information and to coordinate communication. Establish a communication route – use email if practical. Agree on deadlines, and on the method of recording the information.

- Carry out the research in agreed groups. Cooperate with members of the group in sharing information and the burden of recording, so that deadlines are met. Monitor problems with working relationships, to ensure that goals are achieved. Review progress and goals, changing plans by agreement if necessary.

- Hold the debate, inviting others to attend. You could ask a teacher or a fellow student to preside.

- Arrange a post-debate discussion group to give feedback. Encourage this to include positive criticism, with suggestions for improvement. Make a written record of your ideas.

Make a presentation on a given topic of general interest from the syllabus, for example, sentencing. This could be for presentation to the year group.

- Meet as a group and organise the distribution of tasks, for example, there will need to be agreement on pairs or small groups researching different legal aspects of the problem, including obtaining articles and preparing material for presentation, for example, text of an oral presentation, OHP text, OHP illustrations (alternatively prepare text and illustrations for a PowerPoint presentation, if facilities for this are available on the computer network). Appoint a leader to coordinate the exchange of information and to coordinate communication. Establish a communication route – use email if practical. Agree on deadlines, and on the method of recording the information.

- Carry out the research in agreed groups. Cooperate with members of the group in sharing information and the burden of recording, so that deadlines are met. Monitor problems with working relationships, to ensure that goals are achieved. Review progress and goals, changing plans by agreement if necessary. Ensure that the style of presentation is consistent.

- Give the presentation, inviting others to attend.

- Arrange a post-presentation discussion group to give feedback. Encourage this group to include positive criticism, with suggestions for improvement. Alternatively this could be done by a questionnaire completed by those attending.

Problem solving

For this skill you need to follow through a complex activity which involves identifying a problem and providing a solution. The key skills syllabus requires you to implement a solution. You will find this much easier to do during the A2 part of the course, as a lot of the questions that you will practice in the modules of criminal law, the law of tort and the law of contract will involve problem solving.

Some scenario problems are given here for practice, but you will find many more as you continue to A2. You will not, however, be able to implement the solution, since the scenarios provided are hypothetical, not real cases to be taken to court. Your evidence here will be limited to *PS3.1* and *PS3.2*.

- *PS3.1*: recognise, explore and describe the problem, and agree the standards for its solution.

- *PS3.2*: generate and compare at least two options which could be used to solve the problem, and justify the option for taking forward.

Suggested activity

Choose one of the following problem questions and research it in some detail. Compile your answer to the problem, and review the work done, considering any possible practical alternative solutions.

- Jen plays basketball for her local team. She falls during a match and bangs her head very hard. She later becomes confused and dizzy, and when Sam approaches to ask how she is, she thinks he is taking the ball away from her and lashes out at him. Sam dodges the blow, and Jen's hand hits Wanda in the face, cutting Wanda's lip.

   Advise Jen of any criminal liability.

- Henry, while walking past a building site, was accidentally hit by a large piece of scaffolding which was being thrown to the ground by Jake, a builder. An ambulance was called and arrived promptly. At hospital, the ambulance driver, Kelly, did not put the step into position properly and Henry tripped and fell while getting out of the ambulance.

   Henry is found to have sustained head and neck injuries, but these have been made much worse by the fall from the ambulance. Henry is so badly hurt that he is obliged to have several weeks off work to recover.

   Advise Henry whether he should claim compensation and from whom.

Improve own learning performance

To provide evidence of improvement you will need:

- two examples of study-based learning;
- two examples of activity-based learning;
- one example of using learning from at least two different contexts to meet the demands of a new situation.

For this assessment it is important to arrange to meet a tutor who will support you in providing the necessary evidence.

A plan could be drawn up to include the following steps:

- *LP3.1*: agree targets and plan how these will be met, using support from appropriate people.
- *LP3.2*: use your plan, seeking and using feedback and support from relevant sources to help meet your targets, and using different ways of learning to meet new demands.
- *LP3.3*: review progress in meeting targets, establishing evidence of achievements, and agree action for improving performance using support from appropriate people.

Suggested activity

You can monitor progress in many ways, but each should include appropriate feedback, recording of achievement and setting of targets:

- through essay writing and solving scenario-type problems as homework assignments;
- through timed essays;
- through case tests;
- through oral and practical contributions to group activities;
- by extended work on an area of interest or one in which problems arise;
- by attending court or student conferences, and writing appropriate notes and reports;
- by aiming to improve hand written presentation or ICT skills.

Remember that the total portfolio of evidence that you compile for assessing key skills can come from any area of your studies – it does not all have to come from the study of law. Your choice to study law as a subject will, however, provide you with fine opportunities in the above categories.

18 Source-based exercises

When statute law or case law has been used in this book so far, parts of the original source may have been quoted, but they have generally been summarised for the purposes of study for students at AS-level. The original statutes and cases are known as primary sources of law, and this or any other book provides the author's summaries of that law and comments on its operation.

Case law

It is useful to begin to read cases in their original form as these will become important as your studies in law progress. Even at the AS-stage, reading cases will provide a much clearer insight into the operation of judicial precedent and the application of the substantive law, such as criminal law, the law of tort and the law of contract.

When you read a case it is important to make notes. This is especially helpful if you are reading a case in its original format from a law report. Official law reports are long, and making notes will help you to understand and to remember what you have read. It will also make the material useful to you in writing essays and preparing for examinations. For those who have questions in examinations based on original sources, the following exercises will also be very good examination practice.

Figure 18.1

Reading a case

The case below is not an original report, but an author's summary of it, including part of a judgment by Lord Denning. As law reports are often long, it is quicker and easier to find out the mains points of a case from a book. It should be remembered, however, that further points and contradictory arguments may have been raised within the judgment which are only apparent on reading the full report.

Read the account which follows and make your own brief notes under these headings:

- Name of the case, date and level at which it is heard.
- Facts.
- Arguments.
- Decision.
- Summary of legal point(s).

Nettleship v Weston (1971) House of Lords
Mrs Weston was being taught to drive by Mr Nettleship, who was a friend of the family. Mr Nettleship had checked that Mrs Weston was insured to drive the car. During her third lesson, Mrs Weston panicked when turning left at a road junction and failed to straighten the car after making the turn. The car hit a lamp post and Mr Nettleship's knee cap was broken. Mrs Weston claimed that she had reached an acceptable standard for a learner driver and had not, therefore, been negligent. The judge at first instance agreed with this argument and found that Mrs Weston was not liable, but the Court of Appeal found for Mr Nettleship.

Lord Denning quoted the words of Lord Macmillan in *Glasgow Corporation v Muir* (1943) referring to the standard of care in negligence: 'It eliminates the personal equation and is independent of the idiosyncrasies of the particular person whose conduct is in question'. Lord Denning himself then said:

> The learner driver may be doing his best, but his incompetent best is not good enough. He must drive in as good a manner as a driver of skill, experience and care, who is sound in mind and limb, who makes no errors of judgment, has good eyesight and hearing and is free from any infirmity.

Lord Denning also commented that the reason for expecting so high a standard of a learner driver is that she was legally obliged to be insured and by holding her to be liable the court could provide compensation for the injured person. Morally the learner driver is not at fault, but legally she is liable to be because she is insured and the risk should fall on her.

The features of a law report

Law Report
Court

Judges hearing the case
Names of the parties
Date

Judgment

Figure 18.2

- *The factual details* – the court in which the case is held, the judges hearing the case, the names of the parties involved and the date. At first instance the parties to a criminal case will be *R v the defendant*, and in a civil case the parties will be *the plaintiff v the defendant*, but remember that on appeal these may be reversed. The parties to an appeal are the *appellant v the respondent*.

- *The facts of the case* form the basis of argument and the eventual judgment, so you clearly need to understand them. It is therefore useful to read the account and, even if the 'story' seems straightforward, to write the main facts out in your own words or in note form.

    As time is very limited indeed in examinations, it is also important to be able to summarise the facts of a case. Most of your marks will come from *using* cases to illustrate a legal point. You are unlikely to be given many marks for lengthy descriptions of facts at the expense of more useful comment.

- *The arguments raised by a case* should then be noted – points leading one way and points leading another. This is exactly what the judge has to do in his mind when making a decision. Cases which go to court at a high level are rarely simple or one-sided. There are usually good arguments both ways.

- *The decision* is then important. Sometimes it is surprisingly hard to find, and involves reading towards the end of several different speeches. In addition, if a case is an appeal case (as it will be if you are reading a report from the House of Lords or the Court of Appeal) then the decision may be along the lines of 'We would therefore allow this appeal' rather than 'We think that Mr ... should win'.

- *Legal points* which may be established by the case are important to you. You will need to make a summary of these and use them in forming essays on the topics studied for examinations. Sometimes a case results in only one legal point, but others may raise several points. Sometimes there is one main point which is part of the *ratio* (the central part of the decision) with other comments made *obiter* (by the way).

An original case report

The following case is one mentioned in Chapter 10 concerning the immunity of lawyers from being sued in connection with the presenting of cases in court. Cases at this level are often very long (this one is over 50 pages), so there is only room here to include extracts from the judgment.

Read the case and make notes under the same headings as you did with the case above:

- Name, level of court and date.
- Facts.
- Arguments.
- Decision.
- Summary of legal point(s).

There are three appeals against three firms of solicitors being heard as conjoined appeals (being heard together), as they all concern the same legal issue of whether the dissatisfied clients could sue the lawyer presenting the case.

HOUSE OF LORDS
Lord Browne-Wilkinson, Lord Steyn, Lord Hoffmann, Lord Hope of Craighead,
Lord Hutton, Hobhouse of Woodborough, Lord Millett

OPINIONS OF THE LORDS OF APPEAL FOR JUDGMENT

IN THE CAUSE

ARTHUR J.S. HALL & CO.
(APPELLANTS)

v

SIMONS (A.P.)
(RESPONDENT)
BARRATT
(RESPONDENT)

v

ANSELL AND OTHERS TRADING AS WOOLF SEDDON (A FIRM)
(APPELLANTS)
HARRIS
(RESPONDENT)

v

SCHOLFIELD ROBERTS AND HILL
(APPELLANTS)

(CONJOINED APPEALS)

ON 20 JULY 2000

LORD STEYN

My Lords,

There are three appeals before the House from orders of the Court of Appeal in a building case and in two cases involving family proceedings. Clients raised claims in negligence against firms of solicitors. In response the solicitors relied on the immunity of advocates from suits in negligence. In all three cases judges at first instance ruled that the claims against the solicitors were unsustainable. The circumstances of these cases and the disposals are set out in the judgment of the Court of Appeal given by Lord Bingham of Cornhill, LCJ: *Arthur J.S. Hall & Co. (a firm) v Simons* [1999] 3 WLR 873. In effect the Court of Appeal ruled in all three cases presently before the House that the claims were wrongly struck out. The solicitors now appeal …

For more than two centuries barristers have enjoyed an immunity from actions in negligence. The reasons for this immunity were various. It included the dignity of the Bar, the 'cab rank' principle, the assumption that barristers may not sue for their fees, the undesirability of relitigating cases decided or settled, and the duty of a barrister to the court …

In a unanimous decision the House in *Rondel v Worsley* [1969] 1 AC 191 upheld the ancient immunity on considerations of 'public policy [which are] not immutable' at p. 227B, *per* Lord Reid. It is worth recalling that in that case the appellant had obtained the services of the respondent to defend him on a dock brief, and alleged that the respondent had been negligent in the conduct of his defence. It is undoubtedly right, as counsel for the solicitors submitted and nobody disputed, that the principal ground of the decision is the overriding duty of a barrister to the court. The House thought that the existence of liability in negligence, and indeed the very possibility of making assertions of liability against a barrister, might tend to undermine the willingness of barristers to carry out their duties to the court. Lord Morris of Borth-y-Gest encapsulated the core idea by saying (at p. 251D): 'It would be a retrograde development if an advocate were under pressure unwarrantably to subordinate his duty to the court to his duty to the client …'.

I would … dismiss the appeals.

LORD BROWNE-WILKINSON

My Lords,

I have had the advantage of reading the speeches of my noble and learned friends Lord Steyn and Lord Hoffmann. I agree with them and for the reasons they give, I would dismiss these appeals …

Let me initially consider the points on which your Lordships are all agreed. First that, given the changes in society and in the law that have taken place since the decision in *Rondel v Worsley* [1969] I AC 191, it is appropriate to review the public policy decision that advocates enjoy immunity from liability for the negligent conduct of a case in court. Second, that the propriety of maintaining such immunity depends upon the balance between, on the one hand, the normal right of an individual to be compensated for a legal wrong done to him and, on the other, the advantages which accrue to the public interest from such immunity. Third, that in relation to claims for immunity for an advocate in civil proceedings, such balance no longer shows sufficient public benefit as to justify the maintenance of the immunity of the advocate ...

For these reasons, and the much fuller reasons given by Lord Steyn and Lord Hoffmann, I would dismiss these appeals.

LORD HOFFMANN
My Lords,

I have no doubt that the advocate's duty to the court is extremely important in the English system of justice. The reasons are eloquently stated by their Lordships in *Rondel v Worsley* [1969] I AC 191 and I do not think that the passage of more than 30 years has diminished their force. The substantial orality of the English system of trial and appellate procedure means that the judges rely heavily upon the advocates appearing before them for a fair presentation of the facts and adequate instruction in the law. They trust the lawyers who appear before them; the lawyers trust each other to behave according to the rules, and that trust is seldom misplaced. The question is whether removing the immunity would have a significant adverse effect upon this state of affairs.

To assess the likelihood, I think that one should start by considering the incentives which advocates presently have to comply with their duty and those which might tempt them to ignore it. The first consideration is that most advocates are honest conscientious people who need no other incentive to comply with the ethics of their profession. Then there is the wish to enjoy a good reputation among one's peers and the judiciary. There can be few professions which operate in so bright a glare of publicity as that of the advocate. Everything is done in public before a discerning audience. Serious lapses seldom pass unnoticed. And in the background lie the disciplinary powers of the judges and the professional bodies ...

Looking at the other side of the coin, what pressures might induce the advocate to disregard his duty to the court in favour of pleasing the client? Perhaps the wish not to cause dissatisfaction which might make the client reluctant to pay. Or the wish to obtain more instructions from the same client. But among these pressures, I would not put high on the list the prospect of an action for negligence. It cannot possibly be negligent to act in accordance with one's duty to the court and it is hard to imagine anyone who would plead such conduct as a cause of action. So when the advocate decides that he ought to tell the judge about some authority which is contrary to his case, I do not think it would for a moment occur to him that he might be sued for negligence ...

In considering whether such a justification still exists, your Lordships cannot ignore the fact that you are yourselves members of the legal profession. Members of other professions, and the public in general, are bound to view with some scepticism the claims of lawyers that the public interest requires them to have a special immunity from liability for negligence. If your Lordships are convinced that there are compelling arguments for such an immunity, you should not of course be deterred from saying so by fear of unfounded accusations of collective self-interest. But those arguments need to be strong enough to convince a fair-minded member of the public ...

I would therefore dismiss the appeals.

Legislation

It is unlikely that during your study at AS-level you will need to read a whole statute in its original form. You will, however, often need to read an individual section of a statutes and comment on it or apply it to factual situations. Refer back to Criminal law (Chapter 14) to see the importance of the wording in the Offences Against the Person Act 1861.

Figure 18.3

Issues concerning the wording of statutes certainly become very important when answering examination questions on statutory interpretation. The extracts of statute law which you need to read may not be very long, but you will need to pay particular attention to the wording and to the way in which it is interpreted.

Source based question paper on sources of law

You may like to re-read Chapter 6 on judicial precedent before tackling the first of these questions, and Chapter 5 on statutory interpretation before tackling the second. The questions are specimen questions taken from the OCR module, Sources of Law, but are equally useful when preparing for examinations of any board which includes the topics of judicial precedent and statutory interpretation.

The following is a complete paper, and you have the choice of answering **either** the whole of question 1 or the whole of question 2. Question 1 concerns judicial precedent and question 2 concerns statutory interpretation (but in a 'real' examination you could equally have one whole question on European Law). It is important to spend some time reading the source, and becoming quite clear on which aspects of the topic the source places emphasis.

Answer one question, either Question 1 or Question 2

1. Read the source material below and answer questions (a) to (c) which follow.

Exercise on Judicial Precedent

SOURCE A

Their Lordships ... recognise that too rigid adherence to precedent may lead to injustice in a particular case and also unduly restrict the proper development of the law. They propose, therefore, to modify their present practice and, while treating former decisions of this House as normally binding, to depart from previous decisions when it appears right to do so.

In this connection they will bear in mind ... the especial need for certainty in the criminal law. This announcement is not intended to affect the use of precedent elsewhere than in this House.

Extract adapted from *The House of Lords Practice Statement 1966*

SOURCE B

Elliott v C (1983)

C, a 14-year-old and somewhat backward girl spent an evening with a friend and, being unable to stay there the night decided to sleep in a shed. Finding some white spirit and matches she poured the spirit on the floor and set light to it, destroying the shed as a result when the fire got out of hand. The girl claimed that she had no idea that such damage would result.

Magistrates acquitted her under s1(1) Criminal Damage Act 1971 of 'recklessly' damaging property because of her age and lack of understanding. The prosecution then made a successful appeal by way of case stated to the Queen's Bench Divisional Court. This court applied the definition of recklessness given by Lord Diplock in the House of Lords in *Caldwell* [1981]. Lord Justice Goff in the Queen's Bench Divisional Court accepted that he was bound to apply the precedent from *Caldwell* to the case, but felt very unhappy about having to do so in the circumstances of the present case which he felt would be unfair on the girl.

In his judgment Lord Justice Goff said:

> In my opinion, although of course the courts of this country are bound by the doctrine of precedent, sensibly interpreted, nevertheless it would be irresponsible for judges to act as automatons [like robots],

rigidly applying authorities without regard to consequences. Where a judge is compelled to reach a conclusion he senses to be unjust or inappropriate, he is under a duty to examine the precedent with scrupulous care to ascertain whether he can, within the limits imposed by the doctrine of precedent legitimately interpret or qualify the principle in the precedent to achieve the result which he sees as just or appropriate in the particular case.

Extract adapted from the judgment in *Elliott v C* [1983]

Answer **ALL** parts

1. (a)Using the Sources and other cases, briefly explain and illustrate the 1966 Practice Statement. **[15]**

    (b)In a 2002 case of criminal damage an eleven year old boy has thrown down a lighted firework in a shop and this has caused a fire destroying the shop. In each of the following situations consider whether the judges in the case should consider themselves bound by the precedents in *Caldwell and Elliott v C*:

    (i)The judge in the Queen's Bench Divisional Court feels that it would be unfair to convict the boy.

    (ii) All three judges in the Court of Appeal feel that it would be unfair to convict the boy.

    (iii) Three out of five House of Lords judges consider that it would be unfair to convict the boy. **[15]**

    (c)In Source B, Lord Justice Goff suggests that judges should not '*act as automatons* [like robots], *rigidly applying authorities without regard to consequences*'. Using the sources and cases explain and comment on the ways in which a judge can avoid rigidly applying precedent. **[30]**

    [Total: 60 marks]

2. Read the source material below and answer parts (a) to (c) which follow.

Exercise on Statutory Interpretation

SOURCE A

A knife was displayed in a shop window with a price ticket attached to it. The shopkeeper was charged with offering for sale a flick-knife contrary to s1(l) of the Restriction of Offensive Weapons Act 1959 which provides:

Any person who manufactures, sells or hires or offers for sale or hire, or lends or to any other person -

(a) any knife which has a blade which opens automatically by hand pressure applied to a button, spring or other device in or attached to the handle of the knife, sometimes known as a 'flick-knife' ... shall be guilty of an offence.

The court had to decide whether the shopkeeper was guilty of `offering the knife for sale' (he had not actually sold any). Applying the literal rule to the facts of the case, the court held that the display of the knife in the shop window was not `offering for sale' – merely an invitation to treat. Hence the shopkeeper was not guilty of the offence.

Fisher v Bell [1960] 1 QB 394

SOURCE B

'Some may say ... that judges should not pay attention to what is said in Parliament. They should grope around in the dark for the meaning of an Act without switching on the light. I do not agree with this view.'

Adapted from the judgment of Lord Denning in *Davis v Johnson* [1979] AC 264

Answer **ALL** parts

3. (a) Source B refers to Lord Denning's dissatisfaction with the ban on the use of the external aid Hansard prior to 1993. Explain what Hansard is and the circumstances in which courts may make a reference to it. **[15]**

    (b) Read Source A lines 4–9. Using your knowledge of statutory interpretation consider whether any of the following '*sells or hires or offers for sale or hire or gives to any other person – any knife which has a blade which opens automatically by hand pressure applied to a button, spring or other device in or attached to the handle of the knife*' and therefore commits an offence under s 1(1) of the Restriction of Offensive Weapons Act 1959:

        (i) Jane, a youth worker, confiscates a flick-knife from a member o her youth club and gives it to her supervisor.

        (ii) Tony, an antique dealer, displays an old military knife with a spring opening device in his shop window with a price ticket attached to it.

        (iii) Fola buys a 'job lot' box of kitchen utensils from a car boot sale. Without examining the contents closely she donates the box to a charity shop. The box is found to contain a flick-knife. **[15]**

    (c) With reference to Source A and other cases consider the problems that can be created by using the literal rule of interpretation and any advantages to be gained by using the modern purposive approach. **[30]**

    [Total: 60 marks]

Hints on answering the questions

With this kind of question paper you need to have two aims:

- **respond to the source**;
- **demonstrate your knowledge** of the topic to the examiner.

It is important **not** to simply re-write the source material, and neither is it very credit-worthy to write all you know about judicial precedent or statutory interpretation, as if this was a straightforward essay. You need to *use* the material you know in order to *answer the questions* asked.

- **Use your time wisely.** You will need some time to read through the paper, but then notice how many marks are awarded for each section, and divide your remaining time in proportion to the marks awarded. In an examination which should last for one hour, for which 60 marks are available, it would seem that you can write at a rate of a mark per minute. However, time will be needed to read this paper – more than with other more 'straightforward' questions – so you cannot afford to spend quite as much time as this on your answer. In a question worth 15 marks, then, you probably have about 12 minutes to write, and with a question worth 30 marks, you may have 25 minutes to write.

- **Now try the questions**.

1 Judicial precedent

a) You are asked to *explain* in this part of the examination, so this is your opportunity to *display your knowledge* of the Practice Statement. *Referring to the sources*, state the key facts about the way in which the House of Lord is bound by the Practice Statement. You should include:

- the nature of the statement – not a case decision, not a statute, but a statement, read out in 1966 by the Lord Chancellor with the unanimous support of the House of Lords.

- the new power of the House of Lords to move away from previous decisions in circumstances where it is 'right to do so'.

- the recognition of the need to bring about justice in accordance with the state of society, but still maintain certainty by restricting this freedom to the House of Lords alone.

- cases to *illustrate* your answer, e.g. *British Rail v Herrington*, overruling *Addie v Dumbreck*; The *Joanna Oldendorf*, overruling *The Aello*.

b) This part of the examination provides an opportunity to *apply* both your own knowledge and the facts that you have been given in the source. Do not repeat the facts, or cases that you have already used in answering the previous question. You will need to identify that there are facts in the scenario that are similar to *Elliott v C*, and then in each situation decide whether the judge is bound. Remember that the whole of this question is only worth 15 marks, so you have to be careful over time.

- The Queen's Bench Divisional Court is bound by the House of Lords, even if it feels the judgment to be unfair on the boy in the case now before it, unless the situation can be distinguished on the facts.

- The Court of Appeal is also bound by the precedent of the House of Lords in *Caldwell* (see Source B), but (assuming that there was no further appeal in *Elliott v C*) it would not be bound by this case. Even though three senior judges are in agreement, they must follow precedent – and if necessary give leave to appeal to the House of Lords.

- The House of Lords, as the highest English court, with the freedom of the Practice Statement, can make a decision not to follow previous law to prevent injustice.

c) In this part of the examination you have the opportunity to show your knowledge of ways in which an awkward precedent could be avoided. You will also earn marks by *using the sources and other cases* – so you need to discuss why a judge may need to avoid following precedent. This part is worth 30 marks, so you can be fuller here than in the two previous parts. You should include the following key points:

Ways to avoid precedent:

- use of the Practice Statement (for the HL)

- overruling within the exceptions of *Young v Bristol Aeroplanes* (for the CA)

- distinguishing a case on its facts (at any level), e.g. *Merritt v Merritt*

- re-defining a ratio of an older case or one where the facts are unusual

- overruling (if a case is heard in a higher court than the original precedent)

- appeal to the ECJ in appropriate circumstances

Issues to discuss:

- the need for both justice and certainty and the difficulty of balancing these needs – certainty may be seen as a form of justice

- the need for the law to develop to meet the expectations of society

- the reluctance of the HL to use the freedom of the Practice Statement

- the limitations on the CA and the arguments for and against giving this court wider powers

- **Look back at your answer** if you have time left, and check that you have

  - answered the questions asked

  - referred to the source

  - demonstrated your knowledge of judicial precedent and relevant cases

  - produced a balanced answer, bearing in mind the marks given for the sections.

2 Statutory Interpretation

a) You are asked to *explain* in this part of the examination, so this is your opportunity to *show factual knowledge* of the use of Hansard as an external aid to interpretation. You are not asked to discuss whether this is a good idea – just to explain what Hansard is and the conditions when it may be used. Points to mention include:

   - a description of Hansard as the official record of debates in Parliament when a Bill is being discussed.
   - the need to sometimes refer back to the reason for passing an Act.
   - the refusal to allow reference to Hansard as an external aid until the case of *Pepper v Hart* – confirmed later in *Three Rivers v Bank of England*.
   - details from *Pepper v Hart* of the circumstances in which Hansard can be used.

b) This part of the examination provides an opportunity to *apply* both your own knowledge and the facts that you have been given in the source. Do not repeat the facts, or cases that you have already used in answering the previous question. You do not have time here (remember – 15 marks for all three situations) to explain the three rules of statutory interpretation in detail – just apply the rules to each situation. You will not know how the court will decide a case – you merely have to say *whether* an offence would have been committed *if* a certain approach was taken.

   - compare the use of the literal rule with the purposive approach. Jane literally 'gives' a knife to another, but using the purposive approach, the intention of the Act was to punish those who own or sell such weapons.
   - applying the literal rule, as in Source A, Tony would not be guilty. Compare the use of the purposive approach and reference to Hansard.
   - consider how the use of the two approaches would affect Fola. She may be guilty using the literal rule, but was the purpose of the Act to find her guilty?

c) This part of the examination is worth 30 marks and is therefore an opportunity to be fuller in showing both knowledge and ability to analyse issues. You need to show understanding of the literal rule and the purposive approach (remember – you did not have time to do that in part b), and then, referring to Source A, discuss the advantages of the modern approach.

Your explanation should:

   - explain the operation of the literal rule – a definition and an example of its use (Source A, *Berriman*, etc).
   - explain that the rule was applied even where it led to an absurdity (*R v Judge of the City of London Court*).

- Very briefly show how the golden rule did not work very effectively, being limited.
- Show how the purposive approach has developed from the mischief rule – correcting the 'wrong' that existed in society, and looking at the intention of the statute.

Issues to discuss:

- The literal rule can produce certainty, and respects the division between legislators and the judiciary.
- The literal rule can lead to absurdity and injustice (*Berriman, Whiteley v Chappell*, etc) – not a good aim of a legal system.
- The purposive approach can be flexible in taking into account developments in society and bringing about justice.
- The purposive approach is likely to bring about the intention of Parliament when it created a statute.
- The European approach is largely purposive – and this is the approach favoured by both academic critics (e.g. Zander) and the Law Commission.

- **Look back at your answer** if you have time left, and check that you have
  - answered the questions asked
  - referred to the source
  - demonstrated your knowledge of judicial precedent and relevant cases
  - produced a balanced answer, bearing in mind the marks given for the sections.

19 Examination advice and practice examination questions

Examiners set questions to find out what candidates know and understand. As with all sections of this book, however, you are advised to check your specification and specimen question papers/units so that you become familiar with the approach adopted by your particular examining board or group. There are broadly three kinds of questions at AS-level:

- essays;
- problems;
- stimulus response questions – questions where you are asked questions based on source material.

Informed opinion

When an examiner asks for an opinion remember that there is no reason at all why your personal opinion on the state of the law should not be valid or important. It should be an informed opinion, however. A personal view, thrown in almost at random without a lot of previous thought will not, by itself, attract many marks. What the examiner wants is a demonstration of your understanding of the issues involved and the different academic and judicial opinions that have been expressed on the subject, and an ability to form an opinion *having taken the views of others into account*. It really does not matter what your conclusion is, as long as it is supported by valid argument, so it is not a good idea to enthuse about a proposition or institution, such as jury trial, and then to conclude that you are against it. In any case, the examiner will want to see that you can consider the views for both sides of an argument.

The use of authority – cases, statutes, etc.

It is really important to back up legal points with authority – that is, cases, statutes or the writings of others. It is obviously important if you are quoting to be accurate. If you cannot remember something totally accurately, use the information without quoting it. For example, in an essay on statutory interpretation, if you could not remember accurately that in the case of *Maunsell v Olins* (1975) Lord Simon said, 'The first task of a court of construction is to put itself in the shoes of the draftsman', you could say that in *Maunsell v Olins* it was said that the court should put itself in the shoes of a draftsman. The same applies to statute law. Obviously it is better to learn it accurately, but if you forget, at least *make use* of the law.

When you learn cases, you should learn brief summary notes, as you will not have time in the examination to write a lot about the facts of each one. Revision notes should include:

- the name of the case;
- a very brief summary of the facts (perhaps two lines);
- the point(s) of law from the case.

Conclusions

A conclusion is a feature of a well constructed essay. Remember, however, that you should not *begin* with a conclusion, for example, 'I think that magistrates should be replaced because ... . .' or 'Jack will win because ... . .'. Beginning in this way prevents you from considering issues while you answer the question and develop thoughts. It also means that you must have a definite answer, while a more sophisticated alternative may be less definite, such as 'If certain changes were made, such as ... then this area of law would be much more acceptable'. Remember that your conclusion (as with that of a qualified lawyer) may be dependant on the view that a judge would take in a case in court. Sometimes questions are deliberately set which do not have a clear answer, especially when in the form of a problem. Your conclusion in that situation may be 'If the court favoured ... then ... but if the court decided ... then ...'. This is just as valid, and often more thoughtful and accurate, than saying that a particular character will win.

Essays

The first kind of question we will examine is a straightforward essay, for example:

> Describe the role of the jury in a criminal trial and consider whether its use should be continued.

Examiners use different 'command words' at the beginning of these questions, and expect a slightly different response to each one. The one question which you will never be asked is 'Write down everything that you know on this topic'. The questions will expect you to select material, or arrange it in a particular order, and use it in your answer to respond to the particular question asked.

Figure 19.1

- *Describe* means, 'tell me what you know about a particular part of a topic ...'. Here it is important to restrict your answer to the precise topic. In the above example, you are being asked to describe the role of the jury – not how it is selected, who is eligible to serve or many of the other things you probably know about jury.

- To *explain* goes a little further than 'describe'. If the question said 'Explain why it has been proposed to restrict the use of juries in criminal cases', you are clearly being asked something more complex. Your answer should include a description of the role of the jury in criminal cases, but it would also incorporate arguments for and against their use, with particular emphasis on the arguments against and an explanation of why some people believe that the right to a jury trial should be curtailed.

- An *outline* is a fairly short account and will almost always be a preliminary stage in asking you to do something more complex. It means a brief description of the major points on a subject. So, an outline of eligibility for jury service would be little more than a statement that everyone on the electoral register is liable to be called for jury service, together with a list of those who are ineligible, excused or disqualified.

- To *discuss* is to present arguments for and against a proposition and, usually, to come to a conclusion. Your conclusion must be based on your arguments – but it does not matter if you reach a conclusion different from that which the examiner would reach. It is the quality of your argument that gets marks.

- To *illustrate* is an important instruction to candidates in an examination and yet it is often totally ignored. It means that you must support your arguments by reference to decided cases and/or statutes, as appropriate to the subject matter. Even if an examiner has not specifically asked for illustration, an answer is always a better answer if you have supported your arguments by reference to statutes and cases.

- To *consider* is an alternative to the word 'discuss'. In the example above you are asked to 'consider' whether juries should be used in criminal cases. Give the arguments for and against and come to a conclusion.

  A different way of asking you to 'consider' is to ask you 'how far' or 'to what extent' a particular statement is true. What is expected is that you will give the arguments in favour of the statement and those against and then come to a conclusion as to which argument is the stronger.

Sample questions from AS units for AQA

You have to choose **two** question out of five in each of the two AQA papers Lawmaking and Dispute Resolution. Remember, however, that from Summer 2003 you have **one hour** in which to complete each paper. AQA states that they will take the shorter time into account in the marking process.

Lawmaking

1 (a) Describe how the doctrine of precedent operates through a hierarchy of courts within the English legal system. Illustrate your description with cases.   **(15 marks)**

   (b) Discuss whether the doctrine of precedent allows judges flexibility in developing the law.   **(15 marks)**

2. (a) Describe and distinguish between the different types of European Union law. Use examples to illustrate your explanation. **(15 marks)**

   (b) Discuss the importance of the role of the European Court of Justice in assisting English courts to interpret European Union law. Illustrate your answer with cases.   **(15 marks)**

3. (a) Describe the various ways judges approach the task of interpreting statutes. Use cases to illustrate your answer.   **(15 marks)**

   (b) Using examples, explain and comment on the fact that using different judicial approaches (rules) may produce different outcomes in the same case.   **(15 marks)**

Dispute Resolution

1. (a) Alan wants to become a legal executive and Bev wishes to become a solicitor. Outline the steps they would need to follow, after sitting their A levels, in order to qualify.   **(10 marks)**

   (b) 'The work of a solicitor is quite different from that of a barrister.'

      Outline the work of the two professions and consider whether this statement is accurate.   **(20 marks)**

2. 'Jury tradition is not only about the right of a citizen to elect trial but also about the juror's duty of citizenship ...', said Baroness Helena Kennedy (*speaking in a House of Lords debate in September 2000*).

   (a) Explain how jurors are chosen for jury duty.   **(15 marks)**

   (b) Comment on the advantages and disadvantages of trial by jury.
                                                              (15 marks)

3. (a) Outline the differences between a negotiated out-of-court settlement and a civil action for damages.   **(10 marks)**

   (b) Alternative Dispute Resolution (ADR) provides alternatives to the courts for bringing some civil actions. Describe and comment on the different forms of ADR.   **(20 marks)**

Sample questions from AS units for OCR

Specimen examples of questions have been provided by OCR for the two papers, Machinery of Justice and Legal Personnel (remember that the specimen questions for Sources of Law can be found in chapter 18). Each of the papers will be **one hour** long, and you have to answer **three** questions, choosing **two** questions based on factual knowledge from the first section and **one** question based on analysis and criticism from the second section. Some examples follow from the specimen publications. All questions are worth 20 marks.

Machinery of Justice

Section A

1. Describe the sentences available to a court when sentencing a young offender.   **(20 marks)**

2. Police officers on patrol believe that a man that they see, Shane, is a suspect wanted for burglary. Outline the powers of the police to stop and search and if necssary to arrest the man.   **(20 marks)**

3. Briefly describe both (i) the three-track system of civil justice; and (ii) the procedure under Article 234 for making references to the European Court of Justice.   **(20 marks)**

Section B

4. Discuss the aims of sentencing and consider other factors the criminal courts will use to reach an appropriate sentence.   **(20 marks)**

5. Discuss the advantages and disadvantages of using Alternative Dispute Resolution (ADR) rather than using the courts to resolve civil disputes.
                                                              (20 marks)

Legal Personnel

Section A

1. Explain the role of magistrates in both civil and criminal cases.
   (20 marks)

2. Explain the selection and appointment of the different types of judges and identify in which courts they each sit.   **(20 marks)**

3. Describe and explain the training and work of solicitors.   **(20 marks)**

Section B

4. Discuss the advantages and disadvantages of using juries to decide both criminal and civil cases.   **(20 marks)**

5. Consider how appropriate it is that the Lord Chancellor has so many different roles.   **(20 marks)**

Problem questions

A legal problem consists of a set of facts followed by either an instruction to 'advise' one or more parties or a set of questions about the law and its application to the facts. All lawyers, from beginners to experienced practitioners, adopt a similar approach to a factual situation when they are asked to consider its legal implications.

Stage 1

First make sure you understand the facts. For practitioners this involves interviewing witnesses and considering evidence. As an examination candidate you can assume that all the facts you have been given in the problem scenario are capable of proof. You can also assume that you have not been given any irrelevant information. The examiner sits down and decides what topics he or she wishes to include in the problem and then writes a scenario to include those topics. You should, therefore, ensure that you understand the facts enough to carry on with the question. You may want to make a very brief plan of the facts if they seem complicated.

Stage 2

Once the facts are clear, the practitioner decides which area or areas of law are relevant. In a dispute between neighbours, for example, there might be issues of land law and issues of the tort of nuisance. Similarly, you should now decide which areas of law are relevant as the basis of your answer and introduce these in your answer.

Stage 3

The lawyer then researches the relevant pieces of law, making sure they understand the relevant issues. Similarly, you should now explain the relevant law in more detail, giving authority in the form of cases or statute law. You may find (as would as a practitioner) that there is some doubt as to what the law is. You should regard such uncertainties as an opportunity to demonstrate knowledge and understanding, explaining the opposing views, giving authority for each view and expressing an opinion as to which may be the one to be followed.

Stage 4

The lawyer then applies the legal principles to the client's situation, expressing an opinion as to whether the client has a good case. You must do exactly the same. A good examination problem will contain more than one issue and some element of doubt, so it is fine to make advice rather conditional (see the section above on conclusions).

A very important point is that even if it looks as though the fictional client in the examination problem is going to lose on one point, the candidate must go on to consider the other points. Remember, this is an exercise in demonstrating knowledge and understanding and whereas a practitioner may say to a client, 'this point of law is fundamental and goes against you, so there is no point in pursuing your case any further', your response should be, 'whether X is successful or not on point A, points B and C have to be considered'.

An IDEA for tackling problem questions

Identify to yourself, from the facts given, the area of law and the issues which are being examined.

Describe briefly the principles of law concerned.

Elaborate on these principles by explaining relevant cases and/or statutes as appropriate.

Apply this law to the characters in the question and advise them as asked.

A worked example

Consider the following problem.

Alice, a learner driver, was approaching a pedestrian crossing. She was being supervised by a friend, Ben, whose attention was caught by a large sign in a shop window, advertising stereo equipment at attractive prices. Christine, a pedestrian, approached the crossing, looked each way and, believing Alice was

---

> slowing down to stop, began to cross. Alice realised that she had to stop but panicked and pressed hard on the accelerator, instead of the brake. The car shot forward, running into Christine and causing her serious injuries.
>
> Advise Christine.

This kind of problem, which asks you to 'advise', requires you to create your own structure for your answer. As explained above, there is a logical sequence for this.

- Identify to yourself, from the facts, the area of law and the issues that apply to Christine.
- Describe briefly the principles of law concerned – negligence.
- Elaborate on these principles by explaining relevant case law – use cases such as *Donoghue v Stevenson* (1932), *Caparo Industries v Dickman* (1990), *Nettleship and Weston* (1971).
- Apply this law to the characters and advise Christine as asked.

Some examination questions may help you by providing a structure. Be sure to use that help, by giving answers to the precise questions asked. For example, the first question might be: 'Explain which area of law is relevant to this problem and outline the important issues involved'. The answer to that question might be:

> This problem is concerned with the tort of negligence. The claimant will have to prove that she is owed a duty of care by the defendant, that there has been a breach of duty and that her loss was foreseeable and caused by the breach of duty.

You will notice that that paragraph not only answered the question set, but would also be a good beginning if you have to provide your own structure.

Having identified the area of law and described the major issues, you should explain the law. Elaborate on it by using cases you know to explain the concepts of duty, breach and loss.

> The claimant in a negligence action has to establish that the defendant owed him or her a duty of care. this principle has evolved from the case of *Donoghue v Stevenson* where a claim was made against a manufacturer of ginger beer for illness caused to the eventual consumer by a snail in the drink.

In accordance with the House of Lords decision in *Caparo v Dickman*, a claim of negligence involves establishing that the defendant ought to have foreseen the risk of loss or injury to the claimant, that there was a sufficiently proximate relationship between them and that it is 'fair, just and reasonable' to hold that the defendant owes the claimant a duty of care. It is well established that drivers owe a duty of care to other road users and the Road Traffic Act requires that every driver must be insured in respect of injuries to third parties.

The claimant has to prove that the defendant fell below the standard to be expected of the reasonable man. In *Nettleship v Weston* the Court of Appeal held that a learner driver has to reach the same standard as a competent and experienced driver.

The claimant finally has to prove that the loss or injury suffered was foreseeable and was caused by the defendant's negligence. In *Wagon Mound (No 1)* it was decided that defendants are liable only for foreseeable consequences. In that case, the defendant's actions led to a serious fire but there was no liability because fire was not a foreseeable consequence of those actions. The case of *Barnett v Chelsea Hospital Management Committee* shows that the claimant can hold the defendant responsible only for those losses that were caused by the defendant. The claimant's husband died from arsenic poisoning. Although the hospital had been negligent, there was nothing they could have done to save the claimant's husband and they were therefore not liable in negligence because their acts or omissions did not cause his death.

The next step is to apply the law to the facts of the problem and advise Christine. You first have to decide who the claimant and defendant are. The claimant is clearly Christine. It is possible to argue that there might be two defendants, Alice and Ben. Take each one in turn.

As a driver, Alice owes a duty of care to other road users. She has to reach the standard to be expected of a competent driver. Clearly, pressing the accelerator by mistake is not something a reasonable driver would do and she is therefore in breach of her duty of care. The problem states that Christine's injuries were caused by the car running into her and all three elements of the tort of negligence are therefore present.

It is also possible to argue that Ben owed a duty of care to Christine. It is foreseeable that if he does not supervise a learner driver carefully there may be loss or injury to others. As the law takes a fairly wide view of proximity when physical harm is caused, a court would probably decide that there was sufficient proximity between pedestrians and a person supervising a learner.

The court might decide that it is not fair, just and reasonable to hold that a friend supervising a learner driver owes a duty of care because he or she is unlikely to be insured, whereas the driver has to be insured. In *Nettleship v Weston* Lord Denning regarded the insurance position as a very relevant consideration in deciding whether a duty of care is owed. It is possible that a court might decide that it would be fair, just and reasonable to hold that a professional driving instructor owes a duty of care to other road users.

If it was decided that Ben did owe a duty of care to other road users, he is probably in breach by allowing his attention to wander. It is much more difficult to say whether his breach caused the accident. If the car had dual controls, he would have been able to apply the brakes but this was presumably an ordinary car, as it was just a friend sitting with a learner, and it might be decided that nothing Ben could have done would have prevented the injury to Christine.

Christine should bring an action in negligence against Alice with a view to recovering damages in respect of her injuries. An action against Ben seems less likely to succeed. Any damages awarded against Alice would be payable by her insurers.

Further practice problems from the AQA specimen paper Concepts of Liability

This paper is also to be one hour in length from Summer 2003, and because the paper has altered in style, AQA have issued a specimen set of questions. The paper will still examine both criminal and tort law, and sanctions and remedies, and will do so in two separate scenario/problem-type questions. Both questions are compulsory – there is no choice – so you definitely need to learn the whole of the syllabus. You will be reminded to use continuous prose (write in essay style, with complete sentences), give reasons for your answers, and make reference to authority (i.e. use cases and statutes, where appropriate, to back up your arguments). The two questions are subdivided to give you help in both explaining legal rules and cases that you know, and applying that law to the scenario.

Criminal Law

Question I   **Total for this question: 25 marks**

Sophie was driving her car when it stalled at traffic lights.
Edward, who was in the car behind Sophie, jumped out of his car ad started to shout at her. Sophie opened her door and Edward dragged her out of her car onto the ground. He then kicked her in the ribs, causing a fracture and

severe bruising. Despite best advice, she did not go to the hospital.

Two days later, Sophie was rushed into hospital with a collapsed lung that, despite the best efforts of the doctors, had to be removed.

(a) Criminal liability is based on the concepts of **actus reus** including **causation**, and **mens rea**.

Briefly explain what is meant by each of these **three** terms and indicate how **causation** could apply in this situation. **(15 marks)**

(b) Discuss Edward's criminal liability for the attack upon Sophie. **(10 marks)**

Tort

Question 2 **Total for this question: 35 marks**

Polish Limited had developed a new floor polish that they were testing. Jade, a secretary at Polish Limited, did not know about the test and slipped on the highly polished surface of the test area and fell down the stairs. Jade broke her leg and was admitted to hospital.

Whilst in hospital, Jade developed a rare medical complication that was missed by Hari, an inexperienced junior doctor. As a result, Jade's broken leg had to be amputated.

Jade's medical problems have left her unemployed, both from her job as a secretary and as a part-time aerobics instructor. She has also had to give up her hobby of cycling.

(a) Jade is considering suing Polish Limited negligence and will need to prove the three elements of **duty**, **breach** and **damage**.

Explain the relevant rules of law of **each** of these **three** elements and discuss whether Polish Limited would be liable in negligence to Jade.

(20 marks)

(b) Assuming that Hari was found to owe Jade a duty of care, briefly discuss whether or not Hari is in breach of that duty of care. **(5 marks)**

(c) Regardless of whom she sues, explain how the court will calculate the amount of damages Jade will receive in respect of the injuries she suffered, if she is successful in a claim. **(10 marks)**

Stimulus response questions

These are questions where there is an extract, usually from a case or statute, or a piece of academic writing on an aspect of law, with questions based on that extract.

The important points to remember are that you should both respond to the source and demonstrate your knowledge to the examiner. It is not enough just to repeat all that you know on the topic questioned, but equally you must not go into the examination unprepared, assuming that this is merely some kind of comprehension test.

There are examples of these questions for you to practice, and detailed help on how to approach them, in Chapter 18.

Final thoughts on examination and study technique

Use of time

Use your time wisely, both in revising and in the examination. Certainly some short-term memory work can be reinforced on the day before the examination, such as case names. The majority of the material in law needs to be read and understood well in advance of the examination, however. The more that you read and practise, the easier it will become. Active practice is important – try explaining the law you need to know to a non-lawyer, and do have a go at answering the practice questions.

In the examination you will need some time to read through the paper, but then notice how many marks are awarded for each part of each question, and divide your remaining time in proportion to the marks awarded. If you find that you are running short of time toward the end of an answer, finish in note form, rather than ending mid-stream and leaving out some important points.

Practice

None of us was born writing fluent English. The more you practise writing out answers, the better you become. Reading a range of textbooks and articles helps tremendously in forming your own style of writing. You should submit written work for marking regularly throughout your course.

Reviewing

Take a critical look at your own written work to see how it can be improved.

- Read previous essays already written and find better ways of expressing ideas.
- Check the spelling of difficult words in a dictionary.
- Keep your sentences short. It is easier to stick to the point using short sentences and correct punctuation is then much easier.
- Make sure you know how to spell legal words and any words that form part of the subject matter. An AS candidate who cannot spell 'Parliament', 'statute', 'legislation', 'precedent' and other terms may lose marks for poor spelling but is also a less convincing candidate generally.

Participating

Ask fellow students to read your work and agree to read theirs. Make constructive criticism of each other's work, both with regard to the content and the style. Volunteer answers to questions in class, and ask questions of your teachers and fellow students. The more involved you become in legal issues, the more easily you will remember them.

Reading

Lawyers learn by reading and communicating much of what they have learnt in writing. Read as much as you can, from books in your library and other textbooks, quality newspapers, law journals and on the Internet. See the list of resources for help on this. The more that you read, the more you will become confident in your own level of knowledge.

Finally

We wish you well in your studies, and hope that you are indeed successful.

20 Answers guide

Questions may be found on pages 300–302.

Lawmaking (p. 300)

Question 1

(a) • Explain the way *stare decisis* operates – higher courts bind lower, and like cases decided alike.

    • Describe the hierarchy of the courts – ECJ, HL, CA etc.

    • Use cases to show how higher courts bind lower courts.

(b) • Discuss the competing needs: following precedent leads to certainty, whilst being flexible leads to justice in each case.

    • Discuss ways in which judges can avoid the strict confines of precedent, and depart from previous cases: distinguishing, re-defining a ratio, use of the Practice Statement in the House of Lords, etc.

Question 2

(a) • Describe the main types of legislation – treaties, regulations, directives and decisions.

    • Explain the differences between them.

    • Illustrate the different types of legislation using cases.

(b) • Discuss the role and approach taken by the ECJ in interpreting laws, including reference to the court under Article 234.

    • Use appropriate case examples to show areas where the ECJ is useful.

    • Form a conclusion on the importance of the ECJ.

Question 3

(a) • Describe the main 'rules' of interpretation – remember to use cases to illustrate these.

    • Describe the intrinsic and extrinsic aids which courts may use to help interpretation.

    • Describe the presumptions and rules of language.

(b) • Use examples from cases (this is really important) to show that the use of different rules may result in different outcomes, e.g. in *Fisher v Bell* the defendant would probably have been guilty using the purposive approach but was found not guilty under the literal rule.

  • Consider why the courts have used differing approaches – both the historical reasons and where, in more recent times, they had a choice.

Dispute resolution (pp. 300–301)

Question 1

(a) • Outline the main steps to becoming a solicitor (no time for very great detail – part (a) is only worth 10 marks).

  • Outline the route to becoming a legal executive – paid work combined with training.

(b) • Consider the work undertaken by a solicitor and that undertaken by a barrister (outline this so that you can go on to discuss it), including some specific areas, such as conveyancing, criminal defence, civil litigation.

  • Discuss the removal of the monopolies, and the much less clear distinction between the two wings of the legal profession.

Question 2

(a) • Explain the way in which the jury is selected and its compulsory nature. You do not have time, here, to write about other aspects of the jury, such as its role and function or alternative methods of trial.

  • Explain the requirements of qualification of those who serve.

  • Explain the groups of people who do not serve.

(b) • Comment on the benefits perceived by a defendant and the public, e.g. the general advantage of trial by peers, rather than by a single judge, application of the law which may not be so rigid, etc. Remember that you are to **comment on** the advantages and disadvantages – not merely list them.

  • Consider the disadvantages – e. g. the possibility of media pressure, local bias, etc.

Question 3

(a) • This will involved some description of each – the route through a civil court trial – different courts, different tracks, case management – and a negotiation based on precedent.

- Explain the differences between taking action for damages via the court and settling out of court – time, cost, stress, likely outcome, level of compensation, opportunity to appeal.

(b) • Describe the different forms that Alternative Dispute Resolution may take – tribunals, arbitration, mediation, conciliation, negotiation and (briefly) the role of the ombudsman.

- Comment on the advantages of ADR – usually fast, efficient, informal (and therefore accessible), less costly (often no representation), often administered by experts.

- Consider the disadvantages of ADR – lack of funding (and therefore representation for many), unpredictable decisions, lack of appeal structure, low public awareness.

Machinery of Justice (p. 301)

Question 1

- Describe which sentences are available regarding young offenders – see the Powers of the Criminal Courts (Sentencing) Act 2000 – refer to a range of sentences, e.g. detention, community punishment (service), community rehabilitation (probation), curfew (e.g. electronic tagging), fine, discharge.

- Explain detention – adult prison not available but detention for a longer period, e.g. 'at Her Majesty's Pleasure', may be available for serious offences, such as murder.

- Explain that first time young offenders are often dealt with in a less formal manner – e.g. caution/warning.

Question 2

- Explain that the rules of stop, search and arrest found in PACE. Remember that you are only asked to outline the rules, not to comment on their effectiveness or fairness. This is a factual question, not an analytical one. Also remember that you have 20 minutes (maximum) available.

- Explain the powers of stop and search under PACE s1-7 and Code A of the Codes of Practice (also – other statutory rights exist, e.g. in connection with prevention of terrorism and misuse of drugs).

- Explain the powers of arrest under s24 – arrestable offence, and under s25 – general arrest.

Question 3

- Describe the courts available for a civil action, and explain the idea of case management and tracks.

- Explain the operation of the three different tracks – small claims in the County court, fast track for cases in the County court between £5,000 and £15,000, and multi-track for cases in the County or High court over £15,000 or involving complex legal matters.

- Explain that Article 234 references are for rulings of matters of EU law and do not have to be made from the HL – they can be made from any court. Use cases to illustrate, e.g. *Bulmer v Bollinger, Factortame*.

Question 4

- Explain the difference between the retributive aims and the utilitarian aims, and between tariffs and individual sentences.

- Consider the main aims: retribution, rehabilitation, deterrence (general and individual), protection of society.

- Consider the extent to which these can be achieved in setting an appropriate sentence.

- Consider other factors that the court may take into account, e.g. previous convictions, seriousness of this particular offence, circumstances of the offender.

- Consider the balance between these (sometimes) competing aims.

Question 5

- Remember that you do not have to merely describe all of the alternatives, but discuss their advantages and disadvantage. Just describing them will attract few marks.

- Consider the difficulties of using traditional court procedures – time, cost, complexity and inaccessibility.

- Discuss the advantages of ADR – usually fast, efficient, informal (and therefore accessible), less costly (often no representation), often administered by experts, less adversarial, more privacy, use encouraged under the new Civil Procedure Rules.

- Consider the disadvantages of ADR – lack of funding (and therefore representation for many), unpredictable decisions, lack of appeal structure, low public awareness, in some cases dependant on the other party appearing and co-operating.

Legal Personnel (p. 302)

Question 1

- Identify magistrates as being either lay magistrates (and therefore not legally qualified) or District Judges (formerly stipendiary – or paid – magistrates).
- Explain the role of magistrates – mostly criminal, so this 'list' will be longer: granting bail, hearing pleas and mode of trial hearings and transferring to Crown Court, conducting trials, deciding both verdict and sentence, issuing warrants. Civil: licensing (deciding applications for entertainment and alcohol licences), payments for council tax, water, gas and electricity charges, some family proceedings.
- Explain that the role of magistrates may become increasingly important following the changes proposed in the Auld Review.

Question 2

- Introduce the levels of judges and the general principles of appointment.
- Explain the selection and appointment of superior judges and say in which courts they sit: Law Lords (Lords of Appeal in Ordinary) - HL, Lord Justices of Appeal – CA, High Court Judges (Puisne Judges) – High Court and Crown Court.
- Explain the selection and appointment of inferior judges and say in which courts they sit: Circuit Judges, Recorders, District Judges, District Judges (Magistrates' Court).

Question 3

Describe the training route for solicitors:

- Academic – law degree or degree in another subject plus the CPE, or non-graduate route via ILEX.
- Vocational – LPC – concentrates on practical skills.
- Professional – training contract.
- Qualification – enrolment with the Law Society.

Explain the nature of the work of a solicitor:

- Contact with clients, interviewing, listening, advising, preparing cases for court, presenting them in the lower courts unless a certified advocate, or for handing as a brief to a barrister.
- Includes (not necessarily a complete list) conveyancing, family law, contract and commercial law, criminal law, negligence (including personal injury), wills and probate.

Question 4

Remember here that you will not obtain marks for purely describing, for example, the selection procedure. You need to *discuss*, and to focus on *advantages* and *disadvantages* of the system.

- Advantages: peer trial attracts public support and therefore perception is one of fairness – although there is reluctance to serve; twelve opinions better than one, although they need to be reasonably representative, and without pressure; independence and secrecy of the jury's decision enables the law to be 'fitted' to the needs of justice, and not result in oppression or absurdity; jury trial is seen as a right of citizens.

- Disadvantages: unless jury members are selected in a different way and kept apart in accommodation, as in high profile trials in the US, there will always be a real possibility of media pressure and therefore both local and national bias; selection is flawed, resulting in a distorted jury – but Auld recommends reform; jury trial is costly and time-consuming (again – Auld recommends reform to result in less choice of jury trial); no literacy or intelligence tests, therefore jurors may lack understanding of the standard and burden of proof; lack of technical knowledge particularly concerning in fraud trials.

- Civil juries – sitting in the County court as a jury of 8 – useful for defamation cases but not good at assessing damages; not used in personal injury cases for that reason; useful for malicious prosecution in providing some protection against oppression.

Question 5

- Consider whether the roles of the Lord Chancellor conflict with the theory of separation of powers – in all three areas of control, i.e. legislature, executive and judiciary.

- Discuss the role, as head of the judiciary, of appointment of judges – too much to do, lack of openness, not credible in a modern society. Also responsible for magistrates.

- Discuss the role of Speaker in the House of Lords – a full-time post, really, and would still need the support of a deputy. A political role – suitable for the head of the judiciary?

- Discuss the issue of membership of the Cabinet – should legal advice be given, considering the other roles?

- Generally – the LC is a political appointment – leads to perception of bias; too much work for one person; *potential* for corruption – or allegations of it, and lack of public confidence.

Legal resources

Books

A case book provides a selection of extracts from cases, academic articles and other resources on the English Legal System:

Zander, M. (2003) *Cases and Materials on the English Legal System*, Butterworths

The following books, in the same series as this one, will be useful for further reading on the substantive areas of law and for preparation for the A2 part of the course:

Hodge, S. (2002) *Tort Law*, Willan Publishing

Storey, A. and Lidbury, A. (2002) *Criminal Law*, Willan Publishing

Charman, M. (2002) *Contract Law*, Willan Publishing

Newspapers and Journals

The Times (always good for current developments and articles, particularly in the Supplement on Tuesdays, and a good source of recent cases).

Student Law Review: Cavendish Publishing (published three times each year – useful for recent developments – see below for on-line version).

The New Law Journal (the major journal for current developments and academic articles on civil law issues).

See below (The Internet) for journals available on-line.

The Internet

If you have access to the Internet a whole new world of legal information is available to you. You will find here a selection of websites which will be of interest and which should be useful to you in developing your studies and providing current information. They are arranged into categories, very broadly, according to content, although some sites will contain material which belongs to more than one category.

This is a fast developing and changing resource, so the content of a site may not be the same from one visit to another. These addresses were all accurate and operational at the time of publication.

Course details and materials

http://.aqa.org.uk (for specification details for AQA candidates)

http://www.ocr.org.uk (for specification details for OCR candidates)

http://www.stbrn.ac.uk/other/depts/law/ (for course materials)

http://www.e-lawstudent.com/ (for course materials and legal news – subscription needed for full access)

Parliament and legislation

http://www.parliament.uk (for general information on Parliament).

http://www.legislation.hmso.gov.uk (for Acts of Parliament and other legislation).

http://www.swarb.co.uk (for Acts of Parliament and other resources).

Case law

http://www.parliament.the-stationery-office.co.uk/pa/ld199697/ldjudgmt/ldjudgmt.htm (for House of Lords judgments since November 1996).

http://www.casetrack.com (for selected Court of Appeal cases).

http://www.lawreports.co.uk (for sample reports of the Incorporated Council of Law Reporting for England and Wales).

http://curia.eu.int/en/index.htm (for recent cases and information on the European Court of Justice).

http://www.courtservice.gov.uk (for selected judgments and news items).

Articles and news

http://www.timesonline.co.uk/

http://www.lawzone.co.uk (for recent cases and articles).

General interest

http://www.venables.co.uk (for a huge collection of legal resources).

http://www.lawgazette.co.uk (for general legal issues, careers trends, etc.).

http://www.lawcom.gov.uk/ (for reports and information on the Law Commission).

http://www.infolaw.co.uk (for general legal material).

http://www.lcd.gov.uk/ (for the Lord Chancellor's department, giving lots of information on the judiciary, magistrates, funding, etc.).

http://www.jsboard.co.uk (for the Judicial Studies Board, giving information on judges and magistrates).

http://www.ccrc.gov.uk/ (for the Criminal Cases Review Commission).

http://www.justice.org.uk/ (to investigate alleged miscarriages of justice).

Glossary

academic lawyers lawyers who research, teach and write books, rather than being in practice

acquittal a finding of not guilty in a criminal trial

Act of Parliament law made by Parliament

actus reus the act or omission which forms part of a criminal offence

adversarial a style of trial in which each side makes its arguments, the judge acting as a referee

advocate a person who presents an argument on behalf of someone else

advocacy putting forward an argument on behalf of someone else

agenda a list of proposals for discussion

ambiguous capable of having more than one meaning

annulled cancelled

antecedents a summary of what has gone before in a defendant's life, stated in the court before sentence is passed

arbitration a process of dispute resolution in which each party puts its case to an expert who makes a judicial decision

Article a Section of a Treaty

ascertain to find out or determine

assault conduct which causes a person to fear that they are about to suffer violence

authority cases and statutes which state the law

bail the release of a person who has been charged with a criminal offence, pending trial, granted by the police or by magistrates

battery touching or striking a person without lawful excuse

benchers senior barristers with responsibility for discipline within the profession

Bill a proposal for legislation in the form in which it is put to Parliament

case an issue taken to court

causation the link between a defendant's conduct and a prohibited consequence

civil law law concerning wrongs and other issues which are not crimes

claimant the person who sues in a civil case – formerly called the plaintiff

codify to put all the law on one subject into one Act

committal proceedings proceedings in a magistrates' court, for offences which are not indictable, to determine whether there is a case against the defendant which should be heard by a jury

Community Defence Service the new state defence service

Community Legal Service a body established to provide legal funding

community sentence a sentence which is served in the community, rather than in prison

compatible fitting, suitable

conciliation a method of resolving disputes by getting the parties together to discuss their differences and reach an agreed solution

conditional fee a fee that is payable only if the litigant wins the case

consolidate to combine all the Acts on one subject in one new Act

constituency the area represented by a Member of Parliament, Member of the European Parliament or any member of an elected body

constitutional connected with the rules about how a country is run, which body is responsible for what, how laws are made and changed

constraints limits

contentious giving rise to argument

context surrounding circumstances or words

controversial likely to give rise to disagreement

conveyancing the legal work connected with sale and purchase of land

conviction a finding of guilty in a criminal court

CPS the Crown Prosecution Service, the state prosecution body

crime a wrong so serious that society punishes the wrongdoer, aiming to prevent the wrong happening again

criteria standards by which decisions are made

custody officer a particular police officer who has responsibility for those in custody at a police station

damages compensation in the form of money

decision a type of European law that applies to those to whom it is addressed

defamation a tort that is committed by saying, writing or otherwise publishing information about a person that is not true and that may damage their reputation

defendant a person accused of a wrong in court

denunciation public condemnation

deterrence an attempt to prevent people committing offences by convincing them that it would not be a good idea

Directive a form of European law

directly applicable when European law is binding in each member state automatically, without the need for domestic legislation

directly effective European law that gives rights to individuals, enforceable by an individual taking court action

disbursements amounts paid out by solicitors on behalf of the client when handling a case, such as fees to experts or postage costs

disposable capital assets and savings, after an allowance for the individual and any dependants

disposable income weekly or monthly income, after an allowance for the individual and any dependants

distinguish to find material (significant) differences between two cases

detainee a person held for questioning at a police station

dissenting disagreeing

diverse varied

domestic law the law of an individual state, e.g. English law

duty of care a duty owed to others who may be harmed by our actions

duty solicitor a solicitor available to give advice in a magistrates' court or police station

electorate all the people entitled to vote

enactments Acts of Parliament

envisaged expected as a possibility

executive those who run the state on a daily basis, for example the Civil Service

expedient appropriate, convenient

fiscal relating to tax liability

frailty weakness, susceptibility

fusion joining together

general damages money awarded by a court for non-quantifiable losses such as pain and suffering

grievous really serious

hereditary by reason of birth

hierarchy placed in order from high to low

horizontal effect the right to use European law to sue an individual or private organisation

hybrid offences a group of criminal offences which may be tried either way, by magistrates or by jury

implement to put into practice, e.g. making a law operational in this country

incapacity inability to do a job, usually because of poor health

incompatibility where one law is in disagreement with another, inconsistency

indeterminate something that cannot be decided

indictable offences the most serious class of criminal offences, which must always be tried in the Crown Court before a judge and jury

indictment the formal document containing the charge of a serious criminal offence

inferior judges those who sit in the lower courts, including district judges, circuit judges and recorders

injunction a legal order to carry out an action, e.g. to restrict a factory process which makes an excessive noise to a certain time of day, or not to discharge waste into a river

inns of court the institutions which form part of the Bar (the organisation regulating Barristers) and were once responsible for training barristers

inquisitorial a style of trial in which the aim is to investigate, rather than oppose, with the judge taking an active role in questioning

intention a type of *mens rea* which consists either of wanting a particular consequence to occur or of realising that it is virtually certain to occur

interim temporary

interim payment a payment of damages made before the final sum can be calculated in cases where liability has been established but the amount has yet to be decided

judicial review a review of the process that has been followed in making a decision

judiciary the judges

jurisdiction the types of case a court may hear

lay not an expert or a qualified person

legislation law made by Parliament

legislature a law-making body, normally Parliament

liability legal responsibility

litigant a party to a court case

litigation a court case

mediation a process by which a third party tries to get those involved in a dispute to agree

mens rea the state of mind necessary to commit a particular criminal offence

migrant a person who moves from one country to another; immigrants coming into a country, emigrants leaving it

mitigation lessening the severity of conduct

multiplier the number by which the annual financial loss suffered by a claimant is multiplied in order to arrive at the damages payable

nominal in name only

objectively viewed dispassionately, as if by a third party who is not involved

obiter dictum the things said 'by the way', as a matter of opinion, in the course of a judgment

offence triable either way an offence which could be committed in a minor or serious manner, and which could therefore be tried in either the magistrates' court or the Crown Court, e.g. theft

omission the failure to do something which should have been done

opaque material which is not transparent

other jurisdictions areas outside England and Wales where there is a different legal system and, probably, different legal rules

PACE the Police and Criminal Evidence Act 1984

party a person involved in a court case

perceived viewed or believed

perpetrator the person who does something, usually a prohibited act

persuasive precedent a decision which is not binding on a court but which it may choose to follow

plea in mitigation a speech made after conviction, before sentence is passed, explaining any circumstances that make the defendant's conduct less blameworthy

policy a view as to what the law ought to be

posthumous after death

pragmatic practical, as opposed to theoretical

precedent a decision as to the law which becomes binding

prima facie at first sight, on the face of it

pro bono work for which lawyers do not charge, from *pro bono publico* – for the general good

probate the legal work involved in dealing with a person's property after death

prosecuted charged with a criminal offence

protocol the way in which a task should be undertaken, e.g. steps to be followed in a civil action

proximity closeness

Queen's Counsel senior barristers

ratio decidendi the issues which form the basis of a court decision and the reasons for the decision

reasonable grounds grounds for a decision which a reasonable person would regard as appropriate

recklessness a state of mind in which the defendant either realises the risk being taken, or should have realised the risk taken

Regulation a type of European law that is directly applicable

remand holding a person who has been charged with a criminal offence before being tried

representation having a case presented by someone else

repugnant distasteful, unsuitable

retribution punishment, revenge

retrospectively literally, looking backwards, or having effect previously

right something to which a person is entitled

sanction a measure taken, often a punishment, when a person has been found guilty

scrutinise consider carefully

sedition saying or writing something likely to cause people to rebel

sentence the penalty imposed by a criminal court on a convicted defendant

separation of powers　the idea of the three bodies of the legislature, the executive and the judiciary having separate roles

severance　cutting out

specific performance　an order to carry out a duty, e.g. an obligation under a contract

stare decisis　literally, standing by decisions, the concept of a court being bound by previous decisions

statute　an Act of Parliament

statutory　law imposed by an Act

stipendiary　paid a wage, or stipend

strict liability　criminal liability arising solely from commission of the *actus reus*, the defendant's state of mind being irrelevant, or civil liability arising without any requirement that the defendant is at fault

sue　to take a case to a civil court

sued　made the defendant in a civil action

summary offences　the least serious criminal offences, which are always tried by magistrates

superior judges　judges who sit in the higher courts, including Law Lords, Lords Justices of Appeal and High Court judges

tacit　unspoken

tariff　the normal rate, e.g. the usual sentence

thin skull rule　a victim is taken as he is, so if a person harms someone especially vulnerable, e.g. who has a thin skull, the wrongdoer is responsible for the consequences

transferred malice　where a person intends to do harm, but not necessarily toward the person who eventually suffers

Treaty　a fundamental form of European law

tribunal　a body which hears disputes, usually appointed under an Act

ultra vires　outside or beyond the powers of an organisation or individual

unanimous　all in agreement

vertical effect　the right to use a European law against the state or 'an emanation of the state'

void　empty, of no effect

wounding　an injury which is more serious than just breaking one layer of the skin

Index

- References are in simple alphabetical structure for ease of use by students. For major areas of study, sub-headings will also be found under those areas, e.g. *fines* appears both as an index item in its own right and under *sanctions, fines*.
- Readers are also referred to the detailed contents list.
- Where a topic occurs over a spread of pages, the first page number is given for simplicity.